WORLD'S BEST HOBBY

WORLD'S BEST HOBBY

Dave Bell, W6AQ

authorHOUSE®

AuthorHouse™ LLC
1663 Liberty Drive
Bloomington, IN 47403
www.authorhouse.com
Phone: 1-800-839-8640

Published by AuthorHouse 07/01/2014

ISBN: 978-1-4969-1403-3 (sc)
ISBN: 978-1-4969-1404-0 (e)

Any people depicted in stock imagery provided by Thinkstock are models,
and such images are being used for illustrative purposes only.
Certain stock imagery © Thinkstock.

This book is printed on acid-free paper.

Because of the dynamic nature of the Internet, any web addresses or links contained in this book may have changed
since publication and may no longer be valid. The views expressed in this work are solely those of the author and do
not necessarily reflect the views of the publisher, and the publisher hereby disclaims any responsibility for them.

Contents

Foreword

This book is for anyone who ever thought that Amateur Radio might be a fun hobby.

It's for anyone who enjoys helping out in emergencies.

It's for people who like to build things and have them work.

It's for experimenters

It's for adventurers.

It's for communicators.

It's for all ages, men, women and children; a perfect hobby to take into retirement.

Ham Radio is a very tight fraternity with instant friendships and a large common ground. The hobby is so diverse, with so many specialties, that I've never met a Ham who wasn't eager to spend more time in the shack.

Cities and towns large and small have Ham clubs of all sorts, many organized by specialty: Contest, Public Service, Repeater, Digital, Microwave, CW (Morse code), QRP (transmitting using less than 5 watts), and DX (talking to Hams in foreign lands) and on and on.

Hams hold conventions where they learn more about the latest developments, see the newest equipment, search for bargains at the flea market, and meet old and new friends.

In my life I've made friends in high school, college, the military, and in my long career producing television and movies. Virtually all of my good friends, after all of those experiences, are Hams.

Ham Radio is an enjoyable, lifelong learning experience.

Ham Radio is the World's Best Hobby.

Dave Bell, W6AQ

Acknowledgements

Many friends, acquaintances, and family helped get "World's Best Hobby" finished and grammatically sound. So many people have been looking after me, I'll be surprised if you find any grammatical or punctuation mistakes. Principal among my content contributors:

JOHN NATHAN, a non-Ham, my primary editor—many thanks, John.

RICHARD PARSONS, VE2WGH, who did the great cartoons.

JIM SHRYNE, N6DHZ, who created and maintained my website as I was writing.

DON LISLE, K6IPV, who never met a comma he didn't like.

BILL PASTERNAK, WA6ITF, who prodded me forward over many lunches.

ROBERT GRIFFIN, K6YR, whose many suggestions made the book bigger and better.

BRAD FIELD, W8JJO, who jogged my memory from the Showboat to the present.

HAROLD (HAL) TAYLOR, W8CY, who prodded my memory of the early days.

MARK BECKWITH, N5OT, who gave off positive vibes.

PRICE HICKS, a genuine non-tekkie, who asked the civilian questions.

KITTY STALLINGS, my terrific assistant, without whom I couldn't have finished.

AND MY FAMILY:

KRIS BELL, who devoured every chapter and made lots of sensible comments.

KATHY NELSON, who gave me friendly encouragement,

And my two sons, Mitchell and David, who are going to read it when it's on paper.

And of course my wife Sam (W6QLT) who happily endured my hobby all these years.

Chapter 1

The Great Awakening

I remember very clearly my introduction to Amateur Radio, though at the time I didn't realize that such a fascinating hobby had totally escaped what passed for my teenaged attention. Ham Radio, as it is popularly called, had not yet tweaked my consciousness.

Andover, Ohio, in the spring of 1946 was a picturesque if slightly rundown village in the northeastern corner of the Buckeye state, two miles from Pennsylvania and 30 miles south of Lake Erie. Andover's only claim to fame was Pymatuning Lake, a shallow, artificial lake, hardly more than a deep swamp, on the Ohio/Pennsylvania border where "the ducks walk on the backs of the fish." Absurd as that sounds, it's a true boast.

But to a 14-year-old-boy, that boast was old and tired. What else is new? On a Saturday afternoon, with the baseball diamond muddy from last night's downpour, what was there to do? Discovering the world's best hobby didn't appear as an item on my short list of possible activities. But fate intervened.

My father used to say, "if you're bored, you're boring." So I always worked hard at not being bored, but sometimes in this sleepy little town of 1,000 hard working, God fearing souls, boredom provided the best alternative to teenaged angst.

If I still had my BB gun I could have gone out to shoot at squirrels. Uncle Frank had given me the BB gun for my 14th birthday, horrifying my mother. "It was just the kind of thing Uncle Frank would do," my mother said. She called him a ninny. It was years before I realized that if you had a tattoo, rode a motorcycle and were not married to my aunt, you weren't by definition a ninny.

When my mother first saw the BB gun she said, "You won't be happy with that thing till you put somebody's eye out." Every time she saw that gun she said the same thing. She wasn't disappointed, I suspect, that I never lived up to her dire prediction. In fact, the gun was cheap and didn't shoot straight, "just like Uncle Frank" my mother said when she heard my complaint. I could hit the broadside of a barn with it, but that's about all. So when my mother offered to trade me a six tube brown plastic Crosley AC/DC superhet AM radio for my piece-of-junk BB gun, I quickly took the deal. Later I heard her tell my father that with the radio, at least, I wouldn't put anybody's eye out. Little did she or anyone else know that the radio would show me the way to the world's best hobby.

That Saturday I had ridden my bike all over town looking for some action, had my chocolate milkshake at Bloomer's, checked in with my mother at her store and my father at his insurance office above the store. Both suggested that I go home and do my homework if all of my friends were unavailable. I went up to my bedroom to see what I could do to avoid my homework. I reached over, turned my radio on, and waited for it to warm-up. In those early days of the Communications Age, everything electronic had to warm-up before it came on. That warm-up period provided a moment of quiet tension. Would it work or would it be "on the fritz," as my mother used to say? Well, this fateful day it worked—and it didn't. I heard the most overpowering signal my poor little bedside radio had ever uttered.

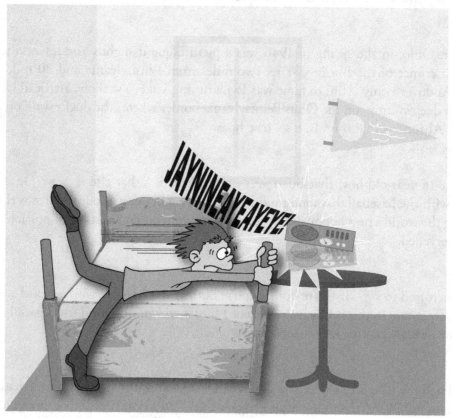

What happened
to the Andrews Sisters!?

It sounded like, "Jaynineayeayeye!" repeated two or three times. When it went off, the piddling little signal of WTAM in Cleveland, 60 miles to the west, appeared playing the Ink Spots or the Andrews Sisters or whatever pop tune fit the moment. Then the eardrum-punishing litany appeared again, sending the poor, distant broadcast station to temporary oblivion.

"Jaynineayeayeye" the deep, male voice shouted. Then he yelled something like, "Doubleyouweightelleyeoh!" I couldn't understand a word of it. What to do? For some reason I decided to unhook the aerial. Remember aerials, those lengths of wire that went from a little clip on the fiberboard back of the radio out the window to a nearby tree or some other handy support?

Now and then they would droop enough to snag some unwary passerby on the neck, causing all manner of new vocabulary to spew out and into the ears of a curious teenager.

For reasons as mysterious as radio itself, unhooking the aerial made the loud voice even more distinct. It said, "J9AAI" a couple of times and then added "W8 London Italy Ocean."

There followed a few seconds of silence before poor distant WTAM regained control of the frequency that it had been assigned by the FCC, only to lose out to the J9AAI guy once again.

I went downstairs and turned on the fancy floor model Philco in the two-tone wood case and the fancy grill-cloth over the big speaker. The mystery signal didn't show up on our big radio. I went next door. They didn't hear it on their radio, a giant 11-tube Zenith with a polished walnut case, dial lights that worked, and a shortwave band that didn't. I went back to my room. J9AAI was still on there, pulverizing the airways. Maybe I could tune it out. I turned the dial. J9AAI was *everywhere*. I listened more. My usually impenetrable curiosity had been severely piqued.

At what point did it dawn on me that I was not listening to J9AAI, but to someone called W8LIO? I got on my bicycle and went searching for the mysterious W8LIO. Who could find a radio signal looking from a bicycle? I could, and I did. It was on the south side of West Main Street, only one block past the small but imposing Andover School, (all bricks and concrete and large windows with dozens of panes of glass, to keep the costs down from the inevitable breakage.) It had a stolid, New England look to it. Grade school was on the first floor with the dreaded principal's office and the auditorium/gymnasium with its molded wood chairs screwed into the sloping concrete floor facing the stage/basketball court. Grades seven through 12 were on the second floor.

A gigantic tower tipped me off to the mysterious W8LIO. And on top of the tower, strands of aluminum reflected the afternoon sun right into my eyes. How could I have missed it before? It must have been put up last night. I rode my bike up the black cinder-and-weeds driveway toward the tower in the backyard of a house that had withstood years of casual neglect. As I got near the screened-in back porch, I heard the familiar chant "J9AAI" begin all over again, but this time it didn't come through the tiny speaker in my plastic radio, but live.

I stood at the screen door and looked squarely at the back of a large man doing his mystic chant into a chrome-plated microphone. Electronic equipment from floor to ceiling surrounded him. I stood at that back door for who knows how long before I summoned the courage to knock. "Come in," said the big man without looking around. That provided my casual invitation to join the ranks of the anointed few. It was my introduction into the addictive world of ham radio.

For many, if not all readers, the preceding will qualify as ancient history. What about today? If a stray thought about Ham Radio lodges for a moment in your curiosity, how would you find those strands of aluminum high in the sky, reflecting sunlight into your eyes? Well, you could go looking on your bicycle, of course, but a somewhat easier and quicker way would be to type "Amateur Radio" into Google, which will tell you that it has millions of references. Somewhere near the top of the millions of possibilities will appear ARRL, which you will learn stands for American Radio Relay League, an organization even older than the time described here in Chapter One, if you can imagine such a thing. Searching the ARRL website will turn up active ham radio clubs in your area, with appropriate contact information. Most, if not all, of these clubs will welcome you with introductions all around and load you with more information than you could possibly assimilate, even if you understood the jargon, which one day soon you'll be spewing as if it were real English.

Chapter 2

Sweet Success

Without turning around, the big man said, "Hi, I'm Jack. Have a seat." He waved at a wicker chair in a corner that had seen better days. He went back to his chant into the microphone with barely a pause. Every time he spoke, two gigantic tubes, each almost as big as my entire radio, turned from grey to bright white. The tubes were in a metal frame about the size and shape of my mom's stove, except it didn't have any sides or top, just a few meters on the front panel, with needles frantically waving every time he spoke. A big fan on the floor blew hot air from around those tubes right toward the chair where I sat.

When he said, "This is W8 London, Italy, Ocean," the word "London" caused the tubes to light the room like the inside of a motion picture studio. "Italy" produced a quick, blinding flash, and "Ocean" was a bright sun appearing for a moment between the clouds. The tubes got bright and the little light above Jack's desk got dim at exactly the same moment.

When he stopped talking, I heard a voice coming out of the big, olive-drab radio on the table in front of him. The little voice was hard to understand. If I remember correctly, and I may not after all these years, the little voice said, "W6AOA this is J9AAI, five/nine." As he listened to a raspy, growling voice say a few words, Jack muttered, "those damn sixes."

In a moment, Jack was at it again. This time he screamed louder. The inside of the old porch glowed brighter than the backyard, naked to the summer sun.

Suddenly, as Jack shouted into the microphone, an unearthly squeal filled the room. It sounded as if someone had stood on the tails of a dozen cats all at once. Jack grabbed what looked like an old rubber hammer and delivered one sharp blow to the dented top of an olive-drab box. The squeal stopped.

Fixing the speech amp.

He turned a little dial on the box down about two degrees and went back to his calling. I watched fascinated as all time was suspended It may have been hours. My host never acknowledged my presence beyond that initial greeting. Every now and then he would say, "Those damn sixes." Now and then he'd add, "Those damn sevens." While I had no idea then what he was talking about, within in a couple of months I had learned that the sixes were all in California and the sevens in Oregon, Washington and a few other far Western states and consequently much closer to the elusive J9AAI than we, in the northeastern corner of the Buckeye State.

After what might have been an eternity, with my severely limited attention span somehow on hold, a little voice came out of the speaker. "W8LIO," it said, "this is J9AAI, five by nine." Jack grabbed his microphone and squeezed the lever on the side of the handle until it bowed. "J9AAI, this is W8LIO. Five/nine. QSL?" "QSL, QRZed," said the little voice, and for the first time I heard what sounded like a swarm of bees which had somehow gotten caught in the speaker.

Jack sagged in his chair and then leaned forward and turned a knob which quieted the room. He looked at a clock on the wall that had too many numbers on it, noted something on a piece of paper in front of him, leaned back again, and rolled his head toward me. All he said was, "OH KEE NAA WAAH." He made it sound like a train announcement at the Terminal Tower in Cleveland, loud and clear yet making me think, "What did he say?" From reading articles in the *Cleveland Plain Dealer* that my father strongly suggested that I read, I knew that Okinawa was a fly-speck in the Pacific Ocean that up until a few months before had been the southernmost part of the Japanese homeland, a territory whose capture mortally wounded the morale of the Japanese people in World War II.

I learned from Jack that afternoon that the operator (yes, that's what they're called) at J9AAI was a ham/GI who had undoubtedly appropriated a large stash of Signal Corps radio equipment, found some official out there to give him a callsign and got on Ten Meters, causing what Jack called a pileup. It seemed to me a massive pileup. Jack sat there looking at his porchful of ham equipment and said, "That was a bitch, wasn't it? Not understanding a single thing about what I had just seen, I said, "Yep." "So, are you a ham?" asked Jack, knowing the answer.

At a loss for words, I said, "I'm Dave."

"Jack," he said, holding out a big, beefy hand.

"Hi," I said.

"Good to meet you, David," he said. He always called me David. While that was my name, everybody else in town called me Dave, except the teachers, and they don't count.

Years later, when I was in college, building scenery in the old house that served as the drama department scene shop, I used to listen to a late-night talk show hosted by Jean Shepherd, who now and then divulged that he was a Ham, K2ORS. Jean, an exceptionally talented guy, did a lot of things, including write the Christmas classic TV movie, "A Christmas Story." When Jean Shepherd talked about Ham Radio, he often divided Hams into what he called, "them" and "us."

"Them" were the guys who ran a kilowatt, give or take a couple of thousand watts, and the ones he called "us" ran a hundred watts, thirty watts, five watts. He referred to the "us" as "barefoot."

Jack and his friends were not "barefoot," and consequently were not among the "us." They were the "them" and since Jack became my mentor in Ham Radio, I quickly became a member of the "them." When I met Jean Shepherd years later at the Dayton Hamvention, we had a really nice chat about a documentary film I had produced about Ham Radio. I never told him that I was one of the "them" though I suspect he knew.

Many Hams told Jack that he had the loudest signal on the band, which made him proud. The phonetics he sometimes used for W8LIO were, "Loudest In Ohio."

Jack told me he "knew there was an FCC rule that says you aren't supposed to use any more power than necessary, but necessary for what? How are you to know that somebody running 10 kilowatts hasn't moved in just down the block? That guy might fire up his rig on your frequency anytime . . . and blotto, there you go." Jack didn't say that the "thems" don't turn off their amplifiers if they overload some guy's receiver so bad that he can't understand what they're saying, but he certainly implied that he would think twice about it, before he did it, just in case it was some kind of trick.

These many years later, I know how Jack viewed me that first time we met, because I have viewed people who showed up in my shack and gotten hooked in exactly the same way. Jack saw me as raw meat. I was his new beef trust. I got to carry all the heavy stuff. I was the one at the top of the tower. I did all the stuff for him then that I won't even do for myself now.

Jack had this thing about antennas. His good friend Sam Harris, W8UKS, coined a phrase well-known to Hams: "If your antenna didn't blow down last winter, it wasn't big enough." A lot of Hams I met back in those early days privately considered Jack and Sam nuts. Since they both became friends of mine, I preferred to think of them as visionaries. Perhaps the line between nuts and visionaries lies in the mind of the beholder.

One of my first "learning opportunities" as Jack called the scut work he had in mind for me, involved helping him put together his soon-to-be-famous 33-element beam antenna. I discovered, by looking up at the top of the tower and counting, that his current antenna consisted of three elements. My teenage mind couldn't conceive of something over ten times as big as what was already up there. "Just imagine," Jack said as we stood in his backyard looking upward, "a 33-element beam for Ten Meters." I couldn't imagine it. What was Ten Meters, for that matter?

Ten Meters, it turned out, was a so called "Ham band"—a group of frequencies above the AM broadcast band which on my little Crosley radio went from 550 to about 1500 <u>Kilo</u>cycles. The Ten Meter band are all of the frequencies between 28 and 30 <u>Mega</u>cycles, which was the first bunch of frequencies returned to Hams at the end of World War II. I say "returned" because it was just one of a half-dozen or so bands that pre-war Hams had been assigned by the FCC and the International Amateur Radio Union. In 1947, as Jack often said, "Ten was hot," so he was happy.

Jack anticipated this restoration of Ham Radio privileges. As he was mustering out of the Army Signal Corps, he somehow managed to take with him a ton or more of aluminum of all shapes and sizes, plus dozens of big rolls of coaxial cable and copper wire, steel cable and almost anything shiny or khaki. He had the original garage that you couldn't get your car into. Jack was way ahead of his time. Clearly, he was a planner. Some would say a dreamer. I acquired these two traits from my friendship with Jack, traits which I have come to really appreciate, not only in Ham Radio, but in life.

The years shortly after World War II were the relatively early days of electronics. During the War, receivers became more and more "sensitive"—meaning they could hear weaker and weaker signals. But when a huge signal like Jack's got into the "front end" of some guy's receiver, it could "overload." The receiver would distort Jack's signal, sometimes to the point that he was unreadable. Some hams, probably including Jack, took pride in the fact that their signals were so loud that they caused some receivers to overload. That's really all you need to know about this topic in order to have a decent on-the-air conversation about it.

Many hams today are as enthusiastic about getting a new country (or entity if you prefer) as there were when I met Jack, in the mid forties. Many more. Probably ten times as many. To get started in Ham Radio you have to find only one. Most of these Hams are members of DX Clubs, DX being an abbreviation of "distance." You can find your local DX Club on the ARRL website, at a local radio store, on the Internet, or even in the phone book. You can also keep on the lookout for big antennas high in the sky. While traveling, I've spent a lot of my life looking off toward the horizon, trying to spot a stack of multi-element beams. Under those beams you will find a Ham on the lookout for new countries. Virtually all Hams like to show off their "shack," even to someone who shows up unannounced and asks if a Ham lives here. "Could you give me a demonstration some time?" is usually the only question you need to ask.

Once, many years later, my wife Sam and I were driving through Switzerland when I spotted a three-element beam on a house by the side of the road. I stopped, knocked on the door, and when the lady of the house opened it I held up my QSL card and said, "Hi. I'm a Ham from America." She held up a finger for me to wait, turned into the house and yelled, "Pierre, there's a friend of yours here."

Jack snagged his prize, the hard to get J9AAI, while I sat in his sagging wicker chair watching in wonderment. He had "worked" (meaning make contact with) the only Ham station on the island of

9

Okinawa, "rare DX" indeed. For Jack, it counted as a new "country" for his log. Some might ask if Okinawa qualified as being a country, being barely an island, but to Hams in those days, this little speck in the Pacific was assuredly a country.

Nowadays most hams call it an "entity," which is probably a bit more accurate, but not nearly as interesting, at least in my opinion. Somehow I can't imagine a DXer going into the shack saying he's going to ". . . look for a new entity."

Whether entity or country, you can bet that at this minute lots of DXers are looking for a new one, or just tuning for an old friend in Finland or New Zealand or a new friend wherever.

"QSL" and "QRZ" (pronounced Q R Zed by all Hams) are two of the dozens of so-called "Q" signals, used originally by telegraphers as shorthand. QSL means "I copy" and a QSL card is a postcard with all of the contact and station information printed on it, confirming a contact. (Nowadays, confirmations can be done on the Internet via a database called "Logbook of the World" but QSL cards still are exchanged, especially for important or unique contacts.) QRZ means "is anybody calling me?"—an unnecessary question from J9AAI, but understood by all, except the unwashed like me.

Chapter 3

The Big Beauty

After Jack worked J9AAI and had the callsign, time, date, and frequency noted in his logbook, he turned to me and said, "If I'd had the Big Beauty up, I would've worked that guy first call." He grabbed a somewhat rumpled sheet of paper from under other rumpled papers on his desk and thrust it in my direction. "What do you think of that?" he wanted to know.

I smoothed out the paper a bit and looked at it.

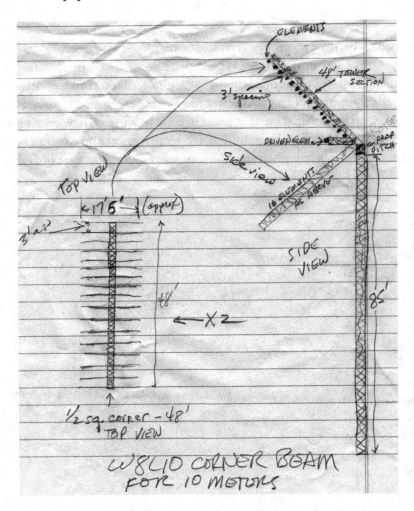

Some sort of tower was on the right margin of the page, stopping at the apex of two other smaller towers joined at a right angle. The freehand drawing showed numerous erasures. Arrows pointed at various dimensions.

"Is that beautiful or what?" Jack asked as he peered over my shoulder at the drawing. I felt like a kid who'd gotten into advanced geometry by mistake.

"It looks complicated," I blurted.

"That's my new 33-element beam," Jack said proudly. A few more optimistic pronouncements from Jack made me realize that his new 33-element beam was little more than a gleam in his eye, a rumpled drawing, and a sag in the garage ceiling where he stored his aluminum tubing.

Jack invited me to come back the following Saturday to help him put his Big Beauty together. Pleased that he trusted me, a teenage know-nothing, I told him I'd be there. He knew I would.

When I wheeled up his driveway the next Saturday, his old "little" antenna was off the top of the tower and leaning against side of the garage. The entire backyard was filled with what looked like small tower sections and piles of aluminum tubing, which Jack called elements, all precisely lined up proving they were equal length. When Jack spotted me coming he greeted me like a long-lost relative and a rich one at that. Jack informed me that I was in time to witness, nay, even participate in, one of the noblest efforts ever undertaken by mankind, the construction and erection of a one-of-a-kind antenna, a 33-element beam for Ten Meters. Modesty was not a major part of Jack's personality.

My parents had lectured me now and then about being more modest. Jack told me one day that modest people usually had a lot to be modest about. That was not Jack.

He called his new antenna a "square corner." Now and then he called it a "corner beam." He never tired of telling me about it. He wanted to be sure I understood it, I guess. I understood the words, but I didn't really get it.

"There will be 16 elements on each leg and in the center a driven element," he said. I decided however driven the element, it wasn't nearly as driven as Jack.

He told me that he could have made it a 51-element beam if he'd wanted to, but decided that if he made it that big, nobody would believe him when he told them about it. But 33, the number 33, struck his fancy, and Hams everywhere, if they really stretched their imaginations, might believe him when he told them the size of his antenna. Others, of course, would not, he predicted. "Them nonbelievers, I won't waste my time on 'em. I'm lookin' for guys with big ideas."

"You got big ideas, David?" he asked.

"I guess I better have," I blurted.

"Good. Good," said Jack. "I don't wanna waste my breath on small town boys with small time minds. What's the point of thinking at all if you don't think big?" he asked as if I had an answer. I agreed that thinking was hard work, so if you had to do it at all, you might as well think big. Jack slapped me on the back and almost knocked me down.

"Right as rain," he said. "Stick with me; you'll be a smart man." That day I got smarter than I had been. I realized that after we bolted them together, each leg of the square corner was a 48-foot long triangular tower, about a foot on a side. On paper it looked small. On the ground it looked huge. Each of what he called the reflector elements was 18 feet long and spaced on the 48-foot tower about three feet apart. All day Saturday we assembled that behemoth on the ground. The unmowed grass in Jack's backyard was trod flat by the end of the afternoon. When it finally dawned on me how big this thing would be, and how heavy, and who had promised to help at the top of the tower, I had a fleeting thought that maybe Ham Radio was way more than I had bargained for.

I have spoken to many ham conventions and meetings over the years and one of my true tales is this story of Jack's 33-element beam. I tell these audiences that instead of doing Jack's bidding I probably should have seen my psychiatrist. Actually, not only did I not have a psychiatrist, I didn't even know what a psychiatrist was. And in the 1940's, there weren't any psychiatrists in Andover, Ohio. For that matter, there weren't even any doctors! Even then, doctors knew where the money was, and it wasn't in Andover, that's for sure. A psychiatrist would have been crazy to settle there. And even a crazy psychiatrist would have quickly discovered that all of those simple folks in Andover agreed with the great movie producer and philosopher Samuel Goldwyn, who said, "Anyone who'd go to a psychiatrist ought to have his head examined." Sam Goldwyn would understand a 33-element beam, because that was show business.

The day of the Big Erection was Sunday. I've noticed that most impossible antennas get put up on Sunday. I think it's because prayer comes easier.

I had no idea how Jack and I would get that monstrous antenna to the top of the tower. And once we got it there, how the hell would we hook it to the rotator? The whole thing would hang precariously off one side of the tower.

I got home about an hour late for supper. After my parents' apprehension subsided, my father asked me what I had been doing all day. How could I explain it to him? I told him I had a new girlfriend. He wanted to know who. Since he knew every family in town, who could she be?

I don't remember how I got out of that one, but clearly at some point I would have to tell my parents that the new love of my life was Ham Radio. I've often thought that if I had really found a new girlfriend, instead of a new hobby, I would've saved a lot of money. But I would've missed out on a lifetime of fun, friendships and adventure.

A parenthetical note is that Ham Radio is more enduring than most girlfriends, and for that matter, many marriages. Lord knows how many spouses have said in a fit of frustration, "either the radio goes or I go." Given that choice, I've observed that the radio is rarely the one to go.

On Sunday morning, my parents went to the Methodist Church for what my father often said were "business reasons, certainly not because of the preacher who is a total nincompoop." Every time he said that, my mother told him to hush.

Per our agreement, I headed off in the direction of the Congregational Church, where I went to Sunday school—when I couldn't think of anything better to do. Today, of course, I *had* something better to do.

At Jack's place I discovered a genuine congregation; a backyard full of true believers. It turns out that other Hams had driven 60 and 70 miles for Jack's big antenna party. If anyone shared my fear that this thing would never get to the top of the tower in one piece, they sure weren't saying so. These grizzled veterans of the antenna wars had seen the best of them go up. And come down.

Sometime between 8 p.m. last night and 8 a.m. this morning, Jack had clamped a long pipe with a pulley contraption on it to the top of the tower. Somebody called it a gin pole. "A big gin pole." A good name, I thought, because you'd have to be drunk to drag that thing up there and bolt it to the top of the tower in the dark. Jack hooked a loose end of the rope from the block and tackle at the end of gin pole to the square corner. Jack and I climbed the tower as a few of the beefier guys grabbed the rope. Up went that gigantic antenna, "like sheeeiiit through a tin horn," as one of the onlookers observed.

As Jack and I bolted the giant antenna to the rotator, he looked at me and said, "See, David; no hill for a climber." No hill for a climber. I learned one of my favorite phrases at the top of a tower, eighty-five feet above a bunch of hams who would have cricks in their necks that night for looking skyward. Up there in the sky that Sunday morning I learned more than I ever had learned in Sunday school: I learned that success is a natural high.

Amazingly, Jack's Big Beauty, our Big Beauty, was rotating before noon. They broke out beer (and Coke) and drank many toasts to the biggest Ten Meter antenna in Ohio—probably the country—maybe the world. Definitely, the world. The biggest. What a work of art. What a wonderful day.

The gang of Hams plus me crowded into Jack's back porch shack for a trial. The rig, as Jack called this porchful of equipment, was fired up. Jack's tubes only went dark when Ohio Edison failed, which in those early days after the war, happened fairly regularly

Jack sat in his big swivel chair and turned up the volume on his receiver. He started tuning the band. The first station he heard was a W6, way out there in California, "the land of fruits and nuts," according to one of the onlookers. The W6 talked and talked and talked.

"He's long winded," said one observer.

"What else is new?" asked another.

Several people commented about those damn California kilowatts as they stood there in front of those huge tubes in Jack's transmitter.

Jack directed all eyes onto the "S meter" of his old Super Pro. The needle, which measured the strength of the incoming signal, hovered up near the maximum reading, hardly wavering in the golden glow. Mostly for my benefit, I'm sure, Jack announced with the solemnity reserved for building dedications and baptisms that his Big Beauty was pointed at California. He began to rotate the antenna and a couple of the old-timers ran outside to watch. The "S meter" began to waver, then slowly move backwards across the scale. When the ends of the antenna were on California, the W6's voice was nearly lost to the band noise. The signal came up a teeny bit as the antenna rotated further, but when the back of the square corner pointed toward California, that long-winded W6 was barely perceptible. All those in the shack knew that none of those damn sixes would ever crack a pileup that Jack was in.

"God!" said the guy with the grey stubble. "That's what I call a front to back!" Jack rotated the antenna back toward California and the long-winded ham's voice pushed the needle to the very top of the "S meter." The W6 was signing off.

"Give him a call," several of the old-timers in the crowd said.

As W6MLZ signed off, Jack spoke into his microphone. The two big tubes in his transmitter turned white hot. "W6MLZed," he said, "This is W8LIO." A nervous silence in the shack. Had the Californian not heard Jack with his new Big Beauty?

Then, the tense moment was broken when W6MLZed came on and said, "God! Where are you? Next door? You knocked me off my chair!" Cheering erupted around the room as Jack told the flabbergasted Californian that he was in Andover, northeastern Ohio and using a 33-element beam.

"I believe it," said the Californian. Clearly here was a ham with an imagination. Jack liked him immediately.

We rotated the beam for the guy in California. Ray was his name, and Ray told us what we had already surmised: This was one hell of an antenna. In those days you couldn't measure what they called the front-to-back ratio, but Jack speculated that it must have been in the vicinity of 100 db, whatever that meant.

I, of course, didn't know what *any* of this meant, or really understand much of what I'd just witnessed, but obviously, it was devoutly to be desired, and I happily shared the occasion. Needless to say, for a gawky teenage know-nothing to gain unquestioned acceptance into this group of veteran Hams was exhilarating. It was my entrance into one of the world's most exclusive clubs. I basked in the glory of the moment.

Alas, the glory was short-lived. For though Jack had QSOs with over 100 countries in the next three days on Ten Meters, the following Thursday night the winds came through Andover as they did every now and then. Winds in Andover weren't measured in miles per hour; they were measured in trees leveled, roofs off, and, in the case of this particular wind, 33-element beams down.

Jack didn't cry over his loss. In fact, in a curious way, he seemed rather proud that his antenna had not withstood the horrendous windstorm. It proved that it was big enough.

The "Big Beauty" had gone up and it worked! It was a glorious if fleeting moment in the history of Ham Radio.

Today as yesterday, when Hams finally get their own "Big Beauties" up in the sky, they get on the air with a new energy, and have a lot of QSOs (conversations/contacts) to see if the antenna lives up to their hopes. Most of the time it does, and often exceeds them! Do antenna parties still happen today? You bet they do, but often a professional "antenna guy" will install the antenna on the tower or roof, perhaps because of local ordinances, city engineers, Hitlerian home owners' associations, or other nosy and/or concerned individuals who worry about more dire consequences than the darkest imagination could possibly conjure. Or perhaps it's because the Ham population is getting older, just like the general population, and the XYL (that's short for ex-young lady IE: wife) won't allow her everlovin' to climb the tower any more.

Even if a pro does the critical stuff, lots of local Hams show up as well, just to take part in the fun and help out by holding ropes, taking pictures, offering advice or working the jin pole. (It's also" jin," incidentally, as well as "gin" as I imagined it as a teenager. "Gin" is the navy spelling, jin is the oilfield spelling. Take your choice. The word gin is an ancient short-form of the word Engine. There's no doubt that Jack's gin pole supplied the power advantage to get that gigantic antenna to the top of his tower.) I've often thought, of all the parties I've gone to in my life, there's no genre more fun than a good, old-fashioned antenna party. Now I know how the Amish feel after they've raised a barn.

The phrase "crack a pileup" is vintage Ham Radio-ese meaning that your signal is unbeatable by any of the hundreds of Hams calling a rare one. With his Big Beauty, everybody just knew that Jack would be the loudest station on the frequency.

Most readers should realize that I now wanted a Ham Radio license. When the Hams who'd come to the antenna party headed home, I asked Jack about getting my own license. He said, "No hill for a climber, David! All you have to do is learn some radio theory, some rules, and the code." "What code?" "The Morse code," said Jack. "Every ham you'll ever meet knows, or at one time knew, the Morse code at least 13 words a minute. I know it; I just never use it."

Jack rummaged around through stacks of old magazines in his full-to-the-brim bookcase and he came up with an ARRL License Manual. "Here," he said. "It's only a couple of years out of date, but the FCC doesn't change things much anyway. Most of this information is probably still good on the test. The code's in here too. You should subscribe to QST, too." He tossed me a couple of smallish, thin magazines, well-read from the look of them. "They only cost eight or ten bucks a year. They've got useful info in 'em."

Now, some 60-plus years later I'm still a member of ARRL which is how you get a subscription to QST as well as a lot of other good stuff. You don't have to learn the Morse code to get a Ham license these days, but for reasons unknown, now that it's no longer a licensing requirement, Morse code is more popular than ever. The radio theory and rules you need to know have become more complicated, like everything else in the last 60 plus years, but it's no hill for a climber.

Chapter 4

I Want A Ticket

When I got home, my mother asked me about the magazine sticking out of my back pocket. It was, of course, the License Manual, which became my constant companion until I got a license. The QST Magazines were under my shirt. Why did I keep news of the new love of my life from my parents? Don't teenage boys always try to keep everything from their parents? And always fail?

I guess I worried about their reaction to Amateur Radio. Obviously, whatever else it might involve, this hobby was not going to be cheap. To my surprise they both seemed pleased with the idea. My father said he had seen that big tower on West Main Street and wondered about it. To him, Ham Radio looked like a lot of fun. My mother leafed through the License Manual and said it looked like a lot of work. They were both right, as usual.

My father told me not to climb the tower.

I went to my bedroom and leafed through the old License Manual that Jack had given me. That made it clear that getting a Ham ticket wasn't going to be easy for a young guy who wasn't much of a student.

From playing baseball against other high school teams in Ashtabula County, I learned about courses called "electives" in some schools, especially those larger than Andover High School with its 300 or so students. My first grade class had 25 kids in it and my senior class had 25 kids in it. Not the same 25, but about half of them I'd known well for a dozen years. A few kids quit school, a few flunked, a few moved, and more than a couple were tossed out. A few new kids came to town, forever known as the "new kids." Several joined us from the year ahead of us. These older kids had taken the art of not studying to its ultimate—all the way to another year in school, certainly an unintended consequence of their sloth.

I looked around Andover School for easy electives. I'd been told that many were easier than the required classes, so reluctant students (my category) could concentrate on important stuff like baseball, girls, and Ham Radio license exams.

My Mother actually discovered the electives before I did. Ninth-graders only had two: typing and Latin, both harder than the standard offerings of woodshop for boys and home economics for girls. I would have gleefully taken woodshop, even though I didn't care one whit about building things out of wood.

But my mother insisted that I take typing and the dreaded Latin. I asked a very rational question: why would anybody study a language that nobody speaks? My father told me that Catholic priests gave their sermons in Latin and the Methodist minister might as well talk Latin for all the sense his sermons made.

My Mother told him to hush. Then she said that good friends of hers taught Latin and typing and they had both told her that future college students would need these classes once they got into a real academic environment.

When I got to the typing class, I discovered that the typewriters didn't have any printing on the keys! How was I to know what I was typing? "Memorize which keys are for which letters," was the practiced response of the very prim Miss Jacobs. How could I memorize radio theory, Morse code, stuff for school tests, and typewriter keys all at the same time? No answer to that one. There was a plus. All of my typing classmates were girls. Girls provided just the kind of distractions that would impede my progress toward a ham license. Even though I carried the License Manual everywhere, the information in that little booklet did not make it from my back pocket to my brain by osmosis or any other means.

Whenever anybody said, "Whatcha got in your back pocket?" I'd pull it out, show it to them, and tell them I was studying to be a Ham. "You can talk to people all over the world," I'd say. "I'm gonna build my own transmitter so I can get on the air as soon as I get my license," I'd say. "I'm gonna have a big tower in my backyard with a big antenna on it," I'd say. "You want to come out to Jack Rodebaugh's place and see his shack? It's really great," I'd say. "It's the world's best hobby," I'd say.

If the person who asked the question started to look sorry that he'd mentioned it, I'd usually follow up with, "How 'bout it?"

It amazed me how often I got an "I don't think so," or a shrug in response to my pitch.

I'd watch, disappointed but not surprised, when the person would make his getaway. "No imagination," I'd mutter to myself, convinced I'd offered the keys to the Holy Grail. Some education critics contend that public school does everything it can to kill kids' imaginations. Fortunately for me, I didn't pay enough attention in school to have my imagination killed if, in fact, that was their intent.

I had no trouble imagining myself a Ham.

Sharing my enthusiasm for a hobby I barely understood prepared me in some small way for the time later in life when I had to sell television program ideas to network executives. I could get hooked on unique programing ideas as easily and quickly as I got hooked on the idea of Ham Radio. The difference is that television programs come and television programs go, but Ham Radio has been with me for the long haul. That's true for a lot of the Hams I've met and I know why. It's MAGIC. When I first realized that it was magic, back there in those days before I got a license or had even taken a test, I added it to my pitch.

And if anyone needs proof that parents are invariably right, Latin and typing proved to be two of the most valuable subjects I ever studied, even though I barely got a "C" in each, and that only because my mother knew the teachers, I have no doubt. In case you're wondering, E Pluribus Unum on the Great American Seal means roughly "from many, one" referring to the 13 colonies joining to create a country. Ubi Ignes Est means Where's the Fire? That's the kind of stuff I remember.

Chapter 5

Another Wannabee In My Wicker Chair

Alas, going over to Jack's and hanging out was a lot easier than studying the Morse code and radio theory, and much more fun. I figured I would learn a lot just by proximity to Jack's shack. He had invited me to come over any time and I took him up on it.

The next Saturday, after I'd done a few chores, I headed down to my mom's store, checked in with her, and got a quarter for my afternoon chocolate milkshake at Bloomer's (actually they only cost 12 cents, and I got to keep the change.) My milkshake was a daily ritual even on days I was too sick to go to school. After slurping it down, I jumped on my bike and headed out West Main Street to Jack's. After pausing to stare at the twisted wreckage in his backyard, I looked up to see that the little three-element beam once again perched at the top of a now somewhat shorter tower.

I figured that Jack hadn't cleaned up the debris in the backyard yet because it gave him an opportunity to wax eloquent about his wonderful 33—element beam for anyone who showed the slightest interest. In those innocent days on the heels of World War II, Hams stopping by for an "eyeball QSO" rarely gave advanced notice of their impending visit.

Not surprisingly, I found Jack in the shack calling faraway stations. I *was* surprised, however, to find Whitey Taylor sitting in my sagging wicker chair. I knew Whitey, one year ahead of me in school, from our Boy Scout troop and the baseball team. His real name was Harold. He got his nickname because of his pure white hair and his light complexion. And I suspect he wasn't all that fond of the name Harold.

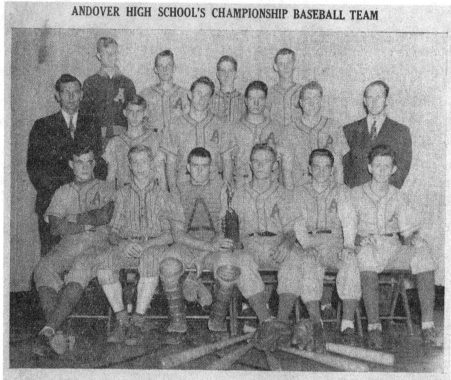

ANDOVER HIGH SCHOOL'S CHAMPIONSHIP BASEBALL TEAM

Pictured above is Andover High School's championship baseball team which went thru the fall season losing only one game in their pre-tournament American League schedule to Dorset. In the elimination tournament which brought Andover their first title in the school's history, they defeated Austinburg 22 to 4, Spencer 3 to 2 in an extra inning and then took the defending champions from Lakeville Rowe 4 to 2, also in an extra inning game. As county champions they will enter the sectional play-off next spring.

Members of the team are (First row, left to right) David Bell, Harold Taylor, Ronald Baker, Roger Litwiler, Paul Mullin, Russell Hall. (Middle row) Supt. P. D. Koeppe, Carl Hartz, Ronald Strait, James Dutton, Coach Walter C. Higgins. (Back row) Bill Sevon, Manager; Dick Daniels, Dean Taylor, Harry Smock.

Courtesy Andover Citizen

Here we are in our team photo, with me front row left staring off into space, and Whitey right next to me. Don't ask me why we're wearing different uniforms. Could be that our school couldn't afford new ones for everybody. Andover High School didn't play football because we couldn't afford the equipment.

It turns out that Whitey, who had been on vacation with his family during the big antenna party, had been studying for some time to get his Ham license.

Hal, which he gave as his handle after he got on the air, lived right next door to Jack and had been working on his radio theory and Morse code. He even had his own shortwave receiver and listened to Morse code every night. I told him that I had a few of the letters memorized—that "A" was dot-dash and "B" was dash-dot-dot-dot, and "C" was dot-dash-dot-dash. Whitey informed me that when speaking Morse code, it was dits and dahs. "A" was dit-dah for instance and "C" was dah-dit-dah-dit. I had remembered the "C" backwards. He knew the whole alphabet and all of the numbers and some of the punctuation. He was working on memorizing the circuit diagrams we'd have to draw on the test and saving up to buy the parts for a transmitter he planned to build so as soon as he got his license, he could get on the air. I suggested we study together. Maybe what he already knew would rub off on me.

We went next door to see his receiver. It was a Hallicrafters S 40. He turned it on and waited for it to warm up. When it did, what we heard, of course, was Jack. Whitey told me that he always knew when Jack was on. He covered up everything on every frequency. For those few moments when Jack wasn't transmitting, Whitey could tune his radio to listen to Morse code, which he called CW. It turns out that CW was short for "Continuous Wave". Some useful information came my way without studying. We heard a CW signal. Whitey said this guy was sending almost slow enough for him to copy some of it. He wrote down a few of the letters that he heard before Jack came on and sent that CW signal to radio hell.

Obviously, Hal was way ahead of me. He showed me his war surplus Morse code key, which had "J-38" etched into its Bakelite base. He had the key hooked up to what he called a "code practice oscillator" that he had built from parts scrounged from Jack. He practiced sending the code with this homebrew outfit. He sent me "dit dah." "A," I said. "Good," he said. I was on my way. Hal was going to be my inspiration and my booster as I attempted to get up to speed.

I decided I needed to build my own code oscillator so I could practice my sending (which is a lot easier than receiving). I knew about a source of radio parts (in addition to Jack's numerous junk boxes) that I had actually discovered years earlier but had no need for until now. Here's how that discovery came about: Sometime during the war, my mother told me that we were having an important visitor who would be staying with us for a couple of days, since Andover had no hotels and motels hadn't been invented yet. Our visitor, Ray Dunham, came from Cleveland. He had contacted my father because he wanted introductions to farmers who owned lakefront property (swampfront I always called it) on Pymatuning Lake. He wanted to subdivide it, whatever that meant.

The much-anticipated day arrived, and I was on the best behavior possible for a ten-year-old and so far hadn't spilled anything on my new shirt. The largest automobile I had ever seen pulled up in front of our house and we all went down the steps off the front porch to greet our visitor. He appeared from behind his car, "dressed to the nines" as my mother used to say, though not at that moment. I greeted Mr. Dunham who was actually about my size. The fancy hat with the feather that he wore made him appear taller, but he wasn't fooling me. We were eyeball to eyeball. I expected someone emerging from a gigantic auto to look, well, gigantic. After our introduction, he asked me to bring in his suitcases, please, both strapped to a chrome and wood rack that had folded down from behind the two spare tires on the rear of the car, which in conversation I learned to be a 1926 Rolls Royce. Its steering wheel sprouted from the wrong side of the driver's seat, I noticed.

After I had deposited the second suitcase in our guest bedroom and came down to join the gathering in our living room, Mr. Dunham arose to greet my return, reached in his pocket and pulled out a wad of bills "big enough to choke a horse" as my father often said, but not on this occasion. He unrolled them and finally got down to a few singles among the 100s and 20s and handed me a dollar. My father had prepared me for this to happen so I dutifully gave the bill back to him, mumbling something like, "thank you, but . . ." when he folded the bill and stuck it in my front shirt pocket. "Young man," he said, "when somebody gives you a dollar, you take it." I looked at my father, who shrugged and nodded, and I thanked our rich visitor so profusely that he ended up having to wave me off. Since then, anybody who wanted to give me a dollar (or any number of dollars for that matter) found a willing recipient. I rationalized that if giving me money made them happy, why should I deprive them?

What does all this have to do with a box full of radio parts? I'm getting to that.

After sitting through several meals on my very best behavior, speaking only when spoken to, I heard Mr. Dunham ask my father if any Negroes lived in Andover. My father thought a moment and said, "No." I blurted out, "What about Percy Johnson?" "Oh, that's right," said my father. "I forgot all about Percy. His family has been here forever. He has a little radio repair shop on the square," referring to the Andover town park, which sat New England style at the confluence of Ohio Routes 6 and 7, ringed by businesses of all kinds. Our dry goods store stood on the southwest side of the square with Percy's tiny little shop on the northeast side, kitty corner from each other, as the locals would say.

As if I'd jinxed it, that night our living room RCA table-top radio with the fancy wooden case quit working, "crapped out" as my father put it, and the next morning I got the chore of putting it in my wagon and taking it over to Johnson Radio Repair for fixing as quickly as possible because Mr. Dunham enjoyed listening to classical music at night.

Naming the town's only African-American family was my sole contribution to the conversation during Ray Dunham's first visit to Andover. Our big RCA radio "crapping out" put me face-to-face with the one local who knew about radio (other than Jack) and who, as it turned out, had a big box of radio junk. I told Mr. Johnson (he told me to call him Percy; everybody did) that my father had an important guest in town and would like the radio fixed as soon as possible. So Percy put it on the bench while I stood there, took the fiberboard back off it, plugged it in and looked inside. It didn't work. He unplugged it, pulled one tube, rummaged around and found a new one, plugged it in, and Eureka, it worked! I decided then and there that Percy Johnson was a genius. He put the radio back in my wagon and gave me a bill to give my dad. I took the radio home, plugged it in, and everyone was pleased. Our town's one African-American had saved the day.

26

After that first visit to Percy's, in the years that followed, I sometimes stopped there following my afternoon milkshake at Bloomer's just to watch him fix radios. It was there that I learned to love the smell of melting solder.

Years later, while attempting to copy Morse code that Hal sent me with his code practice oscillator and J-38 key, I decided that it'd probably be more fun to build my own code practice oscillator like Hal's than to try to decipher Morse. Hal found the diagram that Jack had drawn him for his oscillator, loaned it to me, and I headed over to Percy's place to see what parts he had, since Jack was in Cleveland working at Brush Development Co. Percy looked at the diagram and fished out all of the parts I would need, including an old dead radio, which I could use as the chassis and case. He made a few substitutions he said would be okay, noted them on the diagram, and I headed home with a boxful of parts and a borrowed soldering iron and some solder. It was my first building project, and while the underside of the chassis looked like someone had thrown a handful of wire in it, it worked! I was on my way.

Our rich friend from Cleveland liked me for some reason and one afternoon asked me if I knew how to drive. Since I was going on eleven, the answer was self-evident. He marched me out to the Rolls, showed me the brake, clutch, and gas pedal and started the big old engine. He told me to depress the clutch, which took some muscle, showed me how to put the transmission in first gear and slowly, very slowly let the clutch out while applying some pressure to the gas pedal. So it was, during the war, that I first drove a car, and a Rolls Royce at that! We went around the town square, with considerable help steering from Mr. Dunham, this being decades before the invention of power steering. I wasn't going to tell my parents, but Mr. Dunham spilled the beans that night at dinner, and they seemed pleased, much to my astonishment.

My father actually arranged for Mr. Dunham to buy some lakefront farm land, which made both the farmers and Mr. Dunham happy. Soon Andover had the beginnings of its first subdivision! Ray Dunham stayed at our house fairly often in those waning days of the war. He always gave me a dollar for every little thing I did for him. And I took them. Once, I asked my mother why they approved of me taking money from Ray Dunham. My mother said something I've never forgotten, "It's not about you—it's because he enjoys giving away money."

Years later, U.S. Treasury agents showed up at my mother's store and quizzed her about Mr. Dunham. "Had he ever seemed to have a large amount of cash?" they wanted to know. "Oh, no," my mother said, "in fact we loaned him money a couple of times." My family was suspicious of government and especially the IRS, like most people in this conservative little corner of Ohio. The IRS didn't get what they sought in Andover, whatever that might have been.

I spent many hours sending the code on the code practice oscillator I built, using the J-38 Morse code key borrowed from Jack, who gave it to me saying, "I don't use it anyway." Jack loved his D104 microphone, which was made just 30 miles north of Andover in Conneaut, Ohio (pronounced

Conn'-ee-aught by the locals). Jack was a devoted phone man. So I was destined to become a phone man too and wondered under the circumstances why I had to learn the Morse code 13 words per minute. No good answer to that one, and today I wouldn't have to, but I probably would anyway because CW is such a traditional part of this traditional if cutting edge hobby.

Chapter 6

Radio Row, Street of Dreams

I needed my own shortwave receiver. I knew just the one I wanted. Once every six weeks or so, we three Bells would go to Cleveland's wholesale district to buy stuff for our dry goods store.

Rather than leave me alone in Andover, my parents would take me along to Cleveland, a trip I really looked forward to. They would drop me off on Prospect Street, "Radio Row" as all of the Hams called it, and I was free to roam through the radio stores until time to meet them for lunch at noon.

Radio Row was dream central, Cleveland style. You could overhear Hams discussing potential purchases, wondering if this piece of surplus was better than that other one over there in the corner. These stores contained so much radio equipment that you could hardly get up and down the aisles. In some aisles even my six-foot 110-pound body had to turn sideways to get through. Most of the brand-new post-war gear was in glass cases, to separate it from the surplus stuff and piles of parts. Most of the new gear was receiving equipment of one kind or another, because most Hams in those days built their own transmitters. Some even built their own receivers.

The new stuff cost a lot more than the surplus, so of course I wanted a *new* receiver so I wouldn't have to hope for the best with a surplus one. I knew the one I wanted and picked up a flier about it every time I visited Progress Radio. It was the biggest of Radio Row's stores, and the one which blocked the most public sidewalk with piles of surplus stuff that got wheeled out front every day, rain, snow, or shine. Equipment that had cost the government a thousand dollars sold at Progress for eight or ten bucks. Who could pass up such bargains, even if they were only good for parts?

After a couple hours of poking around, lifting lids, turning knobs, eavesdropping, and picking up fliers and catalogs, eleven-thirty would arrive; time to walk the ten or twelve blocks to Rohr's Seafood House. Rohr's was on Chester Place which dead ended into East 9th Street, right at the Roxy Theater, Cleveland's only burlesque house. I'd take my time walking past the Roxy, because the photos of the strippers didn't require much of my meager imagination. I'd get to Rohr's ahead of my parents, sit at a tablecloth-covered table, and have a Coke while waiting. Sometimes two. And I'd go through the literature I'd picked up at the radio stores, hoping my dad would volunteer to buy some stuff for me. Even he agreed that I needed a shortwave receiver in order to listen to Morse code.

Before lunch, my father would have a Manhattan and my mother would have an Old Fashioned. The service was leisurely as it often is at good restaurants. My father sometimes had a second

Manhattan, especially if my mother had excused herself to go to the Ladies Room. I discovered that the second drink provided a good time to float trial balloons past my father, even outlandish ones.

My father made the mistake of asking me what receiver I wanted. I was ready. I whipped out a flyer I'd picked up at the radio store and put it in front of him. "Hmmm," he said, "an HQ129X. Made by Hammarlund. Is that a Kraut company?" He always asked me a question that threw me off. All I could think of was sauerkraut, which my mother made with pork chops and now and then Polish sausage, a dish I had actually grown to like. Then I remembered that in the World War Two movies I'd seen, sometimes the Germans were called Krauts and I knew that my dad really hated the Germans for starting the war. My mother never said anything when my father took off on the Germans because her maiden name was Fliedner and she had no interest in being lumped in with the Nazis.

Gathering my defense I said, "Hammarlund is in New York City, I think. They made a lot of radios for the army."

My father nodded and asked me how much money I had saved up from my job stocking shelves at the Andover Grocery.

"About 42 dollars and 50 cents," I said.

"That's not much," he said.

"Geez, Dad, I only make 50 cents an hour. That's a lot!" I said.

My mother returned to catch the tail-end of our conversation.

"What do you think, Annette?" He only called my mother Annette when he wanted her to get him off the hook.

"Oh, I don't know Rupert. How much is it?" she asked. She only called him Rupert when this ball was not going to end up in her court.

"One Hundred Twenty Nine dollars," my father read from the flier.

"That's a lot of money," she said. "Dave, if we loan you the money, will you pay it back?"

When my mother lobbed the responsibility ball into my court, I knew I was in!

"I will," I said as solemnly as I could while holding back a big smile. After lunch, we went over to Progress Radio and bought the brand new HQ129X. We lashed it securely in its big box to the roof of the overloaded Ford.

"We look like a bunch of Okies," my father said. My mother didn't disagree. I didn't know what it meant, and didn't care.

That night I listen to Morse code on my own receiver. Every couple of minutes I lifted the lid to watch the 11 tubes glow.

Today as yesterday, a good receiver is an essential part of every Ham radio station (or "shack.") After a good antenna, it's probably the most important piece of gear any Ham can have. These days, receivers are usually in the same box as the transmitter and are of course called transceivers. My HQ129X receiver weighed over 50 pounds and was about the size of a big breadbox. Today, my entire transceiver weighs 9 pounds and is about the size of a loaf of Pepperidge Farm bread. I could have bought an army surplus BC 348 for a third as much money, but the BC 348, like many surplus receivers, only covered the lower of the so-called high frequencies, up to about 18 Megacycles (now called Megahertz, honoring the guy who theorized that radio signals traveled in waves). Ten Meters is at 28 Megahertz and was the first High Frequency band the FCC reopened for Hams after World War Two, on November 15th, 1945, a banner day for ham radio. There had been rumors that Hams weren't going to get their frequencies back, but like most rumors regarding ham radio's demise, these proved far from true.

With my new HQ129X, I could listen on Ten Meters and all of the rest of the high frequency bands. Besides, my receiver was the little brother of Jack's Super Pro, so I thought he'd be pleased by my choice. He was.

One hundred twenty-nine dollars in today's money is probably about $1,500, if you use 12-cent milkshakes as the benchmark. The last time I visited Andover, the chocolate milkshake cost $2.00, and *it wasn't even as thick. For $1,500 today you can get a lot more radio than was even available back in 1946. World War Two revolutionized electronics at a pace undreamed of before. Forty years after World War Two, computers came into their own and brought about a miniaturization of electronic circuitry that revolutionized the size and weight of all electronics, including Ham Radios. From before the war to after the war, the sophistication of electronic circuits grew considerably but the look of Ham stations didn't change much. They were big and clunky and gave off a lot of heat. The computer revolution hastened the miniaturization of Ham Radio, just as it revolutionized all electronic gadgets large and small.*

While virtually everything else has changed, some things remain the same in the Ham Radio world: Morse code, for example. Even though Morse is no longer a licensing requirement, many Hams prefer it to all of the other modes available to them, which include several different types of voice transmissions, various forms of digital transmissions distantly related to radio teletype, slow scan and fast scan television, and on and on. For one thing, Morse-only stations can be simple and cheap. Someone far from other Hams and Ham Radio stores can build a CW transmitter out of a junked TV set or old hi-fi.

I personally think that Morse helps my aging brain—keeps it limber. I have no real evidence for this belief, except various kinds of "brain programs" are being peddled on the Internet, which don't seem as complex as copying code. From the beginning I was never much good at Morse, and I'm still less than great at it. I guess I just don't have rhythm. But I keep trying and I tell myself that I enjoy it.

Incidentally, it took years before it dawned on me that my family was rich, at least compared to other folks in Andover, Ohio. My father pulled out two $100 bills to pay for my HQ129X and I never thought a thing about it.

Chapter 7

Home Sweet Shack

My mother came into my bedroom/shack one day, looked around, swiped her finger through some dust and said that she was going to suggest to my father that I move my junk to what she called the "sun porch" which was just a back porch before it got storm windows and a storm door to keep the weather out. The sun porch wasn't heated as part of its renovation but it was adjacent to the kitchen, which was always warm. The move was certainly all right with me and I knew my father would approve. He approved of virtually everything my mother suggested, unless it had to do with Spam.

Once during the war my mother put Spam on our plates and my father looked at the strangely rectangular piece of something or other and said, "What's that?" My mother of course told him it was the latest thing to help us win the war, called Spam, out of a can. My father took the smallest bite imaginable, chewed it, frowned, and spit it out onto his plate. I'd never, ever seen him do anything like that before. "Oh, Rupert," said my mother, "try it."

He said, "It's god-awful!"

"I've tried it, it isn't that bad," said my mother.

"It's crap!" said my father. "I think we should send all our Spam to the Krauts, that's the only way it'll help us win the war because they'll eat it and croak," he said, pushing away from the table.

"Where are you going?" my Mother asked, knowing better than to argue. (She didn't much care for it either, I suspect. I never tasted it, being the observant spectator in matters culinary.)

"To Meadville," said my Father, and off we went 25 miles to one of my father's favorite, relatively nearby restaurants.

My mother mentioned at dinner that she would like my radio stuff moved to the sun porch. My father thought it was a good idea. It would be easier for him to check and see if I was listening to Morse code.

My HQ 129-X and a couple of surplus CW transmitters from B-17s plus an SCR-522 VHF transceiver plus meters, power supplies, etc., all fit neatly on and under a desk scrounged from the 2nd floor of my Mother's store.

I had picked the biggest desk from the ones stored there and with the help of my friend Ralph Baker (who despite my entreaties, never got bitten by the ham radio bug) got it out to the little, home-made utility trailer hooked to the back of my Model A Ford.

We wrestled it down the outside stairs of the store building and hauled it the block and a half to our house on Chestnut Street, which in those days didn't have a number. Everybody just knew where everybody else lived. And there was no mailman anyway, just Post Office boxes for everybody who lived in the village limits. So the Post Office was kind of a primitive, simple version of the Internet, where the townspeople met, exchanged pleasantries, and picked up whatever missives they might have gotten from out-of-towners.

My mom's so-called sun porch was a great place for a shack. I was one of the few kids anywhere who had a real shack and hadn't even passed his ham radio license exam yet. It took me years before I figured out how to get my priorities straight.

My friend and inspiration, Hal, had passed his code test on his first try, but flunked his theory test because Jack told him that formulas for crystal frequencies would not be on the written exam so he didn't learn them. Guess what? There were ten questions having to do with crystals and frequencies and poor old Hal flunked the easiest half of the exam.

While I was grinding away on the code, I accomplished another diversion. I became an SWL, a Short Wave Listener. I learned that there were lots of wannabee hams in that second-class category, and some even sent SWL cards to ham stations that they heard. I ordered some SWL cards and combed the bands for foreign (DX) stations that I could send my SWL card to, telling them how loud they were in Northeastern Ohio and hoping for their QSL card in return. Quite a few of them sent me their QSLs. More than a few of them said they'd see me on the air.

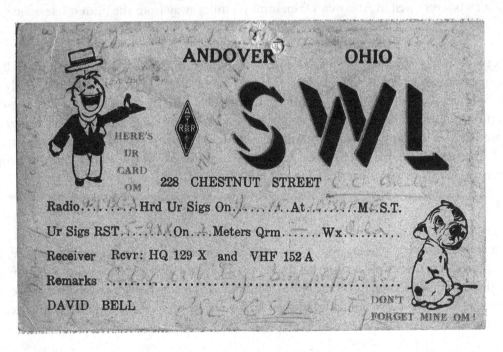

Actually, being an SWL was educational. I'd hear a foreign station and look it up, then check it on a map. Geography for hams comes with the territory. My mother thought ham radio would be educational and she was right, as usual. When my teacher asked the class if anybody knew where Ethiopia was, I was the only one who'd even heard of it, and was able to find it fairly quickly on a map. I took the occasion to remind everyone that I was studying for my ham radio license, and knowledge of geography was essential to hams, otherwise, how would they know what direction to point their antenna? Of course, I didn't have an antenna that was pointable . . . yet. That was to come soon, hopefully. I had actually bought a prop pitch motor for $10 from one of the hams who showed up at Jacks' place, so I was ready to rotate.

Being an SWL offered another benefit. With hours of listening to ham conversations I learned the lingo of ham radio. When I finally got my license, I wouldn't sound like a newbie. And I'd have enough equipment in the shack to impress even ham radio veterans. I spent virtually all of my at-home time in the shack, as even my father began to call my mother's sun porch. I studied out there too, what little studying I had time for, what with everything else going on. Even without studying, I managed C pluses in my favorite courses and C minuses in the rest of them, except for a D in Latin before I got a girl friend who didn't have much to do but study and was happy to try to drill some "Semper Fidelus" into my overloaded brain

The view out the south windows of my shack was of our one-car garage for our one car, with enough room along one side for a workbench, tools and junk of various kinds. The garage was never locked. Neither was the house for that matter, until my Father brought home a television set one day. I helped him set it up in our den because my mother wouldn't have that "ugly thing" in the living room. She was right. It wasn't much in the way of looks, but it had a huge 12 inch picture tube which was round, even though the picture, those few times when we actually saw one, was kind of square. Rabbit ears didn't work very well in Andover, Ohio, some 65 miles away from the nearest television station.

Everyone under seventy will probably have to be reminded that the mid to late 40's was the dawn of television. Every big city had at least a couple of TV stations, which actually had a broadcast schedule of sorts, in between test patterns. The difficulty was that none of these early TV stations ran much output power. Being a kid who was studying radio theory, I realized that if the transmitted signal was weak, the receiving antenna had to be big, in order to detect any kind of a picture. As soon as a television station went on the air in Cleveland, curious people in Andover wanted to watch. That included my father and me.

Since I was the self-anointed electronics expert in our family, my father gave me the chore of finding the biggest, best receiving antenna available so we could see some TV pictures on our new TV, which mostly showed us varieties of snowstorms under its worthless rabbit ears. Every so often, my father would adjust the rabbit ears on top of the Philco, which usually made the snowstorm thicker. Neighbors came over to watch the snow and now and then sat staring at a snowy test pattern, mesmerized.

My research into antennas mostly involved asking Jack what to do. "Get a sixty foot tower and a bedspring," was Jack's advice. "A bedspring?" It turned out that a bedspring was a dozen or so dipoles (remember Jack's driven element?) with what amounted to a wire mesh reflector behind them and looked a bit like a small bedspring. According to Jack it had a lot of gain and at 60 feet would be above most of the trees and could capture the signals from Cleveland regularly. Jack also knew a local handyman-entrepreneur who built towers in ten-foot sections that bolted together. He lived out near Tom Jones' junkyard on East Main Street and his backyard was full of ten-foot tower sections. He had built a jig out of steel, dropped tubing into the jig, and welded it. In fact, that's what he was doing when I found him. A deal was quickly made (he knew my father so payment on the spot was not a problem) and he promised to come over to our house, pick out the best spot, and install the tower complete with a bedspring on the top pointed toward Cleveland.

He came, installed the tower so it ran up into the air right next to the house (but not in front of any windows, my mother insisted) and he bolted it to the highest roof eave to keep it from waving in the wind. With foresight that I wasn't often known for, I asked him to hook a pulley to the top of the tower and loop a long rope through it so I could use it to pull up some wire antennas. He did, and I'd managed to create yet another diversion to learning the code. I could endlessly play around with pieces of wire, hoisting them into the air, and seeing if whatever I got up there received signals better than my last wire experiment. From Jack's big corner beam to my fiddling with all manner of wires and aluminum in the air, I've had a fascination with antennas that lasts to this day. How do they find those signals in the air? It's magic.

With the very first wire I hoisted to the top of our big TV tower I started hearing signals that had been buried in the band noise before. SWLing began in earnest. I heard stations that some stateside hams couldn't hear. What fun. My father was impressed with my wires hanging all over the yard, but most important, he actually saw an okay picture from the Cleveland television stations for the first time—a bit snowy sometimes, but we had created a genuine neighborhood miracle nonetheless. And when the neighbors saw our big TV antenna there on the west side of our house, there was a lot of angling to come over and watch some show, any show at all, please?

Everyone wanted to be in on the dawn of a new age. And as it happens, that's exactly what it was, though I certainly didn't realize it at the time. It was another diversion to keep me from learning the Morse code. My mother didn't actually much care for television. "I'd rather read," was her regular response to my father when he asked if she wanted to watch this or that program.

I wish I could say that I was too busy studying the code to watch television. The truth is what with baseball, basketball, now and then acting in a play and being president of my class plus working some days after school and on Saturdays, and now TV, I had more excuses for not learning Morse than Carter has pills, as my mother used to say.

And then Hal passed his written exam and a few months later got his license from the FCC, W8BGJ. Somehow, that event, which should have inspired me, depressed me. How could he do it and I couldn't?

Hal is now W8CY and is still active on the ham bands, though probably not as much as he once was. He's worked every single "entity" (which both he and I still call countries) that's out there to work. Now and then a new entity shows up, some country splits in half or an island gains independence from another nation, and he's in there chasing the new one just like everyone else. Hal and I see each other for a Polish hotdog and a beer at the Dayton Hamvention almost every year. Obviously, he too is a DXer, just as our mentor, Jack, W8LIO, was. Hams call mentors "Elmers" now, and maybe they did then for all I know, but I never heard the phrase until I became one, in California, years later when a kid from our Sunday school cornered me and asked if he could see my radio station. Pretty soon he was climbing my tower, making adjustments high in the air, as I had done back there in the distant past for Jack.

Mark is now N5OT and is a big time contester, a pursuit akin to DXing, but on steroids. He's also a writer, like his Elmer is every now and then. The term "Elmer" is another ham word whose origin is lost in the dits and dahs and QRM of time, just as the term "Ham" itself is. Amateur radio, with its myriad complexities and specialties, has kinship with many fraternities and sororities and social organizations like the Masons and Kiwanis, so "secret words" and mystery go hand in hand with the hobby. As far as I know though, there's no secret hand shake or sign, but there is the mysterious Woof Hong which any ham can join if he or she goes to an ARRL convention somewhere and can stay up until midnight, when all of the mysterious hocus pocus happens.

W8BGJ came to Hal through intense concentration, constant practice and persistence, three characteristics not used to describe me then and rarely even now. If those characteristics came easily to me, I'd have chosen a profession more demanding of the intellect than producing television programs. I have two excuses for Hal getting his license quicker than I did. He started earlier than I did, and his family didn't have a TV. When my father learned that Whitey had gotten his license, he told me to buckle down. He stopped inviting me to watch television with him (though I watched anyway) and whenever he walked through the shack on his way to or from his car, he'd ask me if I was listening to CW. Whenever I saw him coming, I quickly found a CW signal and turned the volume way up so my dad could hear the Morse code seeping out around my earphones. He'd nod approval whenever he heard that, though I suspect he knew he was being conned.

The "prop pitch motor" I mention in this chapter was a unique piece of war surplus. Originally intended to be on the propeller shaft of aircraft, its purpose was to change the "pitch" (the angle of the blades into the wind) of propellers for speed and power control. With the right voltage on them they turned at about one revolution a minute and were perfect for rotating big antenna arrays.

Of course the term "Spam" now usually is in reference to unwanted flotsam on the Internet. My father would have approved.

Chapter 8

The Comma Curse

Since Hal had been on the air for ages, I had to get my Ham ticket come hell or high water. But first things first. I couldn't hear W1AW's code practice well. Wire antennas are okay, but I decided I needed a big beam—not as big as Jack's big corner beam because I knew if I put one up and it came right down my parents would reconsider the wisdom of their investment in my hobby, which I reminded them as often as possible was very, very educational. And it was, of course, but I don't know how much I was actually learning. However much, the Morse code didn't become a major part of my new storehouse of knowledge, though my code speed had slowly climbed almost into the double digits. I showed my father how I could copy nearly all of what W1AW sent at 10 words per minute, but just some of the 15 wpm transmission. He patted me on the back and urged me to stick with it. "It's no hill for a climber," he'd tell me. He'd obviously been talking to Jack.

The following Sunday we went down to the Kinsman Tea Room, 12 miles south of Andover, for a Sunday afternoon roast turkey dinner with all the trimmings. (That was the only dish on the menu at the Tea Room, so they wouldn't have needed a menu, really, except they had one.) My father was not a huge fan of the place even though it was elegant and the meals were great. Their failing was they didn't serve booze. The Tea Room was proudly dry. My father and mother would have their so-called "cocktail hour" at home after the turkey dinner. During the cocktail hour I told my dad that one of the problems I had with Morse code was that sometimes I couldn't hear W1AW very well and I needed a better antenna. Having listened to a few of my code practice sessions, my father sympathized. He asked me what I needed. I was ready. "A tower and a beam antenna, kinda like Jack's," I responded.

I told him I knew exactly where my antenna tower would go, too.

Beside and behind the garage, our backyard had about a half a football field of grass (that always needed mowing.) At the far end of that grass patch, just on the edge of our very large vegetable garden (which became a Victory Garden during the war) I'd put my pride and joy: the 70-foot-tall tower that I would get our TV tower guy to fabricate for me. My mother said she didn't want me climbing towers, but after seeing Jack's monster tower she understood that towers came with the Ham Radio territory. She still hoped for that slight possibility that I might actually learn something. So she said if I could figure out a tower that I didn't have to climb, they'd help me out with it. (That means pay for it if you've forgotten parental euphemisms.)

So I could have my own tower for my own Ham antenna if I could figure out a tower design that I didn't have to climb. Then it came to me! Inspiration! Why not a tilt-over tower? Imagine one 35-foot tower with a 70-foot tower right next to it! The midpoint of the 70-foot tower hinges at the top of the 35-foot tower, and the big tower tilts right over the top of the little one. I went to the tower guy. Not a problem, he said. He'd just have to reinforce the 70-foot tower in the center so it didn't buckle when horizontal, and up it'd go. Hopefully.

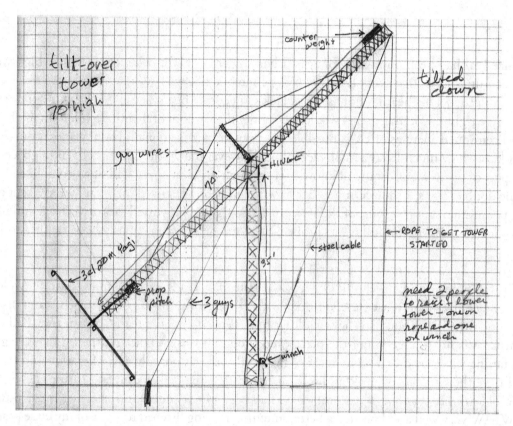

My father looked at both the design drawings and approved. "See, Dave," he said, "you can stay focused if you try. This is really a great idea!" Maybe his only child would become an engineer instead of a lawyer, which he previously pushed for. Either was okay with him and my mother as long as I graduated from college.

The tower guy moved my tilt-over tower ahead of the regular TV tower orders because it was unique and he and everybody he and I knew wanted to see how it would work. While he put my tower together, I built a three-element beam for 20 Meters in the backyard. When my mother saw that it took up almost the entire yard beside the garage, her eyebrows shot up and while I know she wanted to say more, all she said was, "My. That's big." And it was. Bigger than I thought it'd be, but its design came right out of the ARRL Handbook, so I knew that unless I'd mismeasured, it'd work. I went over my measurements for a third time just to be sure that I'd gotten them right. I had used just about every single scrap of aluminum tubing that Jack had given me. He came over to look at my big beam. He was impressed. He said something like, "You're going to burn up the ether with that one, David. As soon as you learn the code. That Morse is no hill for a climber, David, no hill for a climber. Go get it." This, from a Ham who never used Morse and had in fact, given me his Morse code key, my prized J-38.

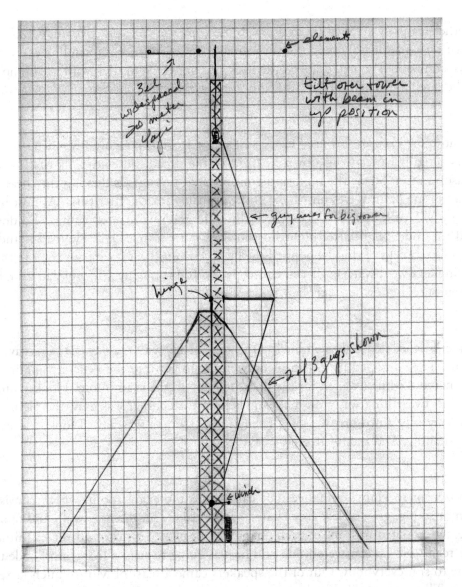

The tower went up just as I'd imagined, tilted over, the 3-element beam was attached to the prop pitch motor, and it all swung up into the sky without a hitch. What a glorious sight. What a miracle! There were no building permits, no engineering specs, nothing but hope and guts. And money. And furthermore, it worked!

After my big beam went up, there was nothing left to buy, so I had no choice but to apply myself and get ready for the big test. It had been years since Hal had gotten his license and by now he had graduated from high school and was out working—making money and making contacts.

Shortwave listening wasn't as much fun as it had seemed. I wanted to talk to these stations that I heard. I really tried to apply myself, out of character as that was.

My father regularly stopped by to listen to me copy the code practice on W1AW, and was pleased that on a good day I could now make sense out of most of the sending at 15 words per minute. Most, not all. He patted me on the back and urged me to stick with it. "It's no hill for a climber," he'd tell me. That phrase was fast becoming a cliché.

I had no more excuses. I'd used every single one I could possibly invent, up to the point that it was actually easier to sit down in front of the dread dits and dahs than to come up with a reason not to. So, as the big beam concentrated the signals, having that beam seemed to concentrate my brain waves on Morse code, probably for the first time. Almost by magic, I could copy W1AW's code practice practically solid at 15 words per minute. I'd done it! I'd conquered the code! Night after night I'd show my copy to my Dad. He read it and smiled. After a couple of weeks of this, he popped the big question: "Isn't it time we went to the FCC?" Suddenly my legs went watery. "If you can copy 15, you can copy 13," my dad said. I felt my eyes balloon out. "I guess so," I replied.

My parents scheduled their next buying trip to coincide with the day the FCC gave amateur radio exams. They dropped me off in plenty of time to get into the Federal Building and get even more nervous while I waited for the doors to open to the exam room. I looked around the waiting room. Everything was grey. The lady behind the counter was gray, the pictures on the walls were grey. The furniture was grey. Even Harry Truman was gray. I looked at my hands. They were shaking. And they were grey.

The dozen or so Ham wannabees got called into the exam room, which consisted of a half dozen or so big, grey tables, grey chairs, grey speakers on the grey wall, and tablets with pencils neatly arranged in front of each chair. We all picked a seat, and the examiner asked if we were ready. No one answered. He said he was going to send a little bit of code to adjust the volume to suit everybody. Out of the speakers came a blast of Morse much faster than I could copy. The grey examiner asked if it was loud enough. Everybody sat frozen in place, petrified. "Relax, everybody," said the FCC guy, a Ham I later learned, "that's about 25 words per minute. I just wanted to get you warmed up." The sigh from the room could be heard down on Euclid Avenue.

Everybody's pencil was poised above their pads when the Morse code began pouring from the speakers. I started copying, barely aware of what letters I was writing down. I would occasionally see a recognizable word but I ploughed ahead, copying every letter as it blared from the speakers. Then it stopped. Immediately the grey man collected the pads and we sat there in stunned silence. Before I let my pad go, I read the first couple of sentences. They made sense! Eureka!

The examiner read the first pad on his pile, counted almost audibly the number of correct letters. (You needed 65 correct letters copied in sequence in order to pass.) The first couple of guys flunked. Then one passed. So it was possible to pass. Then the examiner said, "Mr. Bell, could

I talk to you?" He hadn't talked to anybody else. Why me? I went to the front of the room. He showed me my copy. "You copied this code 100% correct," He said, "except instead of commas, you put double-dashes. This is the first time that anybody has ever copied the Morse perfectly, except for the commas. I'd like to pass you, but you didn't have 65 correct characters between any of your double-dashes. Sorry. Better luck next time."

I found myself back on the street. Dazed. What had happened? I copied the code perfectly, but I flunked because of some lousy commas? I started walking to the usual rendezvous with my parents, Rohr's Seafood House. I felt so bad I didn't even pause at the Roxy Theater to look at the half naked women on the posters. I didn't go by Radio Row. I had every piece of equipment I needed—except commas.

When my parents showed up I was on my fourth Coke. Not a good sign. My father threw his arm around my back and said something like, "Not such a great day, huh?" When he heard the story, he said, "You got perfect copy and that bozo didn't pass you? Who gives a damn about commas? That sounds like Miss Nye to me."

Miss Nye was my English teacher. I was learning to write from her and I liked her, but she wouldn't have taken double-dashes for commas either, that's for sure. She was strict.

I'd buy you a drink if they'd let me," my father said.

The ride home was quiet.

On the ride home, I managed to rationalize my idiocy. Double-dashes for commas, indeed. I realized that every time W1AW's code practice sent a comma, I'd copy it as a double dash. Why? Because ordinary Hams, when conversing in Morse, rarely used commas, but instead, when they are thinking about what to say next they send double-dashes. For the record, a comma is dah-dah dit-dit dah-dah. A double dash is dah dit-dit-dit dah. I've often thought about flunking that code test and decided that I had Morse code dyslexia.

Incidentally, the phrase "Hell or high water" is one of those phrases that everybody uses but nobody knows where it came from, sort of like "Ham." Hell or high water's meaning is clear though; it's something that's extremely difficult, bordering on impossible; sort of like me mastering Morse.

I still have and still use Jack's J-38 key that he gave me so many years ago. The ARRL sponsors an "operating event" on New Years Day called "Straight Key Night" and I still get on and make a few contacts with my prized J-38. My fist is terrible, but on Straight Key Night, it actually doesn't sound so bad.

On that ride home I resolved that I would redouble my efforts to get a Ham license, but as so often happens, resolutions sometimes get derailed.

Chapter 9

And God Created Time

My father used to say that God created time so that everything didn't happen at once. In my life though, in the early part of 1950, while everything might not have been happening at once, there sure were a lot of things going on simultaneously, including graduating from high school, sweating out acceptance to college, getting in shape for the upcoming baseball season and of course the perennial, working on getting my ham ticket, commas notwithstanding. I had to make some decisions. Establish some priorities.

Sometimes my mother stopped by to listen to me copy the code practice on W1AW, and was pleased that on a good day I could copy their transmissions 100%, including commas, at 15 words per minute. I could even copy some of the 20 wpm transmission. Satisfied that I was on the verge of mastering Morse, she asked me whether I had memorized all of those strange circuit diagrams for the written part of the test. I told her now that I had mastered the code, it was time to brush up on all of those diagrams, formulas and rules, no doubt about it.

The only big time distraction was American Legion Baseball, which was just one step down from AAA ball, and rural mythology had it that now and then major league scouts would show up unannounced and pluck some young player out of that amateur league and offer him a pro-contract, no money to speak of, but lots of glory. My father was my biggest fan. He rarely missed a game. It didn't take much for him to hang his "Out to Lunch" sign on his insurance office door, even at three in the afternoon.

When he was 16, he had been offered a contract to play for the Cleveland Indians, but my grandmother wouldn't let him sign because they played on Sundays. That may have explained my father's lifelong disdain of religion. Actually, disdain hardly describes it. After my grandmother killed the Indians, every succeeding job for him was just a job. His dreams of baseball glory got transferred to me somehow, even though all of the old timers who dutifully came to every game told me I was good, really good, but not as good as my dad. Nobody was as good as my dad.

There were no lights at the Andover ball field, so every game was a day-game, which meant that after the games, I was always home in time to copy code from W1AW, and tune around the bands to eavesdrop on CW QSOs in progress, if I could find some loud, slowish senders. Most of the loud ones were up around 20 to 25 wpm. Another problem was that hams' fists were all over the place. W1AW's sending was perfect. Ordinary hams sending was, well, let's say it had character. Sometimes so much character that I couldn't make anything out of it at all.

Probably the most unforgettable day of my life was set in motion when I broke my bat driving in a rally-starting run in the last of the ninth with a bloop single to right field. (At least that's the way I remember it these many years later.) I didn't hit many long balls, but I rarely stuck out. I was the singles guy on the team with a great eye and no arm. I played first base, and couldn't throw on the fly to third. I just never got the rhythm of throwing. It was the baseball equivalent of copying the code.

But breaking my bat was a cataclysmic event as far as my father was concerned and even though I had my own driver's license and my black, 1930 Model A Ford coupe with the rumble seat, my father insisted on driving me to Ashtabula the next day to help me pick out my next Louisville Slugger. He wanted to be sure I didn't get one that was too heavy to get around quick against a couple of tough fastball pitchers who I'd be facing in upcoming games. He told me on the way that he and mom and I would do a buying trip to Cleveland next month on the day the FCC gave amateur radio exams and this time I would come away with a license.

When we got to Ashtabula, we stopped for lunch at my father's favorite steakhouse, which served booze, of course, which, while I'd never tasted it, was probably better than the steak, which I characterized as tasty but tough, a description which made my father smile every time I said it. One reason, I suspect, that my father liked this joint was that everybody smoked, except me of course, at least in front of my father. The atmosphere was just as purple as the inside of my father's rare porterhouse.

The sporting goods storeowner greeted my father profusely, knowing that he hadn't driven up from Andover just to window shop. After finding a 32-inch bat that felt good, I handed it to my dad for his opinion. He assumed a batters-box stance. As he swung the bat at an imaginary curve ball, he fell to the floor. I saw it happen, but all I remember was the clatter of the bat to the concrete.

I couldn't move. What happened?

I remember the doctor who came with the ambulance saying that my dad was dead before he hit the floor. I called my mom's store and my favorite clerk and good friend of my mothers, Matilda, answered the phone and I told her what happened and I said I was coming home and handed the phone to the doctor. I didn't want to talk to my mom. Somebody gave me my dad's keys and his wallet and I took off for Andover in his Buick Special two-door, hell bent for election. I don't remember much about the drive, except on the radio I heard a news report that President Truman was sending our troops to South Korea to stop the North Korean invasion, and that I must have been driving fast because the big Buick seemed to be airborne over the rolling hills of northeastern Ohio.

When I pulled into our driveway my mother rushed out of the house and gave me a huge hug. When we got inside, everybody from the store and a lot of other people were there. Somebody I didn't know was in the kitchen cooking dinner. I sat in the living room with everybody for a while and then went to my room for a nap. My mother woke me up at dinnertime, and I came down and ate something, and when everyone went back to the living room, I went to the shack and listened to W1AW. I noticed that there were teardrops on my yellow copying pad and I wasn't copying very well, so I went to the living room, said goodnight to everybody, got a lot of hugs and words, and finally was released to go upstairs and go to bed. I listened to Amos and Andy on my old bedroom radio. It was my father's favorite show. I thought it was kind of boring, but I often listened with my father, hoping I could figure out what he was laughing about. It wasn't the same without him. I turned it off.

I'm not sure how long it took me to get over my father's sudden death. I may not be over it yet. But I remember the sadness I felt when I realized that my dad would never see me become a ham, never witness my first QSO, never see the fruits of his encouragement ripen.

His funeral was the biggest that Andover had ever seen. Everybody liked my dad. All of his old ball-playing buddies were there along with the Jefferson politicians and Ashtabula business people plus relatives and what seemed like half of the town of Andover. Loudspeakers had to be hastily set up on the front yard of the Methodist Church so that the overflow crowd could hear the nincompoop preacher drone on about a man he thought he knew but didn't know at all. I was asked to say something, and I'm told that all I said was, "I'm sorry I'm not as good a baseball player as you were."

My father's death was a bigger void in my life than I could have possibly realized at the time.

I never played baseball again.

Chapter 10

Headlong into the Unknown

A huge shadow hung over all young men in 1950. It was more than a shadow, really; it was a war. Congress called it a "conflict" so they didn't have to declare it a war, but Americans were dying there and it sure as hell looked like a war to me. If you leave college for any reason, your draft number is sure to come up, and you're conscripted to fight the Commies. Korea was one of the best reasons for the popularity of higher education in the early '50's. In order to stay out of Korea, you had to stay in college. I was apprehensive because college might not be all that easy for a "C" student like me.

Perhaps because my mother told them she'd pay the full $850 per year "inclusive fee"— tuition, room and board—I'd been accepted at Hiram College. I applied there because it was small and I liked the campus, and besides, it was only 50 miles from home. Also, Hiram has a tradition of everybody always saying "Hi" to everybody they walk past. Sounds corny, but it made the place very friendly. Another plus: Hiram allowed freshmen to have cars. And the biggest plus: they ran a showboat on the Ohio River!

My smart girlfriend who got me through Latin in high school went to Oberlin College just east of Cleveland, a really top-notch college then and now. My friends told me that Oberlin was hoity-toity and that the music building didn't need any stairways. I didn't know what that meant back then, but I was considering Oberlin anyway until I discovered they didn't allow students to have cars, only bicycles. I sold my bicycle years ago, thank you very much! And I probably wouldn't have been accepted there anyway. Besides that, Hiram operated the Showboat *Majestic*, the last traveling showboat in America. It plied the Ohio River and its tributaries every summer, presenting old time melodramas and vaudeville to the rubes in river towns like East Liverpool and Dilly's Bottom. According to Bud, the *Majestic's* philosopher/deckhand, Dilly's Bottom got its name because it had huge *piles* of coal and ore along its riverbank, awaiting barges to load them up and haul them up or down river. Bud said, "You can tell Dilly's Bottom by the piles." That's deckhand humor, folks.

When I left for college, of course I took my HQ129X receiver with me so I could keep my code speed up. When the guy the college had chosen as my roommate came into our room for the very first time, he took one look at that big receiver and said, "Are you a Ham?" I smiled. "I've been wanting to get a license too," he said. Jean (Doc) Canaday and I formed an instant friendship. We quickly settled into our room in a "temporary" pre-fab building, which Hiram got from the Fed's war surplus and used for 30 years or more, giving new meaning to the word "temporary." Doc and I walked around the campus looking for Ham Radio antennas on the buildings. It took a half an hour to cover the entire campus. On the walk we got to know each other. I told Doc about my double-dash fiasco.

51

After Doc absorbed my sorrow over flunking the code test, he said, "Well, it puts you ahead of me, anyway." I think he was trying to cheer me up. He did.

Our incoming freshman class included, there were only 450 students total enrolled in Hiram College for the fall of 1950, so it wasn't a big surprise that it had no ham club. Statistically, back in the 50's, Hams ran about one per thousand people. Doc and I decided we'd start The Hiram College Amateur Radio Club and Drinking Society as soon as we settled in. Settling in took a bit longer than we had anticipated. My imagined fears turned out to be prophetic. College was a lot tougher than high school.

Before long, another freshman from just down the hall spotted my HQ129X, walked right through our open door, stuck out his big mitt and said, "Hi, I'm W2FYI." Steve Crawford had passed his Class B exam the year before, after less than a year of study. His father had taken him to licensing classes at a local radio club once a week. He called it a piece of cake. He wanted to be an engineer. Doc of course was pre-med. I was nothing. I had no idea what I wanted to be.

As much as the three of us differed, one night at the Bucket of Blood Saloon, after one beer too many, Doc proclaimed us The Three Musketeers, but to the rest of the dorm I suspect we were the Marx Brothers. We often hung out together and usually talked ham radio, which to the unwashed sounds like Greek, or maybe calculus. We spent a lot of time on the Ham Radio theme when we weren't studying, (or, in my case, trying to get into a class that wouldn't take up every spare minute with homework).

I'd barely squeaked by my high school math classes, except for Plane Geometry, which I aced because I had a great first-year teacher who knew how to make that subject come alive. And apparently I got lucky with the Ohio State test in math, so my college counselor (Andover High School had no counselors, so I didn't know how to deal with one) signed me up for Advanced Algebra, convincing me that with my test scores, Advanced Algebra would be a breeze. At that time, Hiram had what they called the "single-course study plan" which meant that you took one class intensively for seven weeks and got a year's worth of credit. So I started right out with a 9 AM, three-hour class of Advanced Algebra five days a week. The homework the first day took me until midnight and I had no idea what I was doing. How could I go to my counselor and tell him I wasn't as smart as he thought?

After the second day of advanced gibberish, I was as close to depression as I ever get. I told my teacher that I didn't know what the hell he was talking about and I needed to get out of the class. He assured me that I seemed to be doing fine. How would he know? I hadn't said a word in class, we hadn't had a test, I hadn't turned in a homework paper and I didn't have a clue. He asked me a question. I didn't know the answer. He asked me another question. It was like Greek. "Okay," he said. "Go see your counselor."

My counselor told me that all of the easy classes were full, but managed to get me into English 101, which he assured me wasn't too tough as long as English was not my second language. I called my mother and told her I'd gone from Gibberish to English and she seemed okay with that. She probably figured that I wouldn't flunk basic English. She was right, but I had to work like hell to eke out a "C." The only reason I passed college English was that I'd taken Latin in high school. Who knew that you took Latin to learn English? My mother did, that's who.

During that freshman year I learned that Doc was very conscientious. I did what was necessary to get "C's" and an occasional "B," and Steve did a lot of partying. It helped that he was smart, because whenever a car went to the Dew Drop Inn, the liquor-license name of the Bucket of Blood a.k.a. the Bloody Bucket, Steve would hitch a ride and borrow ". . . a couple of bucks for a pitcher of brew." It didn't come as a surprise when Steve let it be known that his parents were very strict. When home on Long Island, he didn't drink, smoke, go out after dark, or carouse. That's how he got his Ham ticket in only a year. He didn't have any fun. At Hiram, he made up for his Puritanical upbringing, and then some. That's disguised advice to parents in case you missed it.

My first year at Hiram I slogged up a steep, rocky, academic hill. Even so, I carved out time to increase my code speed and Doc had time to learn Morse, with a little help from Steve and me.

Dave Bell, W6AQ

While I worked my way through English 101, I brushed up on the circuit diagrams and FCC rules, and felt ready to confront the comma-obsessed FCC examiner for a second (and hopefully final) time. The deal at the FCC was that you take the Morse code test (the hardest half of the test), first; if you pass that, you take the theory test, which, while a headful of circuits, formulas, and facts, was merely a molehill compared to 13 words per minute Morse mountain.

This time Doc came with me to the Federal Building in Cleveland, just to get a taste of what he had to look forward (?) to. Everything was still grey in the FCC offices. That same inspector gave the test. He took one look at me and said, "I remember you. Double dashes."

"What a thing to be remembered for," I thought.

Once again, to set the volume, he sent code at 25 words per minute, but I was unintimidated. Even so, when the test started, the speed seemed fast. I got off to a bad start. I had to concentrate! I couldn't bear to leave that room and have to tell Doc that I'd flunked—again.

Somehow I got focused and started copying. When I turned in my paper it was smudged and covered with sweat. Old comma-obsessed called my name first. I passed! The inspector said, "You didn't copy as well this time, but you did well enough to pass and there are no double-dashes and even a few commas. Congratulations." The other half-dozen or so wannabee Hams didn't know what the hell he was talking about. I sat in my seat, smiling. I'd done it. As one name after another was called, it turned out that I was the only one to pass the dreaded Morse code half of the test. I think to this day that the examiner ran that tape fast. Or that record, or whatever it was. It may have been a wind-up Victrola for all I know, with too tight a wind! Or maybe he was sending Morse on his Vibroplex paddle!

Everybody just kind of sat frozen in his chair after they heard they'd flunked. "You'll get it next time," I said to no one in particular but everyone in general. One older guy who looked at least 50 said, "This is the eighth time I've been here."

"Well, every cat has nine lives," I said to him, apropos of nothing.

I think I blurted out that ridiculous non sequitur from nervousness. My hands were actually shaking—even after I'd managed to get myself pulled together to copy the Morse code—not as well as I could do it at home by any means, but well enough to pass.

The old guy looked at me as if I smelled bad, but then he nodded and smiled. "You're right. I'll get it next time," he said. I hope he did.

The examiner, seeing me shake, asked if I'd like to take a break before sending the code. His suggestion made me even more nervous. Did he think I'd flunk the sending test? I went out into the hallway and had a cigarette. Then I had another. When I went back in I'd calmed down some. I sat down in front of the Morse key and started sending. My sending was really sloppy, but fast enough and accurate enough to pass, though I suspect the inspector wasn't paying much attention, since receiving the code is everybody's Waterloo. I'd never heard of anybody flunking the sending test, although there could always be a first! I took the written test and knew I had passed as soon as I finished drawing my last circuit diagram. I was right. I'd finally done it. I could feel my father patting me on the back, saying, "See Dave; no hill for a climber."

I called my mother with the good news and she was really happy—I had finally done it. I told her I was going to Rohr's Seafood Restaurant for lunch. She thought that was a wonderful idea. Doc and I went to Rohr's and celebrated my nerve-wracking victory. He'd never tasted seafood that good in his entire life! After lunch he told me he'd really never liked seafood before. I'd made a convert.

Five or six months later my license finally came in the mail. I was W8GUE. "Gooey," Jack said as soon as he heard it. He pumped my hand in his ham-fisted shake. "I knew you could do it, David. Congratulations." At least he didn't say it was no hill for a climber.

Ironically, after all of those years eagerly anticipating the moment I'd get a ham license, I was working so hard at Hiram that I had almost no time to get on the air. Even so, every time Doc and I headed up to Andover for a weekend, we'd put the HQ129X and our laundry in the trunk of my bronze 1950 Ford, a going-to-college gift from my mother, who told me that my dad wanted me to have it. (She had never particularly liked my Model A. I'll admit it was a bit of a rattletrap but it was an exciting car to drive because the brakes didn't work very well. They were "mechanical" brakes. Meaning no hydraulic boost.)

All I had at home in the way of a transmitter was a war surplus BC459, which transmitted a pretty good signal on 40 Meters, but it only worked on Morse and I was a phone man. Jack loaned me a much-modified ART 13, a war surplus Collins radio that put out about 100 watts on 20 Meter Amplitude Modulated (AM) phone. Doc and I hooked it to a junk-box power supply and it fired right up! I plugged the Coax from my big 20 Meter beam antenna into the ART 13 and I was off to the races. Even Doc was impressed. He got to say hello to everybody I snagged. I was working Europeans like they were next door. Whoopee!

ANDOVER, OHIO

185 Chestnut Street

W8GUE

Ur____Mc ᴾᴴᴼᴺᴱ sigs RST_____at_____1__EST_____19__
CW

XMTR: _____ RCVR: _____

Dave Bell

*This was a typical QSL card of the 50's. Just the facts.
For a while I sent one to every DX contact I made.*

The HQ129X went back to Hiram every time we did, so Doc could copy W1AW and just listen around for somebody sending slowly enough for him to copy some letters. He rarely missed a night trying to copy those dits and dahs from W1AW. The ARRL Headquarters station sent code practice only five days a week, and a good thing too, since Doc and Steve and I were out at one of the disreputable saloons a few miles down the road from Hiram when we weren't back home in Andover. The village of Hiram was officially, voter-mandated, dry. It was a hangover (no pun intended) from the days when Hiram College was in the iron fist of the Disciples of Christ.

When I attended, the place still sometimes seemed uncomfortably straight-laced, but the veterans from the big war and the generation following (mine) pushed the rigid boundaries with great regularity. The Hiram College student newspaper, the *Advance* pointed out that the "dry" rule only forced its students to drive somewhere to get loaded, and of course drive back. If the town had any sense, it'd let the students drink locally and walk home drunk, not nearly the menace as behind the wheel.

Only a few months after my Ham ticket showed up in the mail, the FCC announced the introduction of a Novice License into amateur radio, with limited operating privileges, but requiring a code speed of only 5 words per minute. Doc was overjoyed. I was dismayed. **Now** the FCC decides that the 13 wpm hurdle was cruel and unusual punishment? Where were they a few years ago when I really needed them? I could copy 5 words a minute in 1947 and I didn't get around to passing a test until late 1950!

But Ham Radio had to take a back seat to staying in College and out of Korea. My Draft Board regularly reminded me that it itched to send me off to kill the Commies. They didn't even care that I made such a tall target! And couldn't hear out of one ear. But after I got a couple of courses under my belt, I had a handle on life at Hiram and there was no way I was going to get drafted unless Washington changed the rules.

In my search for easy classes, I discovered Speech and Diction 101. I took it and learned not only that I could pass without studying until midnight every night, but that I really enjoyed it and it gave me entrée to the Drama Department, run by a pipe smoking Scotsman named Warren Bruce Douglas Sutherland Mitchell whom I instantly liked. I guess everybody liked Doug except the president of the joint, Tall Paul Fall. Everybody called him that, but Tall was not part of his given name. It just proved an irresistible sound-string for a bunch of students who saw him as rigid and unbending—and tall. For me, finding Doug Mitchell was a revelation; a faculty guy who I thought could be a friend. Doug was in charge of the Showboat *Majestic* the following summer, and I applied and was accepted.

Then, unexpectedly, the college lost its bid to get the boat. How could that be? The *Advance* not-so-gently hinted that Tall Paul Fall was asleep at the switch! A surprise bid from Kent State University, a huge factory of a place a dozen or so miles west of Hiram, put in a higher bid to Captain Reynolds, who owned the boat. Cap went with the high bidder. Always.

Doug, my new favorite prof suggested that since there was no showboat during the summer of '51, between my freshman and sophomore years, that I go to summer school and help out with the summer theater on campus. He was putting together an "in the round" theater in a big empty room in Old Main. So I signed up for summer school. I liked college, now that I had the hang of it.

But I missed Ham Radio. Those now and then weekends at home in Andover weren't enough. I asked Doug if he knew of any Hams on the faculty. He said that Eddie Rosser, the chemistry professor, was interested in Ham Radio but he wasn't a Ham. Dr. Rosser told Doc and Steve and me about some surplus radio equipment in a Quonset hut down the hill by East Dorm and said that he had the key. When Doc and I unlocked the rusty padlock on the door to that Quonset hut, we found it stuffed with surplus radio gear of all shapes and sizes, but alas, nothing I had ever seen before. Whoever chose this bunch of radio junk wasn't a Ham, that's for sure. But there was a lot of it and most of it was brand new in the original packing boxes.

Doug suggested that we commandeer an empty room under the auditorium stage in the Administration Building for our clubroom/shack. (Doug enjoyed bending the rules whenever possible.) We took over that basement room, hauled a bunch of the surplus stuff up the hill from the Quonset hut and hooked it up, to see if we could make it work. Miraculously, in no time at all, our commando shack was on the air.

The transmitter we discovered in the Quonset was (I think) a Temco in a tall relay rack. It weighed about 200 pounds, and ran 300 watts on any frequency from the high end of the AM broadcast band up to about four Megacycles. In other words, without modification it covered the 160 and the 75 and 80-Meter bands. We cut a wire dipole about 225 feet long, tuned it to 1.850 Megacycles (160 Meters), strung it up between a couple of the 120-foot-tall trees outside our basement shack, strung the open-wire feedline up to the eave of the Ad Building roof and from there up to the center of the dipole antenna. We used this circuitous route so passersby wouldn't hang themselves on our feedline, and besides, it was less conspicuous, since we didn't really have permission to be there at all.

We fired up the transmitter. After sitting unused in that Quonset hut for years, the transmitter worked great, right out of the box, a testimony to the quality radio equipment that helped us win World War Two! Doc and Steve and I were talking to hams all over the eastern half of the country and now and then in Canada and even Western Europe. My HQ129X didn't have a bandspread dial for 160, but it worked there just fine even though we were never really sure what frequency we were listening on—but we did know what frequency we were transmitting on because the big Temco's crystal told us so.

Having a fairly powerful transmitter on one-sixty, the so-called top band, allowed us to cut a wide swath on that very earliest of the Ham bands. On the home front, it turned out the ART 13 transmitter that Jack loaned me wasn't really Jack's, and the Ham who owned it wanted it back. Jack said he could put the guy off for a few weeks, but I needed to come up with another transmitter for my home shack. The Quonset hut had no other Ham band transmitters or you can believe I would have appropriated one.

As it happened, at that moment in history, the E.F. Johnson Company was selling an all band transmitter kit that used a 4D32 in the final and a pair of 807s as AM modulator tubes that ran about 120 watts, a respectable amount of power. The 4D32 was a "modern" post-war amplifier tube while the 807s were workhorse tubes throughout the war. To give my transmissions some real punch though, I had plans to build a big amplifier—I already had a lot of the parts including a modulation transformer and a power supply from a BC610, one of World War Two's best high-power transmitters. It's obvious to you, isn't it, that to get more output power, you just add an amplifier to whatever transmitter you're running. And more power makes your signal louder. Duh!

I talked my mother into a loan of $209.50 for the transmitter kit and Doc scrounged up some cash for the tubes and crystals. He and I got the whole package up at Progress Radio in Cleveland and stuffed the big box of parts and instruction books into the trunk of my Ford. Doc and Steve and I went home one weekend and by Sunday night we had it built and on the air. My mother was pleased to have all of us home. Hungry, appreciative men to cook for! It turned out to be a great 120-watt transmitter and it was all home-brew. Well, it was a kit originally, of course, so it wasn't literally "home brew" but we built it and it worked! However, being crystal controlled meant that the frequency it transmitted on was changeable only by switching to a crystal with a different frequency, and I only had a limited supply of crystals!

Actually, back in the early '50s this was not the handicap it would be today, because it wasn't at all uncommon after calling a bunch of CQs to end up with, "... this is W8GUE tuning for a call." Meaning that I'd be transmitting on one frequency, 14.240 Megahertz (Megacycles in those days) for example and I might tune across a station calling me at 14.235 MHz, or any other 20 Meter frequency for that matter. If I called CQ DX, as I often did, being a DX hound just like my Elmer, Jack, W8LIO, then I'd be tuning below 14.200 MHz, where most of the non-stateside Hams hung out. Most people, including me, listened on the frequency we were transmitting on first, in case a station calling me had a VFO, a variable frequency oscillator, sort of a crystal on steroids. If you had a VFO, you could of course vary your transmit frequency. When you heard somebody calling CQ, you could "zero-beat his frequency," meaning put your transmitter right on his calling frequency, unless he happened to be in a portion of the band reserved for DX, in those days on 20 Meters was below 14.200 MHz for voice operation.

Sometimes a DX station would call CQ DX on 14.195 MHz and say he was listening on 14.210 MHz. Obviously if I was "rock-bound" (a disparaging term for crystal controlled) on 14.240 MHz, there was no way I could snag this guy who was listening on 14.210 MHz. Frustrating. So we built a VFO for my Viking I. We had a little trouble getting it not to drift (change frequency all on its own, slowly and maddeningly) but then most VFOs drifted in those days so it wasn't such a big deal, however annoying. The station you were talking to just retuned his receiver in order to follow your drifting signal up or down the band. If you drifted a lot, the guy might mention it, causing you to come up with whatever excuse you could for your unintended migration in frequency. The only thing that could be said for our little home-brew VFO was that it performed better than some we'd heard. And then, the Viking guys, probably in answer to customer pleas, came out with their own VFO kit in a little box that sort of matched the Viking I. It was cheap, so I bought one, built it, and wasn't terribly surprised to discover that it drifted too, but not as much as the one we'd built out of a modified military aircraft radio.

Doc and I didn't take the Viking I back and forth to college with the HQ129X because we had the big Temco 160 and 75 Meter transmitter in our shack under the stage, and we were so busy with schoolwork that those two bands gave us our Ham Radio fix every day. But my HQ129X was the receiver at Hiram and at Andover. It was overworked and over-traveled but it didn't complain and it always lighted up when we turned it on, even though it had picked up a few dings to its crackle-finished case.

Ham radio solved my mother's dilemma about what to get me for Christmas and my birthday. She'd ask me what ham equipment I wanted (needed) and if it wasn't out of the ballpark price-wise, she'd buy it. This is how I got what I called the "Elmac Twins" under my dashboard. For a short period of time in the '50s and into the '60s, the Multi Products Company of Michigan made a VFO controlled AM transmitter and receiver covering all of the Ham bands. It passed for compact in the 50's, was state of the art (though I never heard that phrase in those days) and it worked great!

The larger transmitter and the smaller receiver fit under the dashboard of my 1950
Ford Tudor with room to spare. In my view, they made a perfect pair.

Doc and Steve and I built a gigantic antenna for the back of my car, and we made a lot of contacts while driving all over Northeastern Ohio.

*Mobile antennas don't get much bigger than this! It was just high
enough to barely tick most bridges we drove under.*

The first thing any civilian said upon getting into my car and spotting the Elmac twins under the dashboard was always, "what's that?" That question gave me an opportunity to regale my rider with the wonders of Ham Radio, and with a little bit of luck, do a successful demonstration right there from the car, whether the rider (or my dates) really wanted it or not. *Everybody* got the ham radio spiel. One person who became a regular in my car heard versions of the spiel numerous times. Alice Lane put up with a lot to be my steady girlfriend at Hiram. But after a few years, she became Mrs. W8GUE, so tolerance of my other passion worked in her favor—and mine. At least she could never say that my love of Ham Radio came as a surprise to her.

When I'd pick her up for our date, she always knew when I was getting tired of waiting for her to come down from her top-floor dorm room. I'd fire up the mobile rig and while I really wasn't looking for a contact particularly, I came in on all of the AC/DC radios in her dorm. Even more annoyingly, I blotted out reception on the top floor's one telephone, causing her roommates to hurry her along so I'd get out of their driveway and off their phone!

Sometime during my sophomore year at Hiram, we got some good—no, great—news! I don't know how they managed it, but apparently, Kent didn't make their nut with the showboat in the summer of 1951, maybe because they tried to do serious theater for those simple folk down there in Southern Ohio and Northern West Virginia, who came to the showboat to forget their miseries for a while. Not living up to their financial projections annoyed Cap Reynolds, since he got a piece of the gross, so Hiram got the Showboat *Majestic* back in '52. And I was signed up to go!

Undoubtedly, college provided me with the learning experience it was designed to be. Hiram College took a small town boy and opened up the world. The Showboat *Majestic* turned out better than anticipated, much better—it was in fact the experience of a lifetime. I've made a lot of decisions in my years, good and bad, but signing up for the showboat was one of the best—I knew it then and I realize it even more now. I grabbed that Brass Ring and I've never regretted it.

As my roommate, Doc got used to the crazies and weirdoes who hung around the theater, and in fact, rather enjoyed them. They added a little spice to his pre-med life. I even talked him into coming on the showboat one summer, where, like everyone else, he had a blast!

Here I am as the villain, trying to seduce the heroine while the four dim-bulbs at the bar (from left, Brad Field, Stick Steward, Doug Mitchell and Dave Arnold) are trying to figure out how to keep me from my nefarious scheme. In the end, the villain is always defeated by the heroes' collective ineptitude.

My girlfriend, Alice, joined me on the boat and that's where she got the nickname that has stuck with her ever since: Sam. It started with a card game called "Oh, Hell" which required scorekeeping and our pal/pianist/hero Dave Arnold just wrote down "Sam" on the score sheet instead of "Alice," We called her Sam throughout the day-long game and, as it turned out, from that time forward.

Right in here I wanted to include a little bit of cheesecake (every book about Ham Radio needs some cheesecake) but the rinky-dink Ohio River publication that owns the rights to my picture of four of the Showboat ladies strutting their stuff doing a Can-Can while wearing fairly revealing costumes (for 1953) wouldn't give me permission.

Sam was in one photo reprinted in many newspapers up and down the river because it included students *and* Captain Thomas Jefferson Reynolds. It was a blatantly posed picture set up by the college's fearless publicist, Merle Dowd. Merle had trouble talking Cap into posing for the camera, but perseverance won the day! Even Cap liked this shot.

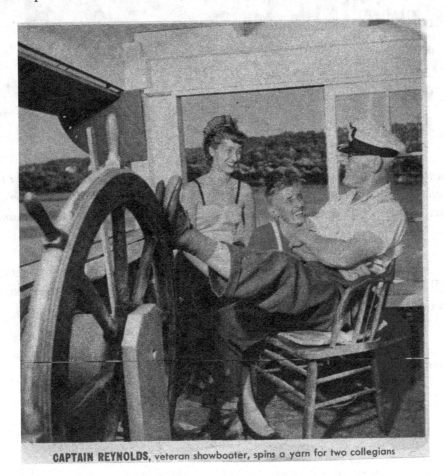

CAPTAIN REYNOLDS, veteran showboater, spins a yarn for two collegians

Here is Sam, with Brad Field, allegedly chatting with Cap. You can tell this is a setup because both Sam and Brad are in costume during the day! Incidentally, two of the three in this photo became Hams later on.

After things on the showboat settled into a routine, I got permission from Cap Reynolds to put a Ham station in the pilothouse. Doc and I strung a dipole antenna for 40 Meters in among the strings of lights that helped the crowds see the boat through the trees that often lined the banks of the Ohio River.

Our dipole antenna was tied to the top of the flagpole on the front of the Majestic, over the top of the pilot-house on a temporary mast, and ran to a pole at the back of the boat. We only operated during the day, since we were in the shows at night, so the antenna went up and came down almost daily.

And how about that line of people in their Sunday finery waiting to buy tickets? We often played to full houses because our shows were great fun. If you don't believe me, take a look at a review from one of the Pittsburgh papers.

ALL'S WELL

Laughter Rocks Showboat

Hiram Players Score Hit Again

Drown your sorrows in the Allegheny, let the river wash away your cares—get ye down to the Majestic Showboat while there's still time to see the spine-tingling melodrama, "Lust, Lucre and Liquor" or "Virtue Unbesmirched."

If you've got one bit of humor in your make-up you'll howl, you'll scream and you'll come away from the shores of the Allegheny a happier person. Even the Allegheny has become a river of laughing waters. No wonder these Hiram College lads and lassies have been filling the ol' Majestic (last of the river showboats) for the past month or so that it has been tied up at the foot of Sixth St. Bridge. This outfit spells their humor with a capital H—for ham, but you'll love it.

After two successful performances of such tried and true melodramers as "Murder in the Red Barn" and "The Drunkard," the thespians from the Ohio College have turned to another epic—"Lust, Inc."

Authorship of this scintillating piece in which "rascality runs amuck" seems somewhat uncertain and it is just possible that we who saw last night's performance were sitting in on a world premiere and didn't know it. It could have been too, but anyway we have seen a flock of world premieres that we didn't enjoy nearly as much.

This melodrama (of uncertain era) has everything . . . a villain, a hero, railroad tracks, garrets, woods and even a saw mill with a whizzing saw.

The program notes tell us that the showboat crew discovered the script while cleaning out the hull of the Majestic in preparation for this season's adventure on the river. Since then Brad Field, a Hiram college graduate has been delving through tons of tomes, 'tis said, trying to trace authorship all the while adapting the script (sly fellow) to the needs of the Hiram players. So it's cheers to Brad Field for his adaptation of what ever you want to call it.

And it's cheers too, with one exception of course, to a fun loving cast of young and talented players who have been doing such a grand job entertaining crowds of Pittsburghers down there on the wharf these past four or five weeks.

This week's performance sees June Eschweiler as the sweet and lovely (with round BLUE eyes as Angeline Lovely and her cohorts include Ray Arnold, Gene Cavanaugh and Jim Moser. Alas and alack (the guy for whom there's no cheers) the hissable villain, Dave Bell.

Last night's audience soundly hissed poor Dave (he must hate himself by now) and cheered stout hearted Ray until the Majestic rocked at its moorings.

As usual the play was followed by six acts of "Vodvil Repertoir" and the usual antics, the candy and popcorn vending.

We were happy with that review of course and we got a lot of them. But nothing got the attention of the folks back in Hiram like the full page pictorial on the front page of the theater section of the New York Times. Whoa! Front page of the Sunday Entertainment Section of the New York Times? That was the big time, my friend! I'd intended to show you that page from the paper, but the New York Times makes reprinting stuff like that page very bureaucratic. You'd think they were an arm of the U.S. Government! Plus—even if I did succeed in buying the rights to that page of photos, the contract would expire in 10 years. This book is going to be on the market beyond 10 years from now. Don't you think?

In addition to critics, all manner of curious folks showed up from time to time at the boat, including some local Hams. One guy stood on the dock looking at the boat for the longest time one afternoon and said to whoever was lounging on the front deck, "Is that a 40-Meter dipole up on the roof?" The Ham was eventually shown up to the pilot-house where Doc and I were operating. After the eyeball QSO in the pilot-house he ran right home and fired up his rig so he could work us and get one of those fancy QSL cards we'd showed him.

The showboat Ham station was like a Field Day operation (more about Field Day in a later chapter) where Hams drag their home stations to some outdoor location, and using emergency power, contact as many other station as possible. Our power came from a gasoline generator that we borrowed from the Quonset hut at Hiram, because the big generator on the showboat only ran at dusk, during the show, and just long enough for the crowd to make its way down the gangplank afterward. On the boat, after the audience cleared the gangplank, it was flashlights or feel your way.

We had juice for the HQ129X and Viking 1 because we found a motor-generator buried at the back of our electronics-filled Quonset hut. We had made our own key for the Quonset because we didn't want to keep "disturbing" Professor Rosser, and we were probably the only ones on campus who cared about all of that old electronic stuff anyway. Incidentally, the generator that supplied the power for the shows along with the big diesel that turned the paddlewheel, were on the bottom deck of our towboat, the *Attaboy*. The kitchen and dining room were on the second deck—ruled over by our chef extraordinaire, Aunt Pearl.

The only downside to our Army Air Corps generator was that it put out, if I remember correctly, 400 cycles at 110 volts AC rather than the 60 cycles that the HQ129X and Viking 1 were designed for.

Doc and I didn't know if a 400-cycle generator would blow up our rig or not, so before we plugged my trusty receiver into it, we asked Jack, who thought about it for a moment, and said it should work. He said, depending on how good our power supply filters were, we might hear a 400-cycle note in our receiver audio, or maybe get a report of a 400-cycle tone on our transmit audio, but it probably wouldn't be a big deal. Some of our contacts mentioned that we had a slight, low frequency tone in our audio, but it wasn't too loud.

Once when the showboat had a big print order for programs, posters and banners, I piggybacked our QSL cards onto the order. We sent a QSL out to every single contact we made. Back there in the Fifties, QSL cards were for the most part pretty simple, straightforward affairs, like my SWL and QSL cards. Our showboat QSL caused a fair amount of comment on the Ham bands. Sometimes we actually found ourselves in a "pileup." It's fair to say that those Hams who contacted us on the Showboat Majestic never again contacted a station on a showboat. While it didn't occur to us at the time, Doc and I were indeed "rare DX." Well, maybe not DX, but rare at least.

We made a lot of contacts from that Pilot house Ham station, but never *after* the shows because the old pilot house hosted romantic trysts for some of our hot-to-trot couples on the boat. Sam and I never headed up there though. We were both pretty private people even then. We would typically head to a bar along Sixth Street in downtown Pittsburgh or to a Jazz joint featuring famed trombonist Tommy Turk, whose claim to fame was that he had played with Stan Kenton, and I didn't doubt it.

Sam and I would see our philosopher/deckhand Bud whenever we ventured into one particularly raunchy saloon. Bud usually sat at a table with a bunch of lowlife women. When I mentioned his choice of companion once, he looked at me, smiled his crooked smile and said, "Oh, Dave, Ya gonna be too fussy, ya gonna miss a lot."

Most of the showboat Ham station's contacts were local, and we invited these local Hams to come down and catch a show and meet us—and some of them actually did!

One of the regular visitors to our pilot house shack was the resident playwright on the boat, and during the regular school year the editor of the school's newspaper, Brad Field. Brad, a couple of years ahead of Doc and me, got the usual Ham radio spiel that I gave all our visitors, Brad actually absorbed the message and earned himself a Ham license.

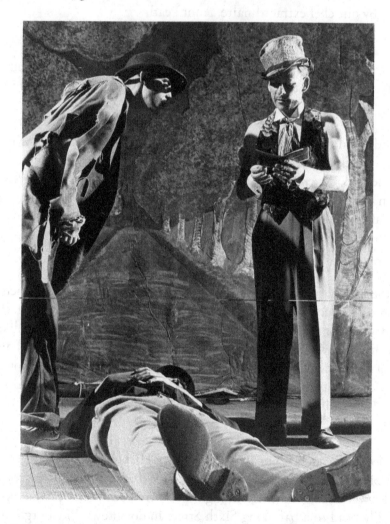

Two of my favorite people on the boat and in life, Brad Field (now W8JJO) on the left playing a bum and the director, Doug Mitchell, as a down-on-his-luck dandy. The corpse is unidentified, but it might be Stick. One day, Doug said to me, "Y'know Davie, you could make it in Show Business." My youngest son's first name, Mitchell, gives you an idea how much I appreciated that unsolicited advice.

Another showboater, Eddie Mark (Rap) Rapaport, one of Hiram's freest free spirits, wore a loin cloth in one song and dance number that he and a lithesome female performed as one of our vaudeville acts (or "vodvil" as we generally spelled it) for our astonished audiences. Amazingly, to me at least, Rap also got a Ham ticket.

So you thought all hams are square?

And to prove that Ham Radio nuts sometimes fall far from the tree, Rap just loved Morse code. In fact he rarely used anything else during his career as a Ham. Rap was an uninhibited dancer and an anything-for-a-laugh actor. One memorable bit he created came at the Villain's (i.e., my) expense. While I did one of my many scene-ending soliloquies, Rap, playing the bartender, was upstage of me tidying up the bar. One memorable night, he blew his nose in the bar towel then went on wiping the beer glasses with it. It got a huge, sustained laugh. I of course didn't know what caused the laugh because Rap was behind me and my speech was exposition, not humor. It took me several performances to figure out how Rap caused the laugh. That bit stayed in the show, of course. Nobody heard the end of my soliloquy over the laughter and nobody cared.

Brad wrote all of the whiz-bang Melodramas that appeared in repertory on the *Majestic's* tiny stage—such memorable shows as *Lust, Lucre and Liquor, or Virtue Unbesmirched* and *The Vengeance of Emory Blacksloth* (that's me), both of which borrowed climactic scenes from some of the greatest melodramas ever written, and strung them all together into "one huge laughfest" as the review in the Pittsburgh paper (humorously) noted.

While some scenes were borrowed, many were original—right out of Brad or Doug's creative imaginations. Some were improbable. Some were impossible. Some were ridiculous. They were all funny. For instance, when looking for a way to get rid of a meddlesome wench, the Villain brought out his trusty cannon and stuffed her into it. Where did the cannon come from? Nobody ever asked. The hapless victim of course was always saved by the slow-witted Hero before the Villain had time to light the fuse. In this photo, that's Alice (Sam) Lane's derriere amusing the audience.

When we rehearsed one of Brad's new scripts during the day, he would sit in the front row of the balcony checking on how we "actors" did with his lines. Every time I'd miss-remember a line Brad would shout out, "Whitefang, you dumb bastard! It's 'My invidious schemes, not my invisible schemes,' you fathead! Get it right!"

At least one of Brad's plays had the heroine being tied to the railroad tracks by a Villain of hideous proportions (me) and in danger of being chopped to bits by a train, and rescued just in the nick of time by the Hero. And, yes, we had a real train (albeit two dimensional) on that tiny 18-foot-wide stage!

While we were docked near the 6ᵗʰ St. Bridge in Pittsburgh, the steel mills went on strike and one day, parked right behind the showboat a huge, out-of-work river towboat (these powerful boats push *dozens* of huge barges full of coal or ore or any big loads that needed moving, up and down the mid-country river systems. They *push,* so why they're called *towboats* is beyond me.) This towboat, named *Lady Rhee,* was one of the biggest on the river system and had one of the world's loudest air horns. We got to know the crew pretty well, and one night we set up a series of elaborate signals between the two boats and just as our little train was about to enter the stage and do in our heroine, *Lady Rhee* blew its air horn. Everyone in the audience raised up at least a foot in their chairs, and the little train chugged across the stage amid much laughter as the Hero ran in and saved the heroine from certain death and the Villain (me) appeared and shouted out over the laughter, "Curses! Foiled again," as the curtain fell.

During the steel mill strike, a remarkable thing happened. The Allegheny River turned from brown to green, and a blue-green at that. It really looked almost like water. You could practically see the bottom. A few intrepid showboaters even swam in it! It was at least a less poisonous stew than it had been.

When the cast lined up on the gangplank after our final show to thank every member of the audience for coming, just as we did every single night all summer long, Brad, Doc, and Erwin "Stick" Steward (the only non-Ham in the foursome) and I piled into my 1950 Ford and headed west for California. We watched Cap Reynolds back the showboat out of its moorings and head home for the winter to his dock in Pt. Pleasant, West Virginia and then we drove off on another great adventure.

My poor old Ford, loaded down with four big guys plus a roof rack full of camping equipment and a trunk jam-packed with food, clothes, and whatever else we imagined we needed for a cross-country odyssey. We bottomed out many times on this memorable, pre-freeway trip.

The fact that three of us were hams made our California trip particularly memorable. There was always a hand reaching for the microphone. We made many contacts, including now and then with a little bit of DX. Even Stick, the non-Ham, got on and talked with Hams, all of whom urged him to get a license.

Our most memorable contact by far turned out to be W6PJ in Los Angeles. When Charley learned that we were traveling cross-country, camping out all the way, he told us that he was building a house in Reseda and while it had no furniture in it yet, the kitchen and bathroom worked, the shower worked (hallelujah!) and we could stay there if we wanted to. Charley's generous offer provided a chance to live and sleep inside at last—after seeing all of those stars in the west's dark skies and dodging all of those raindrops and in some places (like St. George, Utah), freezing our asses off.

BETWEEN REHEARSALS. Three players take time out for a shower

The shower on the showboat consisted of a hose and a bucket.
*And that water was **cold**! (left to right: Donna Rae Willoweit, Jim Dunn,*
and Alice (Sam) Lane.

It was cold showers or no showers on the boat and on the road, so we looked forward to a hot one at W6PJ's new place. As promised, Charley met us at his new house, gave us a key, and said, "Have fun."

Actually, we did have one phone number in Los Angeles. One of our classmates at Hiram lived there. When he learned of our cross-country odyssey he told us to call his parents and say hello. When I called, I was asked if we could come to dinner he following night (one guess at the answer.) We pulled up in front of one of the most elegant houses we could imagine on a street full of elegant houses. We weren't exactly dressed for a house like this, but at least we smelled good (thanks, Charley).

Dinner was formal, complete with a cook cooking and a maid serving the food in a very elegant dining room. We conjured up our very best behavior, refrained from smoking, and only had one or two glasses of wine each. We answered every single question asked about their son (whom we really didn't know well at all) and about Hiram, which we knew a lot about. Since we were just off the showboat, whatever warts Hiram had were swept under the table (where there was not a single crumb), you can be sure of it. What an experience! Our host was an art director in the movies. We saw his Oscars! Wow! I loved LA.

73

Ever since my attendance at the movie theater in Andover, plus acting in plays in high school and college and on the boat, I had dreamed of living in Hollywood, where I eventually ended up. If I'd been *really* smart I would have dreamed of living in Beverly Hills! (Not that I knew it, but the antenna height limit in Beverly Hills was/is 35 feet, so I was probably smart to settle in the Hollywood Hills.)

Undoubtedly, most Hiramites who spent even just seven weeks on the showboat, consider it the highlight of their Hiram education. I spent eight months on the boat, and the glow of that experience manages to erase a lot of the shortcomings of the Hiram College of my time—a college then in a rocky transition from a church school to today's really solid academic and cultural institution.

The heart-stopping nervousness that most of us experienced taking that thirteen words per-minute code test has largely disappeared or at least greatly diminished with the abolishment of Morse code as a licensing requirement. Besides that, tests these days are given by other Hams who have qualified to administer licensing exams. The whole procedure is a lot less intimidating than when we old-timers first got our licenses, and a damn good thing it is too. While there was one Ham per thousand of population when I became W8GUE, today there are over four Hams per thousand in the US. You sometimes hear that amateur radio ranks are dwindling, but "tain't so, McGee." Of course, I did that math, and you already know how I am at math.

It's always fascinated me how Ham Radio makes instant friendships between people who have little or nothing in common, like for instance Doc, Steve, Brad, and me. Ham Radio smoothes over a lot of differences. There's no explaining why my friends Stick Steward and Dave Arnold didn't get their licenses. Many Hams talk about the Ham Radio "Bug" that bit them. Stick and Dave, for all their knowledge about the hobby, didn't get bit. There's no explaining it.

Our original college Ham shack with its transmitter tuned for 160 Meters, was a good conversation starter for the few non-Hams who stumbled into the Ad Building basement. One-Sixty, as you remember, was the original Ham band, 'way back there just after the turn of the century (19th to 20th). In fact, at the dawn of radio, the Government gave Amateurs ALL of the radio frequencies "160 Meters and down" which includes today's commercial AM band, FM band, TV frequencies, cell phone frequencies—in fact, every bit of today's most valuable radio spectrum. It was all ours! A Ham named Clinton B. DeSoto wrote a book called 160 Meters and Down *which, if you're interested in a bit of early radio history, is still available from ARRL. And while I'm on the subject of literature, if you're interested in reading Brad Field's best-known melodrama,* Lust, Lucre and Liquor, *it's available at Amazon.com.*

I mentioned that my HQ129X didn't have a bandspread dial for 160. Most receivers intended for Amateurs in the 40's and 50's had two dials with the left dial calibrated for every frequency that the receiver received and the right one calibrated for the amateur radio bands. The left dial was rough-tuning and the right dial was fine-tuning. For whatever reason, the right-hand dial on my HQ129X did not display the 160 meter band frequencies, so we had to guess what frequency we were listening to.

I hear that Eddie Rosser, our chemistry professor and unofficial faculty advisor, eventually got his Ham license. I hope he enjoyed the shack in the Ad-Building basement. We didn't take the 160 Meter transmitter when we graduated, though we certainly could have. In fact, if we'd had larcenous hearts we could have cleaned out that Quonset hut and nobody would have ever been the wiser.

Building the Johnson Viking I was just the first of many kits I would put together in my Ham Radio adventure. The radio I'm using now I put together from a kit. The Elecraft K3 is both simpler to build and a lot more complicated electronically than that wonderful old Viking.

My entire, incredible Showboat Majestic *career came about because Kent State didn't "make their nut." That is a show-biz phrase that means that you didn't break even, but it's such a strange set of words that I looked it up. Like the word "Ham" itself, nobody knows what it literally refers to or where it came from, though it may be as old as the 6th Century AD, which qualifies it for the Old-Old Timer's Club of words and phrases. Incidentally, Kent State, in case your history is fuzzy, is the school that gained notoriety years later when National Guardsmen opened fire and killed many students noisily protesting Nixon invading Cambodia. Kent is a school best known for a tragedy.*

At the risk of repeating myself, here's a little Ham lingo translated: to call "CQ" is to say to the radio world you'll be happy to talk to anybody who can hear you. A "pileup" is just that, several or many stations calling you on the same frequency, making all of them unreadable. You have an obligation to try to sort them out and "work" them one at a time, especially since you're the one who created the pileup. And "DX" of course is short for distance, usually but not always referring to some country you're not in. And "Elmer" is Hamspeak for mentor. Nobody knows why.

The Vibroplex bug I fantasized the FCC inspector used to send us wannabees the code was a very clever gadget that vibrated on a fancy spring system and allowed the user (once he got the hang of it) to send a sequence of dots just by holding the paddle. Some of its practitioners had a real swing to their sending—so much so that some fists completely flummoxed my meager copying ability. The Vibroplex is still being manufactured and used today, and there are still some fists I can't copy.

The "crackle finish" paint on the case of my HQ 129 X ended up looking as if someone had covered a piece of metal with corn flake fragments and then painted it. It was a rough but popular surface back then for reasons that escape me. While harder to scratch than a baked, painted surface, what it really did well was attract dust. Lots of dust.

These days, many XYLs (ex-young ladies) get Ham tickets for various reasons, especially since now it's a lot easier to do. My wife, Sam, got her license back when it was harder, when she first had to pass the 5 wpm Novice License test, and then she had to pass a 13 wpm code test to get her General license and be able to transmit on the so-called "low-bands" include 160, 80, 75 (the voice portion of the 80 Meter band), 40, 30, 20, 15, 12, 10 Meters and above. The numbers indicate the physical length of one wavelength on each of the various Ham bands. To explain it beyond that would be telling you more than you need to know, at least in an introduction to amateur radio.

Sam's callsign is W6QLT. She's a quilter. She never gets on the air. My fault. I didn't lean on her to sit in the shack operating chair the moment her ticket came in the mail.

When Doug Mitchell told me I could probably make it in Show Biz, that gave me all the boost I needed to pursue a lifelong career for myself producing television specials and series for all of the networks, and a couple of theatrical movies. It's been a great career and it all started on the showboat, where I had the time of my life playing the Villain. Some have said the Villain was a perfect springboard for a career in television, but I think they were kidding. Maybe.

And finally: Brad called me "Whitefang" on the boat because whenever the audience hissed me, as they loved to do, I sneered at them. I could make my mouth perfectly square and all the audience saw were two rows of big, white teeth: thus "Whitefang." Brad still calls me that from time to time.

Whitefang

And finally, my cartoonist friend Rich, VE2WGH, drew a cartoon to remind me of one of the greatest times in my life. Oh, how long ago and far away that experience was.

It's been a while since I've seen anybody that pissed off.

Chapter 11

Just a Born Volunteer

Shattering the predictions of some of my Andover High School teachers and the sour faced principal, I managed to graduate from Hiram College in the late spring of 1954. Not only that, I won a scholarship to spend the summer after my graduation acting at the University of Wyoming summer theater. The only fly in the ointment, as my mother used to say, was that their rehearsals started before my graduation date, so, being ambitious and not caring much about being handed a diploma by Tall Paul Fall, I skipped my graduation ceremonies, much to my mother's consternation I'm sure. To her credit, she didn't say anything. She always applauded enterprise.

As I looked out the windows of my DC-3 approaching Laramie, I could see only a million pine trees, on both sides of the plane. The pine trees kept getting closer and closer as we descended, allegedly toward a runway. We bounced around and while I've never been a nervous flyer, at times, a comforting word from the pilot is, well, comforting. Of course, the way we were swaying and bouncing, he may have been busy. Suddenly the pine trees disappeared and in an instant we were on the ground after a very smooth landing. I guess mountain pilots are used to the bouncing. When I walked down the little ladder to the tarmac, I took a look at the wingtips to make sure there were no pine branches stuck in them. I heard a voice say, "Dave?" On the tarmac waiting for me stood the director of the summer theater program, Charlie Parker (not the famous musician). After perfunctory introductions, his first words to me were, "My, you're tall. How tall are you?"

"About six-three," I said.

"Did you put that on your application?"

"I don't know," I said. "Was there a place for height?"

"The head of your drama department said you were a character actor," he said. "I figured you'd look more like a character!"

I'd sent Charlie a picture, a blurry Polaroid taken in a dorm hallway by Doc—nothing like the kind of glamorous head-shots professional actors send around. But what did I know? I'd never in my life seen a head-shot!

79

I said, "Yeah, well, I'm not sure what a character looks like but Doug gave me a lot of different kinds of parts. I like character parts."

"But you look like a leading man. We have a serious problem," Charlie said.

"Oh, crap," I thought. "They're going to send me home."

Charlie drove me straight to the gigantic theater where our first play was rehearsing with a stand-in for my role. After quick introductions, I replaced my stand-in and while I didn't know the blocking, I faked it. After three or four minutes, Charlie halted the rehearsal and said, "This is just not going to work. The casting is wrong. Dave, I want you to play the lead, and Van, I want you to play Dave's part."

Van came unglued. "I'm the lead," he sputtered. "I know all the lines. You promised! I turned down the Oregon Shakespeare Festival for this!"

I just watched. I'd only been here five minutes and already I was causing pandemonium. Whoopee! It looked like it might be an exciting summer!

Van continued his protest, but Charlie's mind was made up. Van and I were trading roles. Van pouted. Charlie folded his arms. Never having witnessed tempers flaring (other than Brad Field calling me a nincompoop from the balcony when I screwed up one of his lines), I adopted the proper role of innocent bystander.

So I got the leads, not the fun little roles. I explained to Van that I can't help it that I'm tall. I like being tall. As John Lindsay, the former mayor of New York and an ambitious politician, once told me years later, "I'd rather be tall than President." Me too.

Van pouted.

One of the problems about switching from character roles to leads was that I had a lot more lines to learn. As our showboat playwright knew all too well, I'm not "a quick study." Learning lines for me is painful. I was a good ad-libber, but I couldn't get away with that for Brad and I couldn't get away with it for Charlie Parker either. Playwrights have directors brainwashed. They wrote lines to be memorized, not mangled. Somehow they've convinced directors that the exact recitation of what they wrote constitutes the very essence of theater. I wasn't so sure, but what did I know?

We all had Sundays off, this being the west, where piety is up there with patriotism and politics on the scale of priorities. One Sunday I was asked if I'd like to go out to dinner at a restaurant of an admirer of the summer theater. When I asked what time we'd leave for dinner, I was told about noon. "Noon," I said, "for dinner?"

"The restaurant is a ways . . ." was the answer I got.

I discovered that the restaurant was in a town a lot smaller than Laramie and clear across the state. As I sat in the backseat with a couple of other invitees, I noticed a new Lincoln four-door sedan passing us on the right. My eyebrows raised because there was no road on the right, only ranchland. That Lincoln was bobbing and weaving and bouncing along and the old cowboy driving looked as if he was having a helluva good time. When we got to our restaurant, there at the bar sat the cowboy with the Lincoln. I couldn't resist going up to him and saying, "I've never been passed by a Lincoln driving through a field before. Isn't that kind of tough on the car?"

The old cowboy turned around and looked at me as if I was questioning his sanity and said, "Hell, boy, I dunno. Probly. I trade 'em in every year anyway—and they're a helluva lot more comfortable than a pickup or even a horse!" I loved Wyoming.

On those free Sundays I wandered around looking for Ham antennas, and actually spotted a beam on the electrical engineering building, but the shack seemed locked up for the summer. I tried to find a key, to no avail.

While I was there, the University had its big-game barbecue for all of the summer school students and we actors all assumed we fit into that category, sort of. What the hell! We were living in the dorm! We had scholarships!

I had never seen that big a barbecue in my entire life. I tasted meat from animals I thought were extinct. Delicious! It wasn't until after the barbecue that I learned that every bit of that meat was roadkill! The big game hunters in Wyoming turned out to be trucks.

The summer theater season at the University of Wyoming flew by and I had a great time, added to my culinary experiences, learned a lot, and even got some good reviews.

It seemed like I had barely gotten to the wild west and it was time to go home.

Getting home promised to be more leisurely than flying from city to city in a DC-3 because Erwin (Stick) Steward, the only non-Ham on our California drive, had inherited a few bucks the summer after our graduation, bought a fancy red 1954 Buick Super hardtop and volunteered to drive to Laramie, pick me up, and take me home. I was eager to get back to see my girlfriend, Sam, and sit down in front of my half-kilowatt and make some noise on the bands. It didn't take much urging from me to get Stick to really give that big Buick the gas, especially when we were passed by a pickup truck doing about 90. I love Wyoming. In the summertime. I had asked Stick to put a mobile Ham rig in his big Buick, but he hadn't done it, for which I chastised him. He pointed out that since he wasn't a Ham, it was understandable. Stick remains one of my recruiting failures.

We hadn't gotten far from Laramie when I heard a grinding noise of some kind and, looking back down the desolate highway we were traveling, I saw a cloud of smoke. Oh, my. New car, bad news. Stick was oblivious. He peered at the smoke in his rearview mirror with the same sour face reserved for someone who had cut a big one. He decided that maybe going faster would fix the problem. It did. The transmission disassembled itself all over the highway and the big engine lost contact with the rear end. We coasted off the road onto the berm. We debated whether we should go back and retrieve some of the parts on the highway. We picked up the larger pieces and threw them in the ditch. We raised the hood on Stick's new car and leaned against the trunk, hoping someone would take pity on two young guys stuck out on the edge of nowhere. This was years before cell phones of course, and years before hand-held Ham transceivers and repeaters, now ubiquitous.

The first pickup to come upon us stopped. He looked the Buick over and told Stick that it was a beautiful car for sure. He reckoned that the nearest Buick dealer was back in Cheyenne which we'd gone through a couple of hours ago, but he knew a crackerjack mechanic just down the road, and he had a tow truck too! I told Stick that if he'd put a ham radio in the car I could have put out an SOS and we would have been rescued in no time at all. Stick pointed out that we *were* rescued in no time at all. Those Wyoming folks were hospitable. Of course, I already knew that.

The transmission was fixed, free, but we had to get it towed back to the Buick dealer in Cheyenne, a fun town to spend a little time in if you like beer and don't mind the sweetly acrid odor of stockyards to go with your steaks. Good thing Stick and I didn't have a tough schedule!

Home in Andover in the late fall of 1954 was great, lazy fun. I was on the air every day. I drove over to Cleveland regularly to visit Sam. She had a real job, so was only really around on weekends. Every trip I'd be on the air from the car, burning up the airwaves and the highways. Either going or coming from Cleveland, I'd stop to see W8LIO's friend, and by then my friend, Sam Harris, W8UKS. An entire book could and should be written about Sam Harris. Sam went through dental school because his parents insisted on it. When he graduated, he said, "Thank God, I'll never have to look in another mouth." He became a self-taught engineer, going to work everyday for the Brush Development Company in Cleveland, but really doing research into anything that fascinated him.

W8UKS lived on the top of a hill in Burton, Ohio, a dozen or so miles east of Cleveland in a basement home that he had built. He and Helen never intended to spend their lives in a roofed-over basement, but Sam never found time to finish the house. It just wasn't all that important to him. He had too many other things to do. Like design and build antennas. Sam had a 175-foot tower in his backyard. The bottom 100 feet was a free-standing ex-broadcast tower, very husky, and the top 75 feet was a homemade aluminum 4-sided tower, all of which rotated. The rotor of course was a prop pitch motor. That antenna system was a miracle of ingenuity and engineering. The top part probably blew down from time to time, but Sam just put it back up. It held all manner of antennas over the years. They were constantly going up and regularly replaced by another, perhaps better design. He had a huge antenna at the very top for Two Meters, a Very High Frequency band up there amongst the television channels. He talked to hams on the east coast with that antenna with power from a kilowatt transmitter he had built from surplus and scrounged parts. The guy was a genius.

The thing that had earlier created my awe of Sam Harris occurred the day I stopped in to see him, on my way home one weekend from Hiram, and found his kitchen table covered with little three-legged things that looked like tiny top hats. Sam was soldering them into circuits.

"What are those?" I asked.

"They're transistors," said Sam. "They're going to revolutionize electronics. They do the same sort of stuff tubes do. These are kind of like triodes."

"I've heard of 'em but I've never seen one before. What are you doing with 'em?"

"I'm putting them into some fairly common tube circuits, and when I get them to work, I'll draw up the circuit and patent it."

That was Sam, obliviously ahead of his time.

Probably the main thing I took away from my friendship with W8LIO and W8UKS was that they weren't afraid of failure. A lot of their stuff didn't work, blew down, burned up or just wouldn't oscillate or do whatever it was supposed to do. No problem. Just try again.

During weekends my junior year at Hiram, Doc and I had gotten my big amplifier together and it worked great, a pair of 4-125A tubes in the final amplifier and a pair of 100THs as class B modulators—lots of punch. Big signal. It coasted running half a gallon. Only a few shocks from the 1650-volt power supply nabbed me, but not bad because I *always* kept one hand behind my back while near high voltage, a life-saving admonition from Jack, W8LIO, a guy not known for caution.

In that period between graduation and whatever, I was a happy camper. I even got engaged, after only a dozen or so hints from Sam. The way I think of it is, I volunteered to get married, some day down the log. I've thought a few times during my life that popping the big question might have been a result of pre-traumatic stress. At that moment in my history, I was in a holding pattern, and pilots everywhere will tell you that is not a fun place.

The draft board had not pulled my number. They'd been threatening to do it for years, and now that I was ready, they were sitting on their hands. The war in Korea had paused during a flimsy truce, so the need for cannon fodder had diminished for the moment, but I felt somehow frustrated because I wasn't getting on with my life. So I volunteered for the draft. I know, I know, there he goes, volunteering again.

I'll admit that volunteering for the draft was an iffy call. I'm sorry, but I'm just a born volunteer. Somebody need help? Count on me. Time to move beyond where you are? Volunteer.

I couldn't expect to be deferred for several more years if I went to grad school and I couldn't get a job because no employer would hire somebody liable to be drafted momentarily. My mother said I was all at sixes and sevens. I spent the entire fall of '54 floating—just fiddling around. My draft board finally woke up, realized I'd volunteered, and sent me off to Ft. Knox, Kentucky, for basic training. In January.

This was not only the Ft. Knox where they kept the gold (back in the days when this country had some gold), but the Ft. Knox where naïve young men are indoctrinated into the mysterious ways of the military

They say that Ft. Knox is the only place in the country where you can stand in mud up to your hips and have dust blow in your eyes. Why you'd ever want to do that is a mystery to me, but that's the kind of place the army chose for my basic training.

Little did I realize that my first battle as a soldier, barely after I got used to my ill fitting uniform, would be with a 78-rpm record—and the record won! There aren't many people still around who will remember the 78 rpm record, which is to an iPod what a skateboard is to a Rolls Royce.

The 78 rpm record that did me in had Morse code on it—and only three letters at that: an E, an I, and an S. In case you've forgotten your code, the E is one dot, the I is two dots, and the S is three dots (or "dits" as we Hams call dots, as I mentioned before.) On the day I took the test, I knew the Morse code about 15 words a minute, and not just three letters, but the entire alphabet, plus numbers and punctuation, and certainly including the confounded comma!

The corporal who showed up to give the Morse code test was the same guy who, a couple of days earlier, had struggled to read an announcement to us, an announcement designed to get us to donate one dollar of our measly $75 per month salary to help wipe out a crippling disease called polio. After he'd struggled with the paper for a while and it was about to do him in, he said, "All right you sumbitches, cough up a buck so's we can beat polo. That's what he said, "polo." It's hard not to feel superior in the army. At least until the fighting starts.

As the corporal struggled to read the polio paper, he absentmindedly rubbed his left hand over his right arm, over a dark shadow underneath his two corporal stripes, damning evidence that recently he'd gone from staff sergeant down to corporal. That demotion couldn't have improved his disposition much, so I threw a dollar in the number ten tin can he held out for donations.

So Corporal Polo, as I'd begun to call him, showed up to administer the Morse code test, or Morris code as he called it.

When Samuel F. B. Morse invented his code as a means of conveying intelligence from point A to point B, he hadn't figured that the army was going to be involved. If you've ever served your country in the army, you know that it works in mysterious ways. You'd have known that just because I knew the Morse code faster than anybody at Ft. Knox didn't mean that I would pass that test. But me, what did I know?

Corporal Polo graded the tests and solemnly announced, "Not a single damn one of you sumbitches passed this Morris Code test."

Of course, nobody was surprised, except me. As everyone else filed out to go look at yet another V.D. film, I confronted Polo. I told him I knew the Morse code and something was wrong. Before he could react to the affront, I grabbed the 78-rpm record off the Victrola and discovered several colossal cracks across the entire record. The thing was held together by the label! You didn't have to be a genius to figure out that every time the needle hit the crack it skipped over a lot of intelligence.

When I pointed out the big cracks, he didn't even bother to look at them. He just shrugged and said, "Nobody never passes this test nohow, with all them little be-beeps."

I started to argue with him, but he raised his hand in a HALT gesture and said that the code that civilians learned wasn't the same code as the military. Everything is different in the military, he said. That's hard to argue with, I thought, and at the time it even made a certain amount of sense, somehow. And besides, did I want to spend the rest of my time in the army sitting at a desk copying Morse code messages? The answer came back a big Dah-dit, Dah-dah-dah, which, if you remember your code, is NO.

In basic training I learned that the army was not all that bad and not all that difficult if you used your head and trod lightly around the common wisdom, especially if the common wisdom made no sense. For example: One of the eternal verities of army life is "DON'T VOLUNTEER." For anything. Ever.

Almost the moment I settled into the barracks at the very beginning of my basic training, the squawk box came on and asked for a volunteer. "Anyone who can type report to the Orderly Room immediately!" Everybody in my barracks had just gone to bed at about 8 PM if I remember correctly, preparing their weary bodies for the big ten mile double time march the next day. I wondered whether I should volunteer. I wasn't particularly sleepy, so I got up, put on my fatigues, and headed toward the orderly room. "Where you goin'?" asked a fellow inductee, knowing the answer. I told him I could type and in a microsecond the catcalls started echoing off the hard polished wood floor—". . . never volunteer—sucker!" And worse. I ignored them. I've always been a straight-ahead thinker. They asked for a typist and I could type. If they really wanted somebody to clean the latrines, as most of my new comrades truly believed, then I wouldn't volunteer for anything, ever again.

I went into the Orderly Room. The single striper sitting behind the desk closest to the door asked me what I wanted. "The squawk box asked for a typist," I said.

"Can you type?" the PFC asked.

Since he was only a private first class, thus a near-nobody, I said, "I don't know how to type, but I thought I'd come over here and learn."

He looked at me as if I'd just spit a goober on his desk, so I said, "Just kidding. Of course I can type, or I wouldn't have walked over here in the rain." It was what passed for winter in that part of the world and it was always raining at Ft. Knox. That's why Kentucky is so green. If there were a market for mud, Kentucky would be the richest state in the union.

The PFC eyed me suspiciously, pointed to a hard wooden bench near a comfortable-looking sofa and said, "Wait over there."

Keeping his eye on me, he walked to the company commander's closed door, knocked, and entered. In a moment he and the captain came into the reception area and I stood more or less at attention. The captain looked me over. He read my name from the patch over my shirt pocket and said, "Private Bell, can you type?"

"Yes sir," I said. Even I didn't joke with captains. Usually.

"Can you spell?"

"Yes sir."

"Can you actually write?" he ventured.

"I wrote a lot in college, sir," I said.

The captain gave me a small, don't-screw-with-me smile.

Then quickly, I said, "Oh, grammar. I think it's okay sir. Sometimes I have to look something up."

"You know how to use a dictionary?"

"And a thesaurus," I said.

The captain turned to the private who'd been taking all of this in as if watching a python and a rabbit and asked, "Do you know what a thesaurus is, private?"

"No sir," said the PFC, miffed at being called a private.

The captain turned to me and said, "If you can do all that, you'll be the only god-damned enlisted man on this base who can. Let's hope you're half as good as advertised."

He sat me down at an old Remington electric typewriter and handed me a sheaf of paper. He told me to read it all first, then tell him what it was about and what was wrong with it, in my opinion.

I read the dozen or so pages, and even though it was shot full of mistakes and pretty poorly organized, I understood what it was trying to say. I told the private I was ready to talk to the captain. The PFC said, "You read all that already?"

I nodded and he went to the captain's door. In a moment I was standing in front of the captain's desk.

"So what's the gist of that report?" he asked. "If you had to put a headline on it, what'd it be?"

I thought a moment, and said, "Tank missing from Fort Knox."

"That's not bad," he said. "Where would you go from there?"

"You mean what would I write next?"

"Yeah, what would be the first paragraph?"

I thought a moment about the absurdity of this situation, the lateness of the hour, the thought of a tank driving out the main gate of Ft. Knox without so much as a by your leave, and said, "I guess I'd say the tank is easy to recognize because it doesn't have Kentucky license plates."

The captain laughed. He really laughed! I was startled. So was the PFC obviously because he came to the door to see if everything was all right.

"You're gonna do fine here, Bell. Just go easy on the humor on this rewrite. The general who runs this place doesn't think a missing tank is very damn funny. Private? Get Bell anything he needs. A Coke, whatever. He's gonna rewrite this damn report so everybody'll understand it."

The captain turned to me and said, "This may take you a while, but the general is expecting it on his desk by oh seven hundred. That's seven AM to you civilians. Think you can handle it?"

"Yes sir," I said.

"Private, when Bell finishes this report let him sack out on the sofa. I'll check it over at oh six hundred."

"Yes sir," said the private first class, amazed by what had just transpired.

"Do you care how long this report is?" I thought to ask the captain.

"Just get all the facts in and make it readable. Five copies please. G'night."

And with that he was out the door.

I read the dozen or so pages over again and this time made some notes. It was clear that sometime around seventeen hundred almost two weeks ago a person or persons unknown drove an M41 Walker Bulldog light tank right out the main gate of Ft. Knox with hardly a single raised eyebrow. There were hundreds of eyewitnesses, including the MPs at the front gate. While it was a bit unusual for a tank to drive off the base and down the main highway toward Louisville, it wasn't unprecedented, and besides, an MP on duty said the tank didn't slow down as it approached the guardhouse so he opened the red and white wooden arm rather than have to explain to his lieutenant how his gate got knocked off. Again.

That tank drove out the front gate twelve days ago and apparently nobody missed it until early today. The regular driver of the missing tank went out to warm it up for maneuvers and it wasn't where he parked it. There was this perfectly aligned row of tanks almost as far as the eye can see, with this hard-to-miss empty spot where he'd left his tank a couple of weeks before. Apparently, his tank was AWOL. He went to the motorpool. Not there. He looked in all of the obvious places where one might hide a tank, but his baby was missing. With trepidation in his heart, he reported to his commanding officer that his tank was nowhere to be found. A base-wide search was carried out, but no tank. How could a tank disappear into thin air? Even Houdini hadn't tried that one!

Dozens, probably hundreds of GIs were questioned, civilian mechanics were questioned, but as one sergeant charged with finding eyewitnesses reported, "Nobody knows nuttin'." Then someone came up with the bright idea to look through the main gate log of comings and goings. Sure enough, there was an entry at seventeen oh one a dozen days ago noting that an M41 tank had exited the base. There was no evidence of it ever returning.

I rummaged through the drawers of my desk and found my favorite pre-computer recording device, even prior to the IBM Selectric with the little ribbon thingy that let you white out mistakes. My favorite recording device? A yellow pad and a pencil. I sat on the sofa—my bed for the night if I finished the report—read the sheaf of paper again, made more notes, and started to write, longhand, on the yellow pad.

"Hey," said the PFC. "You ain't typin'."

Since just the two of us there, I said, "Professional writers always write their first drafts on yellow pads in pencil. The writer's union requires it, and I wouldn't want to break any rules."

He nodded and went back to his comic book, satisfied with my explanation.

It took me about an hour to get a yellow pad draft that seemed to include everything of any relevance, so I moved to the typewriter, put in five sheets of paper with a sheet of carbon paper between each one, and typed what I'd already written in longhand. I read it a couple of times, was satisfied with it, and looked at the clock on the orderly room wall. It was midnight.

I asked the private if he'd like to read the report.

"Why would I do that?" he asked.

Having no ready answer to that, I put the five copies of the report and the original sheaf of papers on the captain's desk as I'd been instructed to do, left the five used carbon papers on the PFC's desk with no comment and sacked out on the orderly room couch.

I was awakened by the PFC shaking me.

"The captain wants to see you," he said with that you're-going-to-get-it now sneer on his face. I got up, brushed some of the wrinkles out of my perpetually wrinkled fatigues, and went through the open door of the captain's office.

"Ah, Private Bell," he said. "One page? You boiled down a dozen pages to one page?"

"It is single spaced, sir. You didn't tell me how long it had to be, sir, and I think that page has all of the known facts in it, and then some."

"And then some?" asked the captain.

"Well, I mean, a couple of the explanations about who took the tank seem a bit, well, far fetched."

"You don't think the North Koreans swept in here and stole it?" he asked.

"Especially since we signed a truce with them, yes, that's one that seemed out there in left field," I said. "I think somebody on this base probably would have spotted a Korean sneaking around."

"And shot him dead on the spot, no questions asked, truce or no truce," said the captain. "The only problem is that the army never submits a serious report that's less than a dozen boring pages. Twenty is even better. The general will love this. One page. Unprecedented."

I looked at the captain a bit confused and said, "Is it okay?"

"It's great," he said. Then he shouted out to the PFC, "Private. Give Bell a buck slip for the day! Private Bell, your army career is going to be a piece of cake. Whatever we train you to do, you'll end up typing."

He was right.

It's fair to say that I typed my way through basic training, and consequently missed a lot of fun stuff like the 30-mile marches and the infiltration course where live ammo flies above the heads of a bunch of rookies hugging the mud, keeping their weapon dry, and attempting some forward movement. I was sorry to miss it but it couldn't be helped. The paper had to keep flowing.

Some would say that the army has no heart, but I'm here to tell you different. One day when it was cold, windy, raining like hell, and my company had another trip to the infiltration course scheduled, we were marching past company headquarters when a voice from the porch called out, "Sergeant?" The sergeant leading us to our fate called a halt, and the captain shouted, "You got a Private Bell in your company?"

Our sergeant didn't know me by name (because I was rarely with him for all of the fun maneuvers) so he shouted out, "Is there a Private Bell here?"

"Yes, sergeant," I said, raising my rifle in the air.

The captain, seeing me, said, "I want him today, sergeant."

"Private Bell, report to the captain," shouted out the sergeant as he prepared to move his troops-minus-one forward.

I got to the porch, saluted the captain, and followed him into the Orderly Room out of the pouring rain. "I don't have anything for you today, Bell, but this is not a great day to go through the infiltration course. Sit down and read a magazine, or whatever you want to do."

For one of the first times in my entire life, I was speechless. An act of kindness from an officer in the U.S. Army. It changed my attitude for the rest of my time in the service, and probably long after.

If you know what carbon paper is, you're old. Carbon paper was a thin, very thin sheet of plastic-like paper, one side of which was coated with I suppose some sort of carbon film which, when placed between two sheets of typewriting paper, made an okay copy on the second page of paper unless you put it in backwards in which case it made a nice copy on the back of your original typed sheet, an embarrassing situation at best. Five sheets of paper and four sheets of carbon paper was pretty much the limit of legibility on the fifth page. And the typist couldn't make any mistakes, no mistakes, because the "carbons" so called didn't erase. Copy machines destroyed that industry. And not a moment too soon. Carbon paper was a nightmare.

My friend Sam Harris, W8UKS, worked for the Brush Development Company in Cleveland, a research and development outfit that created the wire recorder (remember the wire recorder?) and then because the wire for wire recorders was so difficult to make, they developed magnetic tape and tape recorders. Jack, W8LIO, worked there too. The creative juices must have been flowing down the front steps of that place.

My short stint acting at the University of Wyoming Summer Theater taught me many things, including how difficult if not impossible it is to cast a play without meeting the people you're casting. Van, cast to be the leading man, was about 5'7" and just on this side of plump. He, and the woman they'd hired to be the ingénue (leading lady) had worked mostly in small theaters, and at Wyoming the house (audience area) was 3,000 plus seats with marginal acoustics. I was the only one of the five-person company of out-of-towners who could be heard in the back row. My dad was right. I should have been a politician.

Both basic training and summer stock theater kept me so utterly occupied that I didn't need a Ham Radio fix every day or even every week. But I always knew it was there, waiting for me.

And finally, some definitions: ". . . at sixes and sevens . . ." means in a quandary, in a state of confusion and disarray. It may have originated with Chaucer, or even earlier. My mother described me that way from time to time, and I never paused to think what it meant. I'm sure she knew.

My friend Sam Harris, W8UKS, compared the little transistors he was experimenting with to a triode tube.

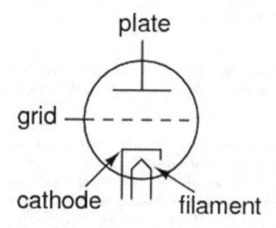

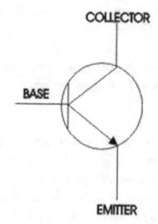

Above is a triode tube. Yes, I know it has four elements, but it's a triode anyway. The cathode doesn't count. Or the filament doesn't count. But see the similarities to the transistor

Above is the diagram of a simple transistor.

If you want more of an explanation than this, it's time you got your Ham license.

A "buck slip" in the army was like a day pass except you couldn't leave the base, but you didn't have to do what you were supposed to be doing, which in my case was marching all over hell and gone.

The phrase "by your leave" is sort of an apology for not asking permission. Certain by-the-book officers in the military like to hear that phrase even though it's almost always insincere.

In theater terms, "blocking" is what the director does with the actors to position them on stage and plot their moves. My cynical friend Brad, W8JJO, the showboat writer who doesn't have a very high opinion of actors, says that blocking is necessary to keep the actors from bumping into each other.

"A fly in the ointment" means something small that spoils the whole, like, well, a "fly in the ointment." It's biblical, when ointments had to do with being anointed and as I'm sure you know, that happened often in various books of the Bible. Finding a fly in the ointment during an anointment was, well, YUCK!

When I told my contacts that I ran half-a-gallon, they knew that I was running 500 watts because a gallon was a kilowatt. The ham radio gallon has nothing to do with a #10 can, which the corporal passed around for donations to fight polio. The can actually held about 3 quarts, and is no longer being manufactured, like most of the great old radios of my career in this wonderful hobby.

And ". . . down the log . . ." is a Ham term referring to the written logbook we all used to have to keep of every contact, and to say that I'll see you ". . . down the log . . ." of course means that we'd talk again.

Chapter 12

Hard Knox

I'd looked all over Ft. Knox for a Ham Radio station but couldn't find one. They had a lot of tanks, but no Ham Radio antennas that I could spot. I missed my daily fix. I missed my fiancée. I missed Mom and Andover and Jack and the freedom of civilian life in general. How long would it be before I could say to someone after a pleasant QSO that I'd see him down the log?

I realized during Basic Training that I had never before been lonely. Back on the showboat, we had a semi-disparaging phrase for elitists whenever an egregious example somehow showed up. We called them EMFs, the E being for Elitist.

Now, a ham hearing EMF would think immediately of Electro Motive Force, which as we all know is an electric potential energy measured in joules per coulomb. Or, more simply put, a potential difference, as found in a battery, i.e.: voltage. Not usually capitalized, EMF is not what we were talking about on the Showboat. Oh, no. Our EMF was much more common: Elitist Mother Fu**er. You figured that out before I told you, didn't you? If you didn't, you come from a much more sheltered environment than any of my buddies on the showboat.

To my surprise, I met an EMF in Basic. He was me. When I realized it I rationalized it. None of my barracks buddies' conversations interested me in the slightest. They loved Basic and talked about it all the time when they weren't talking about loose women they had known. The only interest I had in Basic was how to get out of it.

There was a solution to my loneliness. Get married. For some reason before I headed to Basic, Sam and I had decided to wait until I was out of the Army to get married, but Basic brought me a much more realistic view of my situation which, looked at every which way, was pretty grim. I don't do grim well. I told Sam I wanted to move our wedding date up a bit. "How much?" she asked.

"Right after I get out of Basic," I said.

"That's only seven weeks," Sam said. Being a chemistry major, she was good at math.

"So?"

"My mother won't like such short notice," said Sam.

"I'm not marrying your mother," I said, "What do you think?"

"Okay with me," said Sam.

We were married in a church for reasons known only to our parents. I remember the pre-wedding party better than the actual wedding, perhaps because of the bachelor party.

As Basic ground to the end, my principal task was to get into some sort of specialty training that didn't involve tanks, marching, mud or shooting. I took every aptitude test that came along and did well on the fundamental electronics tests (which didn't have a 78 rpm record associated with them, fortunately, only multiple choice). I always did well with multiple choice. You didn't have to know the right answer to get the right answer. I thought for a moment that maybe I could be the guy who came up with the totally absurd and obviously wrong answers for the Army's many multiple choice tests. Then I heard you needed a Ph.D. to get that job. No surprise.

I applied for radar school at Ft. Monmouth, N.J. and I got it. I couldn't believe the Army offered me that option because radar school was 39 weeks long and it looked to me like a great gig in an interesting part of the country. By the time I got out of there my Army career would be half over. I envisioned heading up to New York from Monmouth over a few long weekends to catch some plays with Sam. I didn't know that radar school would be intense and tough, requiring some weekend homework. (I certainly didn't want to flunk out of radar school, because it'd be straight to the infantry and from there to Korea, which didn't have good scuttlebutt, even during the truce.)

Sam and I flew from Cleveland to New York for our honeymoon. I had booked a nice room at the Edison Hotel because it was in the middle of the theater district. Eddie Mark (Rap) Rappaport (the fearless showboat dancer in the loincloth who, playing the bartender in "*Luste, Lucre and Liquor*," blew his nose on the bar rag) was on the plane with us and in no time everyone on board was buying drinks for the newlyweds! So much for a below-the-radar honeymoon flight.

On our honeymoon, we went to one or two plays a day for a week and ate well. It was Sam's first visit to Sardi's and the Carnegie Deli, two of my favorites in Manhattan. When our theater-filled honeymoon ended, Sam flew home to Cleveland and I got a train to Ft. Monmouth to get the lay of the land, and hopefully then send for Sam to join me. At school, predictably, the first couple of weeks were basic electronics, much of which I already knew. But I also knew (because everybody told me) that after the electronics fundamentals it'd get tough. "They'll separate tuned circuits from dummy loads" was the chatter heard so often it became band noise.

Though I'd spotted ham antennas on a couple of buildings, which you'd expect at a Signal Corps base, I had to keep my priorities straight. First, find an apartment for Sam and me. I found one too, in Rumson, in the converted attic of a big old mansion, now split up as apartment rentals. It was great. Sam drove my Ford (now our Ford) to Rumson and approved of my choice. Rumson was what my mother would have called a toney neighborhood—full of stockbrokers' homes and private schools, yet only a few miles from the Monmouth main gate.

The second priority was to be sure I had radar repair school figured out. Flunking was not an option. And, unlike at Hiram, I took what they told me to take—no easy alternatives. And unlike Ft. Knox, I didn't volunteer to type. Learning all about radar was a lot more fun.

Then, during those few times a spare moment appeared, it was off to the base Ham/MARS station to poach a little bit of time at K2USA.

Photo courtesy Keith, W6BCQ

Inside this typical Army building was a typical (powerful) Army
Ham station using top-of-the-line radio equipment.

When my visits to the station got a little bit regular and I knew when the MARS (Military Amateur Radio Service) boys had their daily schedules, I could work some operating in between their activities. Of course other hams had the same idea so sometimes I'd be at the end of a line of ops waiting. I told Jack the few times I might be on the air and he caught up with me at least once. He called me by saying, "David? Loudest in Ohio here, over." Back in 1955, if the FCC had heard that they would have sh** a brick, as the colorful if anatomically impossible Army cliché goes. Jack would say whatever came into his head, but I always came back saying, "W8LIO, this is K2USA with W8GUE at the mike." I'd worked too hard to get that license to give some FCC flunky an opportunity to take it away!

The antenna on the top of this rather unusual structure was designed for 20 Meters and put out a rock crusher signal. This was obviously pre-OSHA.

I enjoyed my stay at Ft. Monmouth. This base formed the centerpiece of the Army's communications efforts. At one time it even trained courier pigeons, a reliable means of communications when the band conditions were lousy. When the pigeons retired with honorable discharges, they all went to New York City where they are still panhandling the tourists.

On the fringes of Monmouth a couple of huge antennas pointed skyward, the location of Project Diana, so named because the Goddess Diana was the Roman Moon Goddess and she/it became a target of some imaginative Ham-thinkers. One day before my 13th birthday, on January 10th, 1946, before I'd even heard of Ham Radio, one John H. DeWitt, licensed in 1921 with the callsign N4CBC (according to Wikipedia), using a huge radar transmitting antenna, bounced the very first radio signals off the moon. The little returning echo was picked up by a gigantic receiving antenna, a bedspring-like bunch of dipoles. Jack must have known about that when he recommended that I get that bedspring antenna to pick up those weak Cleveland television stations.

Before the first moon bounce attempt, there were, of course, many skeptics. These were the "radio waves won't travel through outer space" folks. They said, "There's no air in outer space and radio waves need air to travel." But Hams, real Hams, they were the true believers, then as now. Not long after DeWitt accomplished his historic feat, Sam Harris, W8UKS, and Jack

Rodebaugh, W8LIO, plus other adventurous Hams, also bounced signals off the moon, using homemade antennas and only one kilowatt, more or less. Watching his gigantic final amplifier tubes get white hot, Jack would describe his kilowatt as, "considerably more of less than less of more" which would leave any FCC inspector scratching his head.

My Sam got a job to help support our little household in the attic of the mansion. Getting married turned out to be a good idea. I was home most nights for dinner, I got chauffeured to work and dropped off at the main gate, and Sam drove herself to the lumber company in nearby Redbank, where she was the bookkeeper. That third floor attic was a nice little honeymoon loft that even had a view. If you strained your neck a little and stood on your tiptoes, you could see Sandy Hook Bay from the upper left pane of one of our bedroom windows.

When graduation from radar repair school came around, I was given three choices of places for my next (and probably last) Army assignment: Korea, Fort Huachuca, Arizona, or 7th Army Headquarters at Böeblingen, Germany, just a few clicks from Stuttgart as the sergeant who told me my choices said. Fort Huachuca, I heard from several sergeants who'd been there, was a desert hell-hole. I'd probably pick up rocks on one side of the base, put them in a truck and drive them to the other side and dump them. Then, next day, I'd do the reverse. Korea, of course, had a porous truce and the fighting might start at any moment, and you couldn't take a wife. So, no surprise, I chose Germany, and after the shock wore off, Sam agreed with my choice.

I said goodbye to the guys at K2USA and a couple of my favorite sergeants/instructors. One of them gave me a piece of valuable intelligence. He told me that if Sam took our car to the Army's port in New Jersey, just across the water from New York City, and showed them my orders, they'd put my car on a boat for Bremerhaven, West Germany, and when it arrived, my company commander would be notified and he'd have to give me a 3 day pass to go pick it up.

I doubted this information. I'd researched it. Sergeants and above could have their cars shipped. Privates were out of luck.

My smart sergeant-intelligence-agent said, "You know that, and I know that, and the Army knows that, but the guy putting cars on the boat doesn't know that. You get your car to that boat with a copy of your orders and it'll be on the boat."

Sometimes military intelligence is accurate. My approach to it was, if you want it to be true, assume that it is.

My father always told me to be on the lookout for the brass ring, because you never knew when it's going to come around. Despite not wanting to be in the Army at all, I kept my senses tuned to opportunities, for indeed there are opportunities in the military. Some came with a little bit of risk. For instance, driving past what I knew to be the Ft. Monmouth surplus equipment warehouse I noticed a really big roll of what looked like coaxial cable right at the end of the loading dock. Curious, I turned around and stopped at the dock and asked one of the warehouse guys if this cable was surplus.

"It's going to the dump," the soldier said.

I looked at the coax. It was an unused, 500-foot roll of RG-8. My favorite.

"Do you mind if I take it?" I said.

"Help yourself."

It must have weighed 200 pounds.

"Would you mind helping me put it in the trunk?" I said.

Into the trunk it went. The poor Ford rode low on its leaf springs which had already put up with a lot through my college years. Would the guard at the gate notice I was driving a lowrider? I didn't have any paperwork on the RG-8, so what I did could be viewed as stealing by some hardass MP (they were all hardasses according to them). But I got waved right through the gate. My next hurdle was that Sam wouldn't be happy seeing that gigantic roll of coax in the trunk, but I don't remember her saying anything about it. She was practicing the stoic resolve that all Hams' wives develop, especially if they want to stay married. I was just doing what hams do.

I got a week off between radar school graduation and shipping out. Sam and I filled our Ford and headed back to Ohio to store our stuff, including, of course, my HQ-129X which I thought I'd use in our little attic apartment, but with K2USA down the road a ways, it just sat there gathering dust on its crackle finish.

It was a whirlwind trip to Ohio to say goodbye to everybody, including Sam, temporarily, and quickly back on a plane to New York City and from there to my shipping out point in New Jersey.

I joined a bunch of GI's at Andrews Army Air Force Base, not far from Ft. Monmouth. I looked around. I saw no one there from my class. The field was filled with Army planes of all shapes and sizes, all khaki, and one Navy plane, all blue. We of course were marched right over to the Navy plane and took our seats. The stewardesses were swabbies, all men, and for a while nobody said anything about the anomaly of a bunch of Army guys on a Navy plane. Most of these guys, clearly, had never flown. My seatmate squeezed my arm so hard during takeoff I thought all blood circulation to my hand had ceased. As we left land behind, he loosened his grip. The sun had set. It was a clear, cool, late fall evening on the East Coast.

After we'd gained some altitude and it looked as if we weren't going to crash after all, the squawk box came on. It had a terrible hum. "I could fix that," I thought to myself. Then the voice: "This is the captain speaking. I know you're wondering why a bunch of GI's are on a U.S. Navy plane. The reason is that while I've been in the Navy over 20 years, this is my first command in the Navy Air Corps. I just transferred over from submarines. My admiral mentioned something about not wanting to risk any Navy men on my first flight while I got used to my new command."

I was probably the only person on the plane, other than the flight attendants, who thought that was amusing. Before anybody had a chance to get too nervous, the box came on again. "Off to your left there is Philadelphia." In the background you could hear some off mike conversation going on, and then, "Correction. That's New York. Our next stop is Frankfort, er, Munich, that'll be tomorrow morning, er afternoon. Sleep well."

I, for one, reclined my seat as far as it would go and went to sleep.

When I woke up, it was about dawn. I looked out my window and could see the Atlantic (I hoped) a couple of hundred feet below me. The wheels went down. The squawk box came on. We got lower and lower and lower. We heard undistinguishable murmurs amidst the hum. The ocean got closer and closer. Then we heard the captain's voice shout, "Well, goddammit, it's got to be around here somewhere!" Everybody panicked just as the wheels touched down in the Azores. The runway extends right out over the beach, unbeknownst to any of us. The flight attendants were laughing. The swabbies got one over on the GIs.

The next thing we heard from the captain was when we were flying past Frankfort. The squawk box came on and he said, "I was kidding about just transferring from the submarine corps. You probably figured that out. And how was that landing in the Azores? Was that great or what?"

Some of the GIs gave our captain a tepid applause. He got a big hand from me.

The captain continued, "Actually, I learned to fly over this part of the world. The only difference was that then they were shooting at me and I was dropping bombs on 'em. Next stop, Munich. I told your CO that I'd be happy to fly into Stuttgart, which is where 7ᵗʰ Army is, but he said he didn't want to spoil you, so you'll be bussing it from München (giving it his best German accent) to Böeblingen, headquarters of Rommel's *Panzerkassern*, which we're borrowing because he doesn't need it any more. One piece of advice for you GIs: just remember we beat up on these Krauts pretty good, and some of them are still pissed off about it. But don't quote me; I'm just a flyboy."

When we rolled into the 7ᵗʰ Army's 39ᵗʰ Signal Battalion Headquarters the first thing I did was look around for Ham antennas, and there, about six feet above the slate roof of the headquarters building, was a 3-element 20-Meter Yagi. Hot dog! I'd be on the air!

This marked the first time I'd ever set foot outside of the United States, and I was eager to explore Germany and Europe, which even from the air looked very different than home. And it was different. As soon as Sam got here, I envisioned heading off on our first big adventure!

While I was in radar repair school, Sam and I lived in Rumson, N.J., in what my mother called a "toney" neighborhood. It could and probably should be spelled "tony" but my mother figured that if it's really toney, then it's "toney."

I really wanted to comment on the Korean War, or "conflict" as the high muckity mucks on the banks of the Potomac had labeled it. It's been called "the forgotten war" because, well, for the most part, it's been forgotten, or perhaps more accurately, overlooked. It was an unpopular war, coming as it did only five years after the end of World War Two. I knew from first-hand accounts that it was an extremely nasty war in a miserable part of the world. You were either freezing or frying. I also know it was, unlike Vietnam, a necessary war, or today the whole Korean Peninsula would be like North Korea, an entire country of brainwashed fanatics who would pose an even bigger threat to world peace than the current North Korea does.

I mentioned a "tuned circuit" which generally is a condenser/capacitor and a coil tuned to one specific frequency, sometimes called the "resonant frequency." You've seen people in old black and white movies frantically turning a couple of knobs while watching a bunch of meters on a transmitter? They were probably tuning for the "dip" which would indicate resonance. I know, I've lost you. If you want to know more, get a Ham ticket.

"München" as our Navy pilot called Munich, is the way the Germans spell it and pronounce it. They didn't know how to spell a lot of their cities as far as we GI's were concerned.

Chapter 13

Army Tales, Tall and Mostly True

I knew instantly that I had made the right choice when I picked Germany over Fort Huachuca and certainly Korea. This was a fascinating part of the world, at least to provincial me. Germany was so beautiful! How could they have started a war? I couldn't wait to get out and explore. And of course there was that big 20 Meter beam up about 100 feet on that roof! I couldn't wait to try that out either.

The enlisted men's barracks at Rommel's old headquarters were elegant, as barracks go. All concrete, two-foot thick walls and floors, windows overlooking a mini-forest outside, and huge porcelain johns. It's no wonder to me that impoverished Germans joined Hitler's army. Compared to home, this place was the Fritz Carleton. (I learned from my friend Gene Cavanaugh that you should never apologize for making a pun. Gene had a distinct punnybone. Another guy who should have been a Ham.)

I was assigned to the 39th Signal Battalion's Radio Repair Company. The army had trained me to repair the latest in radar equipment and when I got to the little repair depot that was to be my workplace for the next year or so, I discovered—guess what? No radar. Not a one. I don't know who got the broken radars, but not this little shop. Only ordinary radios of all kinds. Not only that, the place was deserted! A huge pile of radio junk waited to be repaired with only two guys working at the repair benches.

My boss at the repair shop turned out to be one of the great characters of my army career—Staff Sergeant Cornelius P. Bohan. He had been a master sergeant more times than he could remember, and a private an equal number of times. Bohan's Achilles heel was hard liquor. He was the only man I ever met who downed a pint of whiskey every day before 9 AM.

As I stood before him the first time, he looked over my orders, my record and I guess recommendations from prior commanders and said, "You're a college boy, huh? You can type, huh? We don't have radars but we do have paper. So you got a new job. You're going to be the shop clerk. I'm just assuming that if you got out of radar school at Monmouth with the grades you got, you can probably fix anything with tubes in it, so you can backup these bozos around here, am I right?"

I didn't know what to say so I said, "I guess I can, sir."

"Don't call me sir," he said, "that's basic training bullshit. Call me sergeant or Bohan, but not sir."

"Yes, sir," I said. "I mean, okay, sergeant."

"Any questions?" Bohan asked.

"Yes sir, I mean, yes, sergeant. I'd like to operate the ham radio station whenever I can. Is that possible?"

"You and me and those two guys in the shop and some of the old farts at headquarters are the only warm bodies not in the field—which means chances are, all of the Hams are in the field."

Bohan opened the middle drawer of his desk and pulled out a rabbit's foot with a key on a chain. "Try this key. It'll probably open that radio room and every other door around here. But don't tell anybody where you got it, okay?"

I didn't know it at the time, but this was the beginning of a beautiful friendship. Sarge, as I called him, or Bo, steered me to an apartment that once was the second floor of a German family's house, about 5 or 6 miles, or 10 clicks as Sarge put it, from the base. He knew about it because he and his *schatzi* lived nearby. He'd been in Germany so long that everything was clicks and meters and liters and Marks. We were two of many GIs who were "living on the economy."

Sam drove our car to New Jersey, with my mother for company, and exactly as advertised, the only guy in the army who didn't know that privates weren't allowed to ship their cars to Europe was the guy who put them on the boat. He took a copy of my orders, gave Sam a receipt for the car, and loaded it aboard. Sam and my mom took the train back to Cleveland and Sam made reservations to sail to Bremerhaven, West Germany on the *USS America*. She celebrated New Year's Eve 1955 on a gigantic passenger vessel in the very rough seas of the North Atlantic, one of the few passengers on that huge ship who wasn't seasick, despite the fact that she was rather unexpectedly pregnant.

When I unlocked the door to the 39th Signal Battalion Ham shack in the attic of the Administration Building for the first time, a gust of cold air came out that gave me pause about ever entering. But enter I did, flicked on the lights, fired up a couple of 220 volt electric heaters, and turned on the BC-610 transmitter and a R-388 receiver, also known as a Collins 51-J-3 receiver, two prize examples of American ingenuity and craftsmanship. The BC-610 transmitters had been made by a number of manufacturers during the big war, but the Collins 51-J series was the product of Collins Radio of Cedar Rapids, Iowa. Collins, at least among Hams, was a name revered world-wide because Art Collins, W0CXX, built Ham equipment that was the Swiss watch of radios.

I tuned the big Collins receiver around 20 Meters and didn't hear anything—not even any noise. No signals, no squeals, no nothing, as if the antenna was not connected. I checked. Everything seemed properly and neatly connected and the coax feedline to the big 20 Meter beam on the roof went out through a hole in the window frame and up out of sight, so I decided to try transmitting, to see if I could make the band come alive.

One squeeze of the handle on the D104 microphone filled the room with the ungodly squeal of feedback. Wow! What was that? I pushed it again and watched the meters on the BC-610 go crazy! I sat there, analyzing the problem. Two conclusions: a transmitter problem or an antenna problem. I hoped for the former, since the antenna was on a slate roof five storeys above the ground and it was the dead of the German winter. I looked around the shack for a dummy load but couldn't find one. I couldn't even find any tools or a soldering iron. The operators of DL4USA were just that, obviously: operators. At that moment they were out on maneuvers having a great time in the sub-freezing weather I'm sure. I suspect somebody from our little shop fixed the DL4USA equipment if/when it broke.

The next day I scrounged 4 or 5 hundred-watt bulbs, wired them all in series, soldered a coax plug to the two wires connecting the bulbs, and the next night was back at DL4USA. I unplugged the coax from the back of the BC 610, plugged in my string of light bulbs, and fired up the big transmitter. The string of bulbs lighted up. I spoke into the microphone. The bulbs got brighter as I spoke. I whistled into the mike. The bulbs got a lot brighter than GE ever expected them to. The transmitter worked. No need to fix it. Damn. That meant there was something wrong with the antenna, up on the slate roof. If slate alone wasn't slippery enough, in the midst of winter in Southern Germany, ice and snow made it even slipperier.

The next morning I told Sarge there was something wrong with the big Yagi on the roof and wondered aloud if we had any tower monkeys who could fix the antenna. Sarge said, "Anybody dumb enough to go onto that roof would be too dumb to fix that antenna—except you. You afraid of heights?"

I told him I'd climbed a lot of towers and been on a lot of roofs, but not a steep slate roof covered with ice and snow.

"Oh, hell," he said, "I'd never let you on that roof without my cherrypicker when it's slipperier than eel shit! You fall off; I'd be in big trouble! I can just see all my stripes disappearing. Again!

I'll get Mad Dog to bring over the high basket—that crazy bastard'll have you up to that antenna quicker'n shit through a tin horn." Where on earth did that phrase ever come from?

In an hour, a giant cherrypicker drove up and parked right in front of the steps to 39th Signal Battalion Headquarters. Helpful that the serious brass were in the field. Sarge introduced me to Mad Dog and into the basket I went. I'd gathered up all the extension cords I could find and plugged in a gigantic soldering iron, just in case. I filled my pockets with cutters, pliers, screwdrivers, and every other tool I anticipated needing to fix the antenna.

Mad Dog raised the basket up, up, up, faster than an Empire State Building elevator. When we got to the edge of the slate roof the basket abruptly stopped its rapid ascent. I looked down. OMG, as today's texters exclaim, that's a long way down! Then, looking at that straight boom holding my basket, I came to a chilling realization. But hoping my conclusion wrong, I shouted down to Mad Dog.

"Everybody out?" I thought. "This is it? I've gotta climb up this roof to that antenna? Well, crap, what else could go wrong?"

It was at that moment that I smelled smoke.

Mad Dog had bounced the bucket a couple of times on my journey up and, unbeknownst to me, the soldering iron had flipped out of its stand and was sitting on the floor, a wooden pallet with trash on the bucket floor underneath it. The trash was on fire. Or at least it was smoking, and you know the old cliché. I couldn't step on it and crush it out because the pallet was shielding the fire from my foot. I tried beating it out with a crescent wrench but that only spread it around. I finally did the only thing I could think of—I peed on it. That put out the fire, but now my basket smelled like an outhouse that Andy Gump had neglected.

From down below I heard Mad Dog's voice. "Grab the rope," he shouted. "Rope?" I thought. Then I saw it. About a one inch diameter rope hung over the gutter of the roof, up there five storeys in the air. I grabbed it and gave it a tug, and it pulled up through the ice and snow on the roof. The other end was connected to the little tower section that held the antenna six feet above the roof. Obviously, Mad Dog had been through this before. He gets you to the edge and you pull yourself up to the antenna with the rope. Swell.

I'd gotten this far; I couldn't go back now. Dealing with the rope was a two handed job minimum. The tools were in my pockets, but what do I do with the soldering iron? I picked it up carefully, measured out 20 feet or so of extension cord, and flung the soldering iron up toward the antenna. It sizzled in the snow and ice, but didn't slide off the roof. I tied the extension cord to my belt loop, and hoisted myself up onto the roof. I had never had an interest in mountain climbing, and at that moment I knew why. I took baby steps, squiggling my feet through the ice and snow cover, getting a bit of a foothold on bare slate, which, while slippery, was better than being on ice. I kept one eye on the basket, making sure that it remained directly down the roof from me. Just in case I accidentally became a luge. I'd zoom right down the roof into Mad Dog's basket. At least theoretically.

I'm glad Sam hadn't arrived yet. She'd have killed me if she'd seen this stunt.

Finally I made it to the tower and scrambled to a standing position on the peak of the roof, bear-hugging the tower, which felt good and safe but required both hands. How was I going to get anything done with no hands? What to do? I remembered the soldering iron and pulled it up to me, sizzling in the snow and ice all the way. When it got up to my feet, I tied the extension cord to a belt loop again, and then pulled up 20 feet or so of excess cord, swung it around the tower, and cinched it up as a homemade safety belt. I leaned back a little bit to test it, and it was perfect. Well, maybe not perfect since it had 220 volts in it just waiting to get out, but not bad. Then it occurred to me that I could have used the rope as a safety belt but decided to focus on my mission and not sweat the details, though sweating in Germany in winter wasn't likely. The longer I stayed up there the more likely something would go wrong.

Feeling secure, I inspected the beam. My eyes were two feet from the center of the driven element and what I saw made me smile with satisfaction. My analysis had been correct. The center conductor of the coax had come loose from the driven element. "Cold solder joint," I said to myself. I repositioned the coax feedline so the center conductor was right on the solder lug bolted to the driven element.

I pulled the feedline close to the solder lug, put the center conductor of the coax onto the solder lug, squeezed it tight with pliers out of my pocket tool stash, then pulled the soldering iron up off the roof, being very careful to pick up the handle end of it. Once my friend Brad, W8JJO, picked up the wrong end of a soldering iron in my shack and I remember his days of pain and his nearly useless hand. After the shock of seeing and smelling Brad's catastrophe, I was very careful with soldering irons. I always looked for the wood handle.

The actual soldering was easy—get both parts you're soldering scraped down to bare metal, put the soldering iron on both of them, get them as hot as you can, then apply some solder until it melts over the entire connection, remove the heat, and wait for it to solidify, making sure nothing moves while the solder hardens. Do that and you'll never have a cold (weak, non-conducting) solder joint. I watched it for a minute or so, licked my finger, touched the newly soldered joint, and it was barely warm. I jerked on the coax, and the solder joint held. Lew McCoy, W1ICP, the ARRL's soldering maven, would have been proud.

I unplugged the soldering iron, tied it to the end of the extension cord, and dropped it onto the roof. It sizzled, but not for long. I aligned myself above the waiting cherrypicker basket, grabbed the rope and slowly and carefully walked myself backwards down the roof to the basket, which I carefully sort of slid into gently. After reeling in the now cooled off soldering iron, I yelled a thumbs-up to Mad Dog and in no time I was back on the ground, not much the worse for wear.

After thanking Mad Dog, I made a dash for the shack before reporting back to Sergeant Bohan. I turned on the 51-J-3 and the BC-610 and waited for them to warm up. I knew as soon as the receiver came to life that I'd succeeded because Twenty Meters was loaded with signals. I fired up the big transmitter, tuned it up, and said, 'This is DL4USA, testing." All of the meters read just right. I turned up the gain on the 51-J-3 and found several stateside stations calling me. I got some stellar signal reports and went back to work. Bohan asked me if I fixed it. I wondered if I should admit that I'd already tried out the station when he said, "Of course you did."

Bohan's confidence in my technical prowess came from the first couple of radio "fixes" that I'd made. Unbeknownst to me, Bohan gave me a pair of radios that no one in the company had been able to fix because they both had several things wrong with them, vastly complicating trouble shooting. I fixed them, even though one fix took more than a day. From that point on I was the go-to guy with tough problems. Every time I'd finish a radio, Bohan would ask if I'd fixed it and then answer his own question in the same breath with, "Of course you did."

Bo looked a bit like actor Charles Durning, whom I had a few meetings with way later on in my life about a project that I just couldn't get off the ground. I probably could have used Mad Dog on that one too, but didn't think of him. Both Bohan and Durning were rotund but somehow very light on their feet, and quick witted.

One afternoon I was in the DL4USA shack running pileups of stateside Hams when the door opened and three GIs entered, obviously surprised to find an interloper (me) in their shack. Their surprise, however, turned to joy when they realized they'd left the shack with the transmitter and receiver on the fritz and returned to find them fixed.

One of them said, "You fixed the modulation transformer. Great!" They had assumed since the room was filled with feedback every time they pushed the mike handle that the problem was in the transmitter's audio system—thus their assumption that the modulation transformer had gone south. I never told them what their real problem had been. Instantly they made me a card-carrying member of their radio club. They, of course, spent a lot of their time in the field on maneuvers—couldn't trust those Russkies not to invade, so we had to look ready, you know. Never having been out on maneuvers, I didn't know if we were ready or not, and somehow figured that the Russians had probably had enough of war for the moment, at least of the fighting kind. The war of words of course, was fierce.

Most of the radios that came into our little shop were simple and after 39 weeks of radar school, I could fix them faster than the rest of the crew. Even so, I mostly did paperwork, because Bohan appreciated my typing speed more than my repairing speed. Now and then Bo would kid around with me—tell me that I was really running this place and I'd reduced his job to that of a fancy man—all smoke and mirrors and no real job. While that was true, I didn't think he had noticed.

Just to keep me sharp, now and then he'd give me a real problem radio to fix, like the one he dropped on my desk one day which had been run over by a truck. I found an identical one in our "parts" morgue, basically rebuilt it, change the serial number plate, and gave it back to him as the crushed radio resuscitated. We both enjoyed that kind of horseplay. When Bo gave the radio back to the motor pool, fixed, they couldn't believe it. Bohan had a sign made to hang over his desk: "Impossible repairs may take an extra day."

Now, all I needed was my wife and my car and life would be about as good as it gets—in the Army.

Schatzi is German for girlfriend, I guess. I never learned any German while I was there. No aptitude for languages. I tell people I'm still working on English.

Russkies was a derogatory term for Russians. A lot of saber rattling went on in the late 50's and beyond and they earned their derogation as far as we GI's were concerned.

111

The Panzerkassern *HQ had 5 storeys—that's British for "storys." It just seems to me that "storey" is appropriate for buildings and "story" is appropriate for fiction. It may be an idiosyncrasy but my Mother would approve.*

The BC-610 and Collins 51-J-3 are of course the big transmitter and receiver known to all (old) Hams as the workhouse pair of the Signal Corps, still in use in a lot of Hamshacks around the world whose owners prefer Amplitude Modulation to the much more modern Single Sideband. When it was first devised, SSB (as single sideband is known), was called Single Sideband Suppressed Carrier, partly because that's what it was and mostly to distinguish it from Amplitude Modulation which transmitted a radio frequency signal (the carrier) and two sidebands. AM took/takes up a lot of radio spectrum space, at least compared to SSB and CW (Morse Code) and a lot more than PSK 31, an interesting teletype-like mode favored by my friend Brad, W8JJO and lots of others who'd rather read their QSOs on a computer screen than listen to them in headphones. More on PSK 31 and other oddball Ham Radio creations later on in the book, if I remember them.

Collins Radio, while the company has been gone for decades, is far from forgotten. A national Collins Collectors Association and clubs still exist in cities worldwide. I even have a Collins transceiver in my office. I never use it, but I'm sure it would work. After all, it's a Collins.

I mentioned that I was "running pileups" from DL4USA, which means, as you've probably guessed, that lots of people called me and I was giving them signal reports as fast as possible. The DL4USA QSL card was a prized piece of wallpaper for a lot of Hams.

The "Dummy Load" I built to test the BC-610 is just that—a substitute antenna. I wired the five 100-watt bulbs in series so when I transmitted 500 watts into them, they'd light up but not blow out. If I'd wired them in parallel, they'd only be able to handle 100 watts total and not only would have burned out but possibly blown up! Best to know your series from your parallel. See what fun Ham Radio can be?

I mentioned that Lew McCoy, W1ICP, one of the more entertaining guys at ARRL Headquarters, would have been proud of my solder joint. One of his pet peeves was cold solder joints, which often look good but don't work, like a lot of people you hire to do a job for you these days. Cold solder joints happen because the solder on one part of the connection wasn't hot enough or the wires weren't clean enough, or whatever. They result in weak and just plain inferior connections.

Lew was first and foremost an antenna expert. I never missed an opportunity to hear Lew speak at the various Ham conventions we attended. I learned a lot about both antennas and speaking to Hams from observing Lew. Keep it fast, keep it funny, and never mind if the subject of your talk gets lost in your digressions. "Life is just a series of digressions," Lew once told me. I believed him and tucked his phrase into my handful of eternal verities.

Chapter 14

Car and XYL,
Not Necessarily In That Order

When I told Sarge that my wife was coming into Bremerhaven on the giant ocean liner *America*, he said that our company commander didn't like GIs bringing their wives over (though the Army itself rather encouraged it) and he wouldn't give any free time off to go pick up wives. But when the hard-ass CO got a notification that my *car* had arrived in Bremerhaven, he called me into his office to ask how I, a mere GI, and a draftee at that, had managed to get my car shipped to Germany.

"How, sir?"

"Yes, how?"

"Well, my wife took it to the port in New Jersey with a copy of my orders, and . . . well . . . here we are."

The Captain sighed. He'd been beaten. "Here's your three-day pass to pick up the car. Get out of here."

I took the train to Bremerhaven, found the car, gassed it up at about 10 cents per litre, courtesy of a rebate from the US Government. Germans were paying over $2.00 a litre. One more thing to piss them off. It was great to get behind the wheel of my Ford. No mobile rig though. The army wouldn't allow non-standard accessories to be shipped. That way they couldn't be stolen. Of course since they weren't shipped, you didn't have them. So either way, you didn't have your gadget. That's what's known as Army logic.

I found the dock where the *America* was scheduled to tie up in a couple of hours, looked out to sea, and sure enough, saw a gigantic ship headed my way. Hallelujah! In no time at all, Sam was in the car, her two big trunks were in the back seat, her suitcase in the trunk, and we were off for our new home in Sindelfingen.

Although the Army won't give you time off to pick up your wife, it will give you time off to pick up your car. If you were a phenomenal planner or just plain lucky, the wife and the car would arrive together. As so often with me, luck prevailed. Even though she got picked up perfectly, when Sam heard that the car rated the three-day pass and she didn't, she shook her head and said, "SNAFU! That's the Army."

When we arrived in front of the house on the knoll in Sindelfingen and I shooed away the guard geese who patrolled the yard honking and hooting at each and every intruder, I took Sam up to see our second floor apartment. She approved, though it was a far cry from our digs in Rumson, N.J. It did, however, have a great view of a long straight road that went right past the little hill our neighborhood was on. Look straight down that road a couple of miles or so and you saw the main gate of the Mercedes factory, and along that road, parked on the wide shoulder, new Mercedes with their hoods up and men in white coats with stethoscopes listening to the engines. If you looked closely inside the chalk circles on some of the cars, you might detect a tiny flaw in the paint that would have to be redone. Was I impressed? You'd better believe it! I'd been to the Plymouth plant and never noticed anybody with a stethoscope!

The apartment I rented was actually just the second floor of a typical German house. The family lived on the first floor, and the displaced son lived in the attic, which I suspect he wasn't too happy about. It got very cold up there in the wintertime. We kept our milk on the inside steps to the attic, and it froze now and then. Even the beer, with a lot of alcohol in it, froze. I felt sorry for the poor guy in the attic but he seemed okay with the situation and tried his English out on me at every opportunity. I gave him five Marks to climb a tree in the yard and hook one end of my antenna to it.

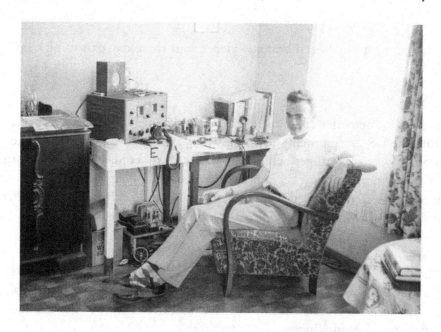

The HQ-129X had survived yet another trip. That it continued to work at all was a continuing surprise and delight. It did go to the shop in Böeblingen once for new tubes and an alignment, but it didn't really need it.

A small table by a window was perfect for the shack. The HQ 129 X had come over in one of Sam's trunks. I hooked it to a wire out the window and was listening to signals from everywhere. It was a terrific location! I built a little 20 Meter transmitter at the shop out of junked radios and in no time I was on the air from our digs in Sindelfingen. If I'd operated CW, I would have made a lot more contacts, but I, like my Elmer, was a phone man.

—— DEUTSCHE BUNDESPOST ——

AMATEUR RADIO STATION AND OPERATOR LICENSE
for Allied Personnel in the US Zone of Germany and US Sector of Berlin

Pfc David L. Bell   W 8 GUE

(Title and name of licensee)   (Call sign of FCC-license)

176 Sig Co (Repair), APO 46, Sindelfingen,
Sonnenbergstr. 50

(Address and location of station)

DL 4 NV

(Call sign)

is authorized to install and operate an amateur radio station under the licensing provisions given by Military Government (Bipcom) **for a period of one year** from the date of issuance, unless sooner terminated or suspended by the appropriate authority.

Deutsche Bundespost

27/1/56 Oberpostdirektion Stuttgart ,27 Jan 1956

(Date of issuance)   For the President

Druck Moser, Darmstadt — 2000 — 8. 53. (F 633)   FTZ — IV K — Nr. 1

My ticket from the German version of the FCC. Much faster service than the FCC back stateside.

My little homebrew transmitter ran about 50 watts of AM Phone on 20 Meters and, being crystal controlled, didn't drift too badly, no worse than the HQ-129X anyway. I worked stations all around Europe. It was remarkable how quickly Hams whose countries had been all but destroyed got back on the air after the war. Getting a station on the air might not be a Ham's first priority, but on the other hand, it might be too.

In the late 50's sunspots were abundant, usually in the dozens, day in and day out. Twenty Meters was open to many parts of the world seemingly 24 hours a day. Not that I could take advantage of it. I had to go to work every day. Not only that, but in one of Germany's worst winters ever, I had kind of volunteered to pick up Bohan every day and schlep him off to work with me.

It never got above freezing for 30 straight days, and was around zero most of those days. The only car that started every day, without fail, was my Ford. Before I left Germany, that car was legend. I'm sure nobody ever put a stethoscope on that V8 engine, but it didn't need one. It was very healthy. Other GI's with dead cars requested rides to the base. If Bohan okayed them, they got a ride.

Even before Bohan got to know me well, he asked if he could have my monthly liquor ration. He'd do me a favor down the line he said. He was already doing me a favor. As long as I got my paperwork filed with 7ᵗʰ Army, I could do pretty much anything I wanted to. Sam and I couldn't really afford booze anyway, so we gave him our ration.

Germany is where I really got my taste for beer and wine, especially wine, because Hiram had gotten me very well acquainted with beer. Every little German town had at least one brewery, and winery, and often several. On weekends, Sam and I would drive out from Sindelfingen exploring. Lunch was never complete without at least one "local" beer or wine for me and a wine for Sam. This was long before anybody worried about how wine would affect a fetus. I think our little fetus Kathy liked it. She does now anyway.

My father taught me to be an adventuresome eater, and when Sam and I got far off the beaten path, exploring tiny little German towns that had seen few if any American Fords navigating their narrow streets, we'd sometimes stop at a restaurant with no one who could (or would) translate the menu. Once I ordered Steak Tartare.

"What's Steak Tartare?" Sam wondered.

"I haven't the foggiest," I replied.

What came was a ball of very lean, uncooked hamburger with little piles of spices around it. I just sat there and looked at it. The proprietor came by, mixed the meat and the spices together and nodded satisfaction at his creation.

"So," he said.

"Danke Schoen," I said, and ate the Steak Tartare. It was good. Strange but good. I think Sam, to this day, is surprised that I scarfed it right down. My father would have been proud.

Sam was getting a little big in the belly, causing some waitresses and other German females to try feeling the bulge and attempting conversation. Sam spoke a bit of scientific German, but here in Southern Germany, the pronunciations were too earthy for her to get much. In any event, none of the strange German food seemed to do our fetus any harm. In fact, daughter Kathy today is an adventuresome eater. Sam's German pediatrician seemed pleased with her progress, which might have been because he didn't speak much English and she didn't speak much German. If we'd been in a German hospital this wouldn't have been particularly unusual, but this was at a U.S. Army hospital.

Before Sam got to be too obviously pregnant, we decided to take our leave while we could, and go to Paris, the Riviera, Northern Italy, Liechtenstein, and Switzerland—all in less than two weeks, driving our Ford, often on roads designed for horse and buggies. I kept my eye peeled for Ham antennas but saw very few. I spotted some wires that might have been Ham antennas, but being a big-signal guy, I was looking for Yagis. The one in Switzerland was the only one I spotted.

In Paris, Sam, using her very best high school French, tried to get us into a hotel by saying, "Un chambre pour deux, sil vous plait?"

Looking Sam up and down, the proprietress of the little hotel said in English, "Not for you, madame." As this was happening I thought, this is Paris? Where anything goes? And we're even married! Oh. Maybe that was the problem. We moved on to an innkeeper with a memory long enough to know who saved his ass in World War II.

In Italy, after being challenged at several traffic lights, Sam dragged a Ferrari, and won, but then she got smoked in the mountains, though she had our tires squealing. Way further down the log, our two sons, David and Mitchell, regularly demonstrated the Sam speeding gene, leaving skid marks in places I'd be sure to notice on my way to work. I remember a couple of new tires lasting about a month. Son Dave was a professional race car driver for a while—until his winnings failed to meet his expenses. Son Mitch collects cars.

I saw my first Thunderbird in the showroom window of a Ford dealership in Zurich. I loved it. It was beautiful.

Back in Germany, a local Mercedes driver tried to force Sam off the road, but he ended up in the ditch. I don't quite know how Sam accomplished that one. I was too busy hanging on to have it really register. Sam had not had her share of time behind the wheel since she got to Germany because I took the car every day, and she had been housebound taking it easy "because of the baby." At least that's what she thinks her doctor told her. Our leave was great fun, if a bit more exciting than I anticipated.

Every morning on our drive in to the base, Bohan asked how Sam's pregnancy was coming and every morning I'd tell him she was fine but a little bored since she couldn't get a job. One day he told me he was going to get me a free three-day pass.

"Really?"

"You're going to be the 39th Signal Battalion's Soldier of the Month."

I almost choked. I hadn't polished my boots since I left the States. I never stood with the rest of the troops for inspection. Bohan needed me at the shop, or so he told the CO. My fatigues were perpetually wrinkled. I only shaved every other day, if that. From a spit and polish standpoint I looked like Joe Btfsplk from Li'l Abner.

"C'mon, Sarge, I'm the last guy in this Battalion who they'd choose as Soldier of the Month," I said, quite correctly. Of course I wasn't taking Bohan's connections and due bills into account. Much to my astonishment I was announced as Soldier of the Month. The only downside was I had to put on my dress uniform, polish my boots, get a haircut, shave, and look like a real soldier. A formal ceremony took place on the front lawn of the Headquarters Building, and I got not only my coveted three day pass, but a plaque, which I have to this day, hanging in the Dave Bell Memorial Bathroom of our home in the Hollywood Hills.

It's rusted and scuffed, but is a testimony to the power of politics. I hereby apologize to whoever should have gotten this plaque. Once he thought of it, Bohan would not be deterred. It's one more proof that sergeants run the Army.

Sam and I thoroughly enjoyed my free three-day pass. We jumped on the Autobahn, and barreled off toward Vienna, Austria, for an overnighter and a tour of the city. I don't remember anything about Vienna from that visit, but I do remember coming to a halt on the Autobahn while a tow truck tugged and tugged to get a crashed motorcar up a steep hill, out of a stand of young trees. I expected to see a totaled vehicle once it made it back to the Autobahn, but was surprised to see a Mercedes 300 SL Gullwing appear on the berm. The owner of the car walked around it, inspecting all of the dents, scrapes and scratches, raised the rider's door and slammed it, raised the hood and slammed it, raised the trunk and slammed it, opened the driver's door, jumped in, started the magnificent car, and zoomed off down the highway as if nothing had happened.

I could have bought a new 300 SL for about $6,500 U.S., but I didn't have that kind of cash in 1956. That car in good shape today would probably bring several hundred thousand dollars. It's just as well that I couldn't afford it. I wouldn't have been smart enough to hang onto it, anyway.

One day Bohan burst into my office. (Yes, I had an office in the shop so I wouldn't be disturbed by techs asking pesky questions.)

"Hot damn," he shouted, "the flyboys have a radar for you to repair! Maybe. That dumb-ass lieutenant over there doesn't think it's broken but a new radar operator is sure that it is. I'm bettin' on the operator! Your big moment is here!"

An Army airbase that was just a few clicks down the Autobahn from Böeblingen was experiencing an unusual confluence of events. They had a new radar operator in the control tower who insisted that their PPI scope wasn't working and their electronics repairman was on leave. What to do? They did what everybody in Southern Germany did when they had an electronics problem. They called Bohan. So the very next morning a Jeep and a driver showed up at our little repair shop and I was whisked off to the airbase to solve their problem. Hopefully.

Finding the airport control tower was not a problem since it was the tallest structure on the base. Once introduced, I was led to the Plan Position Indicator scope where I met the new operator, fresh out of Ft. Gordon, Georgia. Now, the PPI scope is the indispensable piece of equipment in every control tower that movie directors love because the lighted line sweeps around a cathode ray tube with its fixed point in the center of its round display.

I took a look and the sweep line was rotating, the red pilot light was on, and it showed images on the tube made by nearby buildings.

"So what's the problem?" I asked the new and by now defensive radar operator.

119

"Look at this," he said, putting his finger on what looked like a building. "What do you think that is?"

"Looks like a building," I said.

"Watch for it on the next sweep," he said, leaving his finger on the CRT.

Sure enough, the next sweep around produced no building under his finger.

"Aha," he said.

"Aha, indeed," I said, "the case of the disappearing building."

The tower's second lieutenant was watching and said, "I never got a complaint from the two operators prior to Private, err . . ." he sneaked a look at the complaining private's name above his breast pocket, "err, Bergman telling me it wasn't working. His predecessors certainly thought it was working. They stared at it hour after hour." He looked at me, reading my pocket and said, "What do you think, Private Bell?"

"Well, sir," I said, "it looks to me like it's not working." I put my finger on what these radar operators called a target as the sweep line went by.

"Let's see if this building or whatever is still here on the next pass."

We all waited the minute or so for the sweep line to make it around 360 degrees and sure enough, the object on the screen, there only a minute ago, was gone.

"This scope shows you phantom buildings," I said.

The new radar operator looked smug.

The Lieutenant said, "Can you fix it?"

"Probably," I said. "How do I get around behind these relay racks?"

The tower was designed so that all of the radar and radio innards were in 6-foot relay racks built into a wall. None of those messy wires showed. There was no apparent way to get behind them. The lieutenant pointed to a narrow door in the wall, which I entered. There, hidden from the tower occupants, I found the inner workings of a control tower. Wires and cables everywhere. I located the PPI radar rack, opened the back door, and noticed first that all the tubes were lighted. Each chassis was plugged into the one above it with a cable or two or three.

Getting on my hands and knees to look at the bottom chassis, I pulled out a few instruction/installation manuals that had been stuffed in among the electronics, for safe keeping no doubt. I pulled the manuals out and noticed that one plug hadn't gotten plugged into its socket, probably when the thing had been installed. Or maybe the books had pushed it out. I put one hand behind me, reached inside the radar rack, and plugged the plug into what was obviously its socket. Immediately I heard Private Bergman yell, "Yea, you fixed it!"

I closed the back of the relay rack and emerged into the tower, ready for my medal. The PPI scope was filled with images. You could even see airplanes taxiing around the airport, just the way God intended.

"See, sir," said Private Bergman, "That's the way it's supposed to be!"

The lieutenant handed me a 10 Mark bill. I waived it off, about to say that fixing this stuff was my job, when he said, "Private Bell, please give this to Sergeant Bohan."

I smiled, "Yes sir," I said. "I'll be happy to do it."

When I got back to my little repair shop, Bohan said, "Well, did you fix it? I dropped the 10 Mark bill on his desk. "Of course you did," he said, with as big a smile as he ever managed. "Only fools and second lieutenants bet against Bohan," he said.

The Army had invested I don't know how many tens of thousands of dollars in my radar repair education just so I could put a plug into its socket. I rationalized that it was a good investment, because now that airfield could see its runways, planes, vehicles and buildings, and perhaps keep them from bumping into each other.

Actually, I saved the army a lot of money during my stint in the service. When I got to Bohan's shop, I was busy every day with nothing but paperwork. Every piece of equipment that showed up needed a piece of paper when it came in, when we worked on it, when we fixed it, and when we shipped it out. All of those reports and more were sent to 7th Army, properly filled out, every day. What was broken? Could we fix it? Etc., etc., etc. Every day a pile of paper left my typewriter heading for 7th Army. After I'd been on the job a week I realized I'd spend my entire European tour of duty buried in paperwork. Not my idea of fun. I called the guy who got all of this paper at 7th Army and asked him what he did with my gargantuan output.

"I file it," he said.

"Does anybody ever look at it?"

"Never," he said. "I'm about out of file cabinets."

The next day I tossed one particularly annoying set of blank forms into the wastebasket. Each week thereafter, in the vivid phrase the army loved, I shitcanned yet another category of fill-in-the-blank forms. Shortly after my paperwork downsizing began, Bohan noticed me spending more time fixing stuff in the shop. He was curious how I found the time to both fill out the forms and fix equipment. "Seventh Army doesn't need all of the forms we've been sending," I said with as innocent a look as I could muster.

Bohan then told me his theory about how we won the war, and he of course was talking about World War II, "the big war" in the parlance of most of the older non-coms in 7th Army.

"We won the war because the Germans were the only army in the world that had more paperwork than we did," he said.

And there you have it. In that one sentence, Bohan proved to me that the paperwork reallocation program that I had created was indeed patriotic, and probably even heroic. It was justification for my receiving the Solder of the Month Award. The fact that only two people in 7th Army, both enlisted men, knew about it, only added to its importance. It was a stealth program before the word had achieved notoriety. The "need to know" list for the paperwork reallocation program was the smallest in Army history—only one person—me. Of course my pal at headquarters who used to spend all day filing the crap I cranked out was now catching up on his reading, and keeping mum. We were both draftees, and as such, innocents. "Who, me?"

With Bohan's "anything goes; just don't get caught" attitude, one day when all of the troops were once again out in the field and the base was deserted, I told him the Ham station needed a 15-Meter beam, because I was getting a lot of requests from Stateside stations to "meet them on 15."

"What's it going to take?" he said with his usual we-can-do-anything scowl.

"Well, I need a tower and a beam," I said. "I can build the beam if I can scrounge around a bit."

"How about a telephone pole?"

"That'd be fine if it's tall enough."

"It will be," Bohan said. "I'll get the pole and Mad Dog and you can do a midnight requisition of the antenna parts."

The next day, a humongous wooden pole lay on the 39th Signal Battalion front lawn. That day I got six tank whips from the motor pool, and for five bucks had a guy in carpentry build me a double 2x2 12-foot-long wooden boom which I planned to nail to the top of the pole and point toward the States. I'd looked all over, but had been unable to find a prop pitch motor or any other kind of antenna rotor.

Grabbing the *ARRL Handbook* off the shelf of tech manuals at the shop, I checked the element dimensions and spacing for a 15-Meter beam, trimmed the tank whips a bit, bolted them onto the boom (wood isn't a great insulator, but it's not awful) and in one day, when all of the brass was in the field, built the beam on the front lawn of Battalion Headquarters.

Mad Dog showed up with a hole-digging truck, dug an eight-foot hole where I had put my chalk "X," took that truck away and brought in a crane. He picked the pole up just toward the top from center, I nailed the beam on it and he carefully picked it up and dropped it in the hole. He nudged it around a little bit so the Yagi was pointed the direction I wanted it, held the pole vertical while a couple of guys I'd recruited filled in the hole, cleaned the excess dirt off the grass, and planted some flowers around the base of the mast in a kind of instant flower bed. That'd been Bohan's idea. Keep 'em looking down at the landscaping and they won't be looking up wondering who authorized the humongous antenna. What I saw was a three-element 15-Meter beam pointed stateside, 55 feet off the ground. It was a thing of beauty. I heard that the CO told his lieutenant to thank whoever was responsible for the new flower bed.

Anytime I had a free moment I'd head to the shack. I'd always tune the receiver around the band a bit, usually on 15 Meters since I was understandably proprietary about the antenna for that band. I'd spend a little time looking for someone who sounded interesting, so I could have more than a "... hello ... you're Q5, S9 ... goodbye ..." QSO. Often I'd look for weaker signals, guys not running much power or without a big antenna. Little Pistols, as they are known, appreciated the DX contact more than the full gallon boys. One day I heard a mobile station signing off with another station in the States. The mobile's callsign was K6IPV, and he told the other guy his handle was Don, and his QTH was San Diego. That was a long schlep from Southern Germany. When Don said his final 73 to his contact, I called him.

"K6IPV mobile," I said, "this is DL4USA. How copy, Don? Over." That was all. No long call from me. He either got it or he didn't. I was ruthless. There was a pause. "DL4USA, DL4USA, well, that's a surprise. This is K6IPV mobile in San Diego, California. I don't get called by a DX station very often." And we went on to have a nice QSO, with Don requesting my QSL card, please, to prove that he'd worked Germany from his mobile station. I was happy to oblige, particularly since DL4USA was an official government installation and we didn't have to put stamps on our stateside mail.

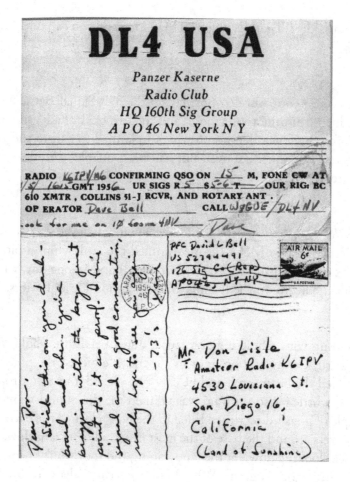

*The DL4USA QSL was a typical QSL card of the day. The Government not only
paid for the card, but the postage. Nowadays, QSL cards border on works of art.*

One day, reading some of the official communications that settled on Bohan's desk, I noticed that the Army had come to the conclusion that higher education was a good thing. Anyone currently in the Army accepted to an accredited college or university could be released from active duty up to three months prior to the official end of his or her time left to serve. I could get out in the fall instead of in the winter, and all I needed was enrollment in a college class that began up to three months before my mustering-out date. I'd already graduated from Hiram, but didn't I need another class in something or other? You bet I did.

I was accepted at Hiram (no surprise) and the Army, not knowing how invaluable I was battling the paperwork logjam at 7th Army, decided they could do without me, so I got an early discharge. Hallelujah! It wasn't that I really disliked the army; actually, I was having a pretty good time. It was that I wanted to get on with my life. The fact that I didn't precisely know what I wanted to get on with might be seen by some as a pitfall, but for me it wasn't a problem—some brass ring would come by and with a little bit of luck, I'd grab it.

While we didn't know that the future Kathryn Anne Bell was a girl, we did know that she was overdue. We also knew that she couldn't fly until she was 30 days old, and she showed no sign of making her debut. She could screw up our early discharge! Sam discovered that her German doctor wasn't going to speed up the birth so we could only worry and wait. All of my carefully laid plans and the mountain of paperwork I'd filled out for the early release could be derailed by an infant, or lack of an infant, in the case of our reluctant baby.

Kathy was due on August 1st. She arrived on August 13th. If she'd dawdled around much longer I would have lost my early discharge and her name would have been Mud.

We sold our wonderful Ford to friends and for the first time in my adult life, I didn't own an automobile. We had a going away party at which I got rip roaring drunk and told Bohan I'd never forget him. While I may have made a bit of a fool of myself at that party, I didn't get thrown in the brig, and I was together enough to gather up my little family the next day and somehow get to the airport. Our household goods, including my HQ 129 X and the spare-parts transmitter, got sent home by ground, and arrived about three months later.

The commercial charter DC-6 that brought a bunch of us GIs home was forced to stop in Gander, Newfoundland for what the pilot called, "mechanical problems." When the three of us, plus a hundred or so other GIs, wives and children, got off the plane, we discovered that we were in the middle of a huge puddle of oil. As we tippy toed through the oil slick I thought, "Why does he park in the middle of a big puddle?" Then we learned that the big puddle was all of the hydraulic fluid that had recently been controlling our airplane. Mechanical problems indeed. If he'd lost any more fluid over the North Atlantic we would have been coasting to our stop in Gander, maybe with the help of a few pine trees.

Even though Newfoundland wasn't home, it had some of the trappings of Ohio, and we knew that if we had to, we could take a train the rest of the way. My army career lacked only one piece of paperwork from being over: my honorable discharge. Actually, it was many pieces of paperwork as it turned out. I could simplify the discharge process paperwork, I thought, but then realized that it was no longer my job to save the army's ass.

They tried to get me to join the Army Reserve. Are you kidding?

I had done my duty and was now a proud veteran. And no, I'm not joining the American Legion.

A few reminders and definitions: A QSO you probably remember is an over the air conversation, one of the many "Q" signals used by Hams with great regularity.

I mentioned "Little Pistols" as being small stations, usually low power, so-called because the rest of us were known as "Big Guns."

More sunspots appeared at the tail end of the 1950's than any other time in recorded history for reasons that nobody really knows. As I mentioned earlier, that meant that worldwide communications via Ham radio was a piece of cake. At the time, I had no idea how good those conditions actually were. I explained sunspots before, didn't I? If not, I will later, despite the fact that they are inexplicable.

I mentioned that if I had used CW (Continuous Wave, you'll remember, better known as Morse code) I would have made more contacts. That's because it's easier to make weak signal contacts with CW than with Phone (Voice). You can figure out why, can't you? You can hear tiny tones in a lot of noise that would total obliterate speech. I became a phone man was because Jack (my so-called Elmer) was a phone man. Didn't I explain all of this before? Oh, well, repetition is the soul of education.

Looking for more than a Q5, S9 signal meant that I wanted to get into a real conversation, not just exchange reports. Q is for quality or readability, and S is for strength. S meters on receivers top out at 9. After that it's db above 9. More than you need to know.

As all GI's who served in Germany know, a "click" is a kilometer, roughly 5/8th of a mile, I think—something like that. Since my Ford speedometer showed only miles per hour, I knew if the speed limit was 50 kilometers per hour and I went 50 miles per hour, I was speeding. But I quickly learned that Europeans take speed limit signs merely as suggestions.

I mentioned that I hadn't taken Bohan's "due bills" into account when it came to base politics. In the financial world, due bills are always written proof of a certain kind of debt. In the Army, due bills are never written but always cashable anyway.

When I stuck my hand into the radar set at the Air Force control tower, I kept one hand behind me, not to scratch my ass as one cynic suggested, but to keep any voltage that my working hand might inadvertently find from looking at my body as a short circuit, what some observer might correctly consider a "dead short."

My cynical XYL (wife) considered many Army happenings a SNAFU, a popular acronym meaning Situation Normal—All Fu**ed up!

Sergeant Bohan said his Achilles heel was booze. We all know that the phrase "Achilles heel" connotes a fatal weakness, but did you know that the original Achilles had only one vulnerable part on his body, his heel? That was because his mother dunked him into the River Styx as a baby and she held him by his heel, causing all parts of his little body except his heel to become indestructible. How his mother got him to the River Styx and back is a mystery, at least to me.

The 1955 T-Bird that I saw in that Zurich showroom may as well have been in a museum. It was the only car on display. I loved that car. But I couldn't afford it. Now I can afford it. I have a T-Bird, a yellow 2002, the only year they made that color. Mine is just like the one that Bob Heil, K9EID, has. Bob is the great audio guru of Ham radio. Almost every headset you see in pictures of Ham operators at their rigs has the word HEIL on it. Bob was honored by the Rock and Roll Hall of Fame not too long ago. Sam and I and a lot of other hams were there to share in the moment.

At my drunken farewell party I told Bohan I'd never forget him. Obviously, not all drunken pronouncements are forgotten.

I realized years later that the Army bureaucracy prepared me for life in California, a state that never met a ridiculous regulation that it wouldn't enact and try to enforce.

Whatever else it was, the Army was certainly a great source of tall tales—many of them even true.

Chapter 15

No Time for Ham Radio?

There was never no time for Ham Radio—at least for W8GUE (me). Friends of mine have let their licenses lapse because of extreme inactivity, but not me. I worked too hard getting my license ever to let it go. In the 50's you had to be ready to show the FCC that you were active—on the air, in order to renew your license. While I doubted that the FCC ever checked any Hams for their activity level, should they ever get around to checking me, I would be prepared. I hadn't endured the Boy Scouts for no reason at all. I appropriated their motto, and applied it, at least when it came to government entities.

When Sam and Kathy and I got back to Ohio after mustering out, civilians again, an overwhelming number of things needed doing, including getting on the air—but I couldn't do so because my HQ-129X was traveling again, on its way back from Germany with the rest of our stuff. Since the receiver is the most important piece of equipment in anyone's shack, what to do? I'd figure that out, but first I had to do my duty.

And my duty was fulfilling my obligation to the Army. When they came up with the "we'll let you out early if you go to college" scheme, it seemed an invitation to get on with my life. While I didn't know what I wanted to get on *to*, I knew it *wouldn't* be the Army. I had experienced both the Army and college and believe me, college is better, especially with Korea still simmering and liable to blow at any time. It was safer on the hill at Hiram than anyplace in the Army. To the Army's credit, they worked like hell to get me to join the reserves, but I had done my bit.

Back at Hiram College, I felt too old for the dorm (they still had rules like no alcohol in your room and besides, I didn't want any roommate other than Sam) so I rented a room for six weeks at what today would be called a B&B. It was in one of the many houses that ringed the campus and the breakfasts alone were worth the rent.

The class I took required little homework, so I could dash up to Cleveland and visit my little family with great regularity.

I checked out our old Hamshack in the basement of the Ad Building. It had been turned into a storeroom. Ignominious. The big old Temco transmitter was gone. Somebody had stolen it before I had a chance to. Damn.

My pal, the head of the Drama Department, Doug Mitchell, was no longer around. He moved to Vermont or New Hampshire, one of those original 13, and opened a bookshop.

When I left Hiram for the second time, I rejoined my little family, living with my in-laws in Cleveland while I looked for a job. My mustering out pay and savings allowed me not to take the first job that came along. On weekends we were back and forth to Andover in the 1955 Pontiac 4-door that my mother got almost as a gift from one of her Andover friends whose husband had passed to his reward. The widow couldn't drive and the car had been in her garage some three years or more. My mother regularly picked her up and drove her downtown, a distance of maybe 300 yards.

When I opened her garage and took a look at my new car, under the dust it actually looked like new if you discounted the flat tires and the dead battery. The straight-eight had five thousand miles on it. Not in the slightest stylish, but oh my, was it ever practical. It had a trunk the size of Yankee Stadium. And it was free. My mother and her friend gave it to us as a gift. Mom wanted us to have it particularly because of her granddaughter, so we could get Kathy down to Andover regularly and her nibs would travel safely in that gigantic tank of a car.

Even though I'd been out of circulation only a couple of years, Ham Radio had undergone some big changes. Single Sideband Suppressed Carrier got all the headlines in *QST* and *CQ Magazines*. I didn't have an SSB transmitter, only my old Viking One, still among the best AM transmitters around. But alas, AM was "ancient mode."

Single Sideband had replaced Amplitude Modulation in many Ham shacks and was gaining adherents daily. When Jack, W8LIO, succumbed to SSB, I knew I would be a short-timer among the diehard AM guys.

An odd-looking SSB receiver that they built right over in Miamisburg, Ohio, had been on the market a couple of years and I decided I needed one. It looked like a mailbox as some of its detractors noted but it delivered superior reception of SSB signals and weighed less than half as much as my HQ-129X. A lighter, smaller receiver made sense to me, since I figured my immediate future would probably involve traveling to catch those brass rings wherever they appeared.

As rationalizations in favor of the Drake 1A kept accumulating, I capitulated. I got one. Don't ask where I got the money for a new receiver because I never question my own Ham Radio purchases and as a consequence have no idea. I do know that my new daughter, Kathy, didn't miss any meals.

So it looks like a mailbox! Ham Radio is changing constantly, but hams know what equipment is supposed to look like, and this mailbox didn't look like a receiver. I loved this radio, and I talked up its unorthodox shape.

The Drake 1A received AM, fortunately, though you had to hold your mouth just right while tuning in an AM signal. My Viking One worked as well as it had when I left it on my back porch shack a couple of years earlier, but it was still just an AM transmitter (and CW of course, but we've already covered that). I hankered after an SSB transmitter, and the one I wanted and was almost affordable was the Central Electronics 20A.

I landed a job in downtown Cleveland at the Industrial Publishing Company. I started out as what the movie business would call a gofer but was promised a promotion to assistant editor if I played my cards right.

I would have preferred a job at one of the local television stations, but they weren't hiring—not even college grads with showboat experience and an honorable discharge!

I interviewed with the number three guy at the Industrial Publishing Company and the number one in editorial, an intellectual dynamo named Bud Goodman. He'd read some of the stuff I'd written in Miss Vincent's Advanced Comp class at Hiram and I guess was impressed. If he wasn't, he didn't say so. And at least I could type. At the end of the interview he said, "You're hired."

And that was that, other than filling out a bunch of forms that reminded me of the Army, and being shown how to punch in and out on the time clock. I had to punch in and out on a time clock? What kind of a sweatshop had I signed onto?

After getting the corporate paperwork and the time clock routine finished, I headed back to Bud's office to get my first assignment. He pulled a book out of a stack of a dozen or so copies, handed it to me, and told me to report for work the next morning ready to answer questions about the book: Rudolph Flesch's *The Art of Plain Talk*. I am a slow reader. Always have been. And I didn't have time to take a speed reading course. *The Art of Plain Talk* is not a thick book, but it's a whole book, and he expected me to get it read in half a day! This guy was a slave driver! My first day on the job and I had homework!

When I finally closed the book in the middle of the night, I understood why Bud wanted me to read it. His magazines, with titles such as *Applied Hydraulics, Industry and Welding* and *Aeronautical Purchasing*, demanded "plain," interesting, and easy to read writing.

When I was handed my first paycheck, I celebrated by heading over to Prospect Avenue in downtown Cleveland to see if any of the radio stores had a Central Electronics 20A kit, since the kit was fifty bucks cheaper than the factory-built version. As so often was the case, my timing was perfect. A disgruntled purchaser had just returned a 20A, complete with what looked like a commercially made outboard VFO. It was a sweet package, exactly what I'd hoped for. It looked just like new, and was $50 off the original price. It was the kit price, but I wouldn't have to find the time to build it. And they'd throw in the VFO for free!

"How come somebody turned this in?" I asked. "It looks like new."

The Ham behind the counter leaned forward as if to impart a military secret. "It's one day from new. You know that gang of old farts who hang out on 3875? All AM kilowatts? Or more!"

"I'm a DXer," I said. "Not much DX on 75. Besides, except down in Andover, I haven't had room for a 75 Meter antenna. Am I missing something?"

"Yep," said the Ham-clerk, who always seemed to have time for a chat as well as a sale. "You're missing the biggest bunch of hot air on a band full of blowhards. This bunch of old drunks is on there every night and god help you if you try to break in. They wouldn't hear you if you were ran ten kilowatts. Selective deafness. They got an exclusive club. They haven't realized that nobody in his right mind would want to join. That helps keep it exclusive. Windbags of the world unite on 3875."

"So what's that have to do with the 20A?" I asked.

"One of the gang came in yesterday first thing and said he wanted to get on Single Sideband. I tried to talk him out of it, but he insisted on giving it a try. I told him that there wouldn't be a big carrier bang when he transmitted, but he said he'd already built a big linear amplifier and he was eager to try it so I, of course, sold it to him."

"What happened?"

"I listened on 3875 last night so I'd hear it for myself," the clerk-Ham said. "When my customer called into the group on Single Sideband, nobody acknowledged his call, maybe because none of them wanted to bother trying to tune in a single sideband signal, but more probably they viewed him as a traitor. Amplitude Modulation is the only modulation as far as those old farts are concerned. A couple of them made comments about some duck quacking on the frequency and one of them said 'Polly want a quacker?' and it went downhill from there. This morning first thing he was in here trying to return the 20A, but we don't take stuff back unless it's broken, so I offered to sell it for him as used equipment. That's why it's 50 bucks off. And a free VFO. It's a real bargain."

"I'll take it," I said and the clerk-Ham smiled. Another tough sale accomplished. It only took him a half hour to talk me into it. He even cashed my Industrial Publishing Company check.

Photo courtesy N5BU

If I'd managed to keep my 20A throughout my ham career, this is what it would look like: rusty.

When I got home that night with two boxes and cash instead of a check, Sam took the cash and looked at the boxes, knowing that she wouldn't have to listen to any more of my subtle whining about wanting to get on sideband. I was the breadwinner, after all. If I wanted to spend part of my paycheck on the transmitter of my dreams, well, she understood. The fact that 'homemaker' was the harder job was also understood, though left unspoken. Daughter Kathy recognized me when I got home from work—sort of—so I'd pick her up and give her a kiss and a hug, and that was about the extent of my domestic duties unless Sam was otherwise occupied with cooking dinner in which case Kathy and I would play pattycake or other equally stimulating game.

On one visit to Andover, Sam and my mother got busy doing something so my ten-month-old daughter and I took a ride out to W8LIO's new QTH in Dorset, about three miles north of Andover. A couple of towers were up, sprouting antennas, but the surprise was a 30-foot dish right in the middle of the front yard. A screen door slammed and Jack's booming voice said, "Moonbounce!"

Kathy was introduced to Jack, who shook her hand and told her she was pretty. She looked overwhelmed. Jack was nothing if not an imposing figure. At 10 months, Kathy was in what I came to call her sponge mode—she seemed to absorb everything her eyes and ears encountered. She babbled, but not often. She could stand but wasn't interested in it. Sitting was her thing.

After the small talk subsided and I'd carefully examined all of the equipment that Jack had built during my Army career, we got around to the practical purpose of my visit; converting final amplifiers from AM to Single Sideband. Jack drove his big amp with a Central Electronics 20A, which he liked, so that pretty much confirmed that I had made the right choice of SSB transmitter.

We discussed how Jack had converted his big AM amplifier to a big SSB amplifier. He made it sound simple.

"A lot of guys are using grounded-grid amplifiers," Jack said, "but what with the 20A only putting out 20 watts PEP, it wasn't enough power to drive a grounded grid amp, so I decided that I'd make my old amp grounded cathode, just like it was originally when I was running the Ancient Modulation mode. That hot grid was hard to tame, but I finally got it damped down pretty good."

"I'm gone for a year and a half and already AM is 'Ancient Modulation?'"

"Have you been on SSB? It's great," said Jack.

"I've got the 20A on barefoot," I said. "Not much time."

"Barefoot! You're trying to get out with 20 watts? "Life's too short for QRP, David."

He grabbed a crumpled sheet of yellow paper he'd ripped off his ever-present tablet, turned it over to get a clean surface, and quickly drew a diagram of how I should rewire the old AM amplifier I'd built a few years ago. Jack showed me what he called his special damper circuit for hot grid amps.

"No hill for a climber," he said.

Through it all, Kathy sat in the big wicker chair that had survived the move from Andover to Dorset, not making a peep. She found a lot to absorb in Jack's shack.

"She's a good kid," Jack said. "She know the code yet?"

"Not yet," I said, "She's still working on 'Daddy'."

"Daddy!" Kathy said.

"She's got that down pretty good," said Jack.

I was at the publishing company less than a month when Bud promoted me to Assistant Editor, and in two months I was an Associate Editor. Some people who had been there for years still hadn't made Associate Editor. I got the reputation of being Bud's fair-haired boy, but I was really just good at what I did, or so I told myself. What I did was to read articles submitted by people who wanted to be writers in addition to being welders. Not many welders could write. Hydraulics guys and purchasing agents weren't much better.

I, of course, had no idea what they were writing *about*; my job was merely to make the writing readable using as few words as possible. The company paid authors by the word, so words were money. The authors were not paid for *their* words, but for *my* words. Their articles after my editing sometimes only ran half as long as originally submitted. I had authors whining about my editing. My standard question was, "Have you read *The Art of Plain Talk*?" And then while they were sputtering to come up with an answer to that one I'd say, "Did I leave out anything critical to the message of your article?"

I had one big pet peeve about my job, in addition to fairly low pay; the damn time clock. I hated the time clock. I complained to Bud about it. It wasn't fair that an Associate Editor with his name on the masthead should have to punch in and out. Besides, I forgot to either punch in or out with great regularity, causing consternation among the green eyeshade gang. Bud would have to straighten out my derelictions and it annoyed him.

One day I told Bud if he couldn't get me off the time clock, I would have to quit. The time clock was corporate policy, he said for the hundredth time. He could do nothing about it. I gave him one-months' notice. Bud was surprised. And disappointed.

Then, I told Bud the truth: I wanted to get into television production. I'd been accepted into Syracuse University's twelve-month Master's Degree program, which allegedly guaranteed you a job in TV.

Bud told me that television was for kids, not adults, that the print business was where the intellectuals were, and that TV didn't pay well. He should talk, I thought.

He told me he was starting a new magazine and he'd mentioned to the boss that he wanted me to be the editor—well, co-editor of it.

"Is the new magazine about Ham Radio?" I asked.

I'd talked to him several times about starting a magazine about Ham Radio. I suggested a chattier, less technical magazine than either *QST*, which was pretty formal and like reading a tech journal, at least to me, or *CQ*, an only slightly less stiff version of *QST*. He said he had researched it, and came to the conclusion that there'd be no money in that enterprise.

"Not enough advertisers," he said. All Industrial Publishing Company magazines were 100% advertiser supported, and circulated free to readers in their particular field.

My deal with Bud was to work until just before leaving for Syracuse. He tried numerous times to get me to stay and even gave me a raise when I was a short-timer, but he couldn't get me off the time clock. When the final day came, I said goodbye and gave a somewhat emotional thanks to one of the smartest guys I'd ever met. Bud Goodman had taught me a lot. That short stint in publishing had turned out to be a genuine brass ring with lots of lessons learned. One was this: anything written can be improved; and the second was: time clocks are for slaves, and riding a bus to work was not for executives, however junior.

On my bus ride home that final day, I told myself: no more time clocks and no more busses.

We packed the Pontiac full of our junk, which kept accumulating, plus my Drake 1A and Central Electronics 20A and accompanying VFO, and headed toward our academic adventure.

"Our big-ass Pontiac is stuffed," I said.

"Big Ass," Kathy said, plain as day.

Sam looked at me—one of those looks. Then she laughed.

We were off.

I mentioned speed reading. It reminded me that years later I made a series of films featuring prominent educators and I got to know Dr. William Glasser, author of "Reality Therapy," "Schools Without Failure" and other books. He told me once that he had taken a speed-reading course. He said after that he had to read everything twice in order to get it.

"The Art of Plain Talk" may be the best book ever written for people who attempt to write non-fiction. If you have such ambitions, it's still available here and there and I recommend it to you without

137

reservation. Its author, Rudolph Flesch, an Austrian by birth who had English as a second language, also wrote "Why Johnny Can't Read."

I also mentioned the Boy Scouts' motto, which is, of course, Be Prepared. Hal, W8CY was in my Boy Scout troop. (Andover being the size it was, we were lucky to have even one troop). He remembers getting a Merit Badge in radio. I don't, which may be why Hal got his license so much faster than I did.

When my mentor at Hiram College, Doug Mitchell, was fired for fraternizing with a female student on the showboat, they gave up theater and opened a bookstore in a small New England town. I know for a fact that they lived happily ever after. Another lesson courtesy of Doug: getting fired is not the end of the world.

Our red Pontiac three-speed, four-door sedan was as durable as it was unstylish. "Built like a tank," as either of my boys would say these days. "Bullet proof" they'd call that straight-eight motor that cranked out all of 95 horsepower. I never put a mobile rig in that car because I didn't think I'd keep such a behemoth for any length of time. When the transmission finally froze up on it, I didn't cry, though I should have because I didn't have any money.

The Drake 1A receiver I bought was a remarkable piece of equipment. Single Sideband transmitted on either the upper or lower sideband and in those early days, sometimes both. Either way, the carrier was "suppressed" so getting SSB tuned in just right was a bit tricky. Bob Drake came up with a variable passband tuning arrangement so you could adjust a signal to make it sound pretty good without changing your listening frequency. Or if you couldn't get someone's voice to sound as you knew it should, you at least knew that with this receiver you were hearing it as good as it was ever going to sound. The problem was on the transmitting end, which in the early days of Single Sideband wasn't in the slightest unusual.

The Ham magazine I wanted Bud Goodman to start came along years later in a publication known as "WorldRadio" which was very chatty and informal and generally not very technical at all except sometimes for an antenna Q&A column by a person whose nom de plume is Kurt N. Sterba. A Sterba Curtain, in case you've forgotten, is/was a complex bunch of wires high in the air that some Hams claimed to be the best antenna ever designed. You hardly ever hear of them these days. WorldRadio was started by Armond Noble, N6WR, who became a friend of mine, and not just because he published a bunch of my random musings from time to time. WR, as it was known, is now an online publication owned by CQ Magazine and Kurt N. Sterba is still dispensing the truth as he sees it to all antenna experts, which would include me and most other hams.

At each of the magazines I edited in my short publishing career, I was listed on the masthead, which in television terms would be called the credits. No one ever read them on TV, either, but they were given in lieu of raises.

I sometimes called daughter Kathy "her nibs" which actually means a person in authority. While Kathy really couldn't talk much, there's no doubt that she was the boss.

The "carrier bang" happened when a particularly loud AM transmitter first came on the air. For some, the louder the bang the better. With Single Sideband Suppressed Carrier, there was no or little carrier, thus no bang. Old timers missed the bang.

Duck Quack comments came from people listening to SSB signals who didn't know how to tune them in. Improperly tuned, SSB modulation could indeed sound like ducks quacking. It was one more reason that the transition from AM to SSB was painful for some hams.

The Central Electronics 20A had one shortcoming. It didn't have a VFO, which you'll remember is a variable frequency oscillator that allowed you to change your transmit frequency just as your receiver allows you to change your receive frequency. That's why I was so happy that the "used" 20A that I found had an outboard VFO with it.

Jack talked about his "hot grid" amplifier, which he said was hard to tame, meaning that sometimes it thought it was an oscillator and if you weren't paying attention it could commit hara-kiri right there in front of you. The guts of your big tubes would turn red, then white, then melt while you were trying to get them turned off. It's too complicated to explain here, but to stay on the safe side, opt for grounded grid.

And finally, I rarely got on 75 Meters, not because of all the hot air floating around that band, but because a dipole antenna for 75 is about 135 feet long. The lower the frequency, the longer the wavelength. Remember? And the longer the wavelength, the more wire you need to create a half-wave dipole, the length of all dipoles. All right, some dipoles are not half-wave but those are anomalies beyond your need to know. And anyway, outside of Andover, who's got the room? In addition to all that, back in the days when I was just cranking up in Ham Radio, there wasn't much DX on 75, and that's what I was looking for, as you know. I'm a DXer.

Chapter 16
Miracles Sometimes Happen

Miracles actually do happen now and then, especially if they are accompanied by lots and lots of elbow grease.

My biggest concern about television graduate school was not whether I'd like it or whether I could do it, but where my little family would live. (Married student housing sounded faintly ominous to me for some reason, and of course what kind of antenna could I put up there?) Sam and I decided to make a weekend scouting trip to check out our new digs.

Fortunately for us, Kathy wasn't talking much yet, or she would have raised holy hell about being left with her maternal grandparents, who loved her dearly but had rather Hitlerian ideas about child rearing: You *vill* eat your peas!" Poor Kathy. Poor us too, as we viewed what Syracuse University foisted off on its married students as housing. From the outside, it looked pretty drab, understandable since these were slapped together by the military as temporary buildings nearly 20 years earlier.

And not a single nearby tall *anything* to hang an antenna on. Why do housing developments of every kind cut down every damned tree?

Sitting in the big Pontiac staring at the middle unit in a prefab type building divided into thirds, I said, "Well, what do you think? Do I plead with Bud Goodman for my job back or do we move to the slums for a year?"

"It'll probably be better inside," said Sam. "And if it's not, we can paint it. And it's the middle unit so it'll be warmer in winter than the end ones."

Sam's positive attitude came in part because she wanted to get out from under her parents. If we didn't go to Syracuse, we'd be stuck living with them until I could get a major league raise from the Industrial Publishing Company, an event that would be way, way down the log. As it turned out, Sam was right. Our little house's interior was oddly inviting, and a little paint worked wonders. At times in our marriage I thought that Sam's mantra was, if it's not moving: paint it.

A quick look at the backyard convinced me that I could put my old Hiram-era mobile antenna on the little roof of the back porch, drive a copper ground rod into the sandy-ish soil and I'd have a nice little vertical radiator—at least I hoped it'd radiate, because there weren't many other options. Besides that, the little antenna would be stealth. Nobody would notice it. Since I wasn't planning to ask anybody permission to put it up, I didn't want it to provide what some esthete could call an eyesore.

To seal our resolve on the new digs, Sam and I went out and bought a bed, the only new piece of furniture that would grace this place in the next year. It was the first bed we'd ever owned.

Then back to Cleveland to rescue Kathy and cram the old Pontiac full of necessities, and head back to Syracuse to get our adventure going.

It might be cockeyed optimism to call searching through used furniture stores an adventure. But it was kind of fun looking for anything a little bit stylish and not totally trashed that was in our price range. We actually came up with some very nice stuff and in no time at all our little house became a candidate for "House Beautiful" (if you kept the lights down low).

I found a small desk and a typewriter table and a comfy office chair that I could slide from my study desk right over to my Hamshack, which consisted of a tiny table with the Drake 1A and the Central Electronics 20A single sideband transmitter and my outboard VFO.

Me working as captured by the class caricaturist, Dani Aguila,
a student in "Sequence Ten" from the Philippines.
And yes, I smoked. Like everybody else. Except Sam.

My office was in the dining room along with the shack. There wasn't much room for dining in the dining room, but we had dinner there every night, except for the few times we splurged and went out.

If we had guests for dinner, as we did fairly often, I'd unplug five wires and move the shack into the bedroom. And since it wasn't really a dining room anyway, but a dining area, we could rotate the table 90 degrees, causing some of it to extend into the living room, so everybody could be seated if we could rustle up enough chairs. You've heard of BYOB? At our place it was BYOB&C.

The living room had an old black & white TV (it was old even then), a sofa that pulled out into a lumpy, uncomfortable bed, so we could welcome overnight visitors firm in the knowledge that their stays would not last too long. One of our first visitors was our old Showboat pal, Brad Field, who in those days was K3LRV. When Brad arrived, Kathy, pushing two, flirted with him shamelessly for someone who was handicapped by her vocabulary of only a few dozen words. Even when loquacious, she generally chose her words at random. Brad considered Kathy's use of the language creative and decided it was time for her to learn to read.

Brad spent a lot of time sitting on the back stoop under my antenna pointing out simple words to my attentive daughter and though he did not teach Kathy to read before she was two, it was not for want of trying. Kathy was very patient with Brad, and tried to ignore his occasional curse word.

Whatever fun transpired at home, I never missed a class.

That doesn't sound like the old Dave Bell, but early in my Syracuse University career I heard an interesting rumor. The Dean of the Television School was the point man for job offers coming into the university, one of only two television graduate schools in the country (Iowa being the other). He got job openings from the three broadcast networks and local stations. Did he know which student was the best prospect for the available job? Hell no. He just gave the best job offer to the student with the best grades. Made sense to him, and what made sense to me was that I was going to be the student with the best grades. That would be my miracle.

I got straight A's in grad school, with one B+. That blot on my record was handed out by none other than the dean himself in the one class that he taught. He prided himself in rarely giving A's. Since I got the highest grade in the class, I rationalized it up to an A—which of course was the same as an A.

My "wet noodle"

Getting straight A's was a time-consuming job, but I got on the air anyway. I heard lots of signals on 20 Meters on my little mobile antenna with the gigantic band-changing coil in the middle, but not many of those signals heard me. "I hear somebody in there but I can't copy you," became the typical come-back that I heard time after time after shouting my lungs out. Running 20 watts into an antenna that Jack would call a wet noodle was a new experience for me, and not one that I much cared for. Sam heard me calling and calling and calling and said I needed an amplifier. She was getting smart about Ham Radio.

I would have gone out and bought an amplifier but I didn't have any spare cash. Not only that, but early in our tenure in the little apartment we learned that Kathy was about to become an older sister to somebody, and before we left Syracuse too. The GI Bill check was already spread pretty thin, and a pending new arrival made frugality a necessity. So what to do? Even Sam knew I needed an amplifier! So I decided to build one.

My new amp would have to be small, because embarking on a career in TV would probably require a lot of moving around, and the huge, homemade amp I had on the back porch shack in Andover wouldn't travel well unless I was accompanied everywhere by Tom Swift and his electric wheelbarrow. I decided to build my new amp out of an old Command Set, so called—a ubiquitous piece of radio surplus that had been converted into almost every kind of radio equipment imaginable. The BC 459 was small and quite light. The aluminum case and chassis was exactly the same size as the VFO for the Central Electronics 20A, so the VFO and amplifier would match perfectly. I figured I could jam a 200 watt grounded grid amplifier into an old Command Set.

144

Two views of a WWII BC459 Command Set, made as aircraft radios; thus the aluminum chassis. Every Ham had at least one of them after the war.

One solid contact I made was with a Ham a few miles from Syracuse, a "local" in Ham parlance, who said I should be louder than S-5 at his place and suggested I get an amplifier. I told him my wife suggested the same thing. When he heard I was thinking about building one on a Command Set transmitter chassis, he said he had one of those gathering dust at his place that he'd be happy to give me. Not wanting to let so much time go by that he forgot his offer, I went out the following weekend and picked up the guts of my new amp and relaxed for a couple of minutes in a real shack with non-stealth antennas.

That eyeball QSO was great fun, but as I left with the ARC-5 under my arm, I knew it'd take me a while to get my new amp built, because straight A's pretty much precluded anything except hitting the books.

One of my classmates, Les Martin, also after straight A's, and was breathing down my neck. Because we led the class, when an opportunity arose for two students to go to New York City and observe production of *Wide Wide World*, a very classy, live Sunday afternoon program, Les and I were the chosen pair. All day Saturday we toured NBC, met the *Wide Wide World* staff and host Dave Garroway, and watched segment rehearsals, prepping for the live show the following afternoon.

We left NBC about 10 pm Saturday night and discovered that it had been snowing all day. Les talked me into coming with him to meet an actor friend of his from their old hometown, Danville, Illinois. I slogged through snow and slush in my new loafers over past 10th Avenue, and climbed five or six flights of stairs in a cold, dark tenement building. Les knocked on the door and a voice said, "Come in." There, in bed with his wife was Les's friend Gene. We had a nice chat, the two of them caught up on their lives and I tried to stay warm in what was quite apparently a cold water flat. No surprise to me that Gene and his wife never got out of bed! It was the only slightly warm place in the building!

I hadn't caught Gene's last name so on the way back to our hotel I asked Les.

"Hackman," said Les. "He's a really good actor looking for his break."

"Never heard of him," I said.

At eight A.M. Sunday, Les and I showed up at NBC for the 90 minute live show tech rehearsal, dress rehearsal, and live broadcast.

During one of the pauses in rehearsal to get some technical glitch fixed, I got into a conversation with one of the control room techs who was a Ham. I got around to asking him why mobile whip antennas don't work as well at home as they do on a car. "Because the car makes a ground plane that gives you a pretty low angle of radiation," he said. "How many radials have you got under your vertical?" he wondered.

"None, but I've got the base grounded," I said.

"Pick your favorite band, cut a bunch of radials about a quarter wave long and string 'em out under your vertical. It'll be like night and day," he predicted.

I thanked him and he got back to work.

Wide Wide World was a phenomenon because it took you to various places around the country, all live. Today, and for the past 50 years or so, cutting around the country for live "feeds" is commonplace. In 1957, it was a technical marvel, and all in Living Color! Of course, virtually no homes had color TVs, but NBC was owned by RCA and RCA manufactured color television sets, so NBC broadcast as many programs as possible in color, which wasn't just "color," but "living color." OMG what an exciting world television was in those early days.

Getting back to our tiny TV studio in the basement of the library at Syracuse was a shock. Getting back to reality usually is.

As soon as I had a free moment, I cut four radials for my little vertical, soldered them to the shield side of the coaxial cable feeding the stealth vertical, and laid two of them on the roof of our little house about 90 degrees apart and ran the other two to the hand railing of my neighbors' back porches. Radials should be all the same angle from each other but in Ham Radio as in life, perfection often takes a back seat to reality.

After I attached my four radials for 20 Meters, I went inside and turned on the rig. The signals seemed louder. A station in Nova Scotia was calling CQ. I called him. He came right back and gave me a Q5, S5 signal report. I gave him a Q5, S9. When I told him I was running 20 watts PEP he said I had a good signal for 20 watts. I told him about the NBC engineer and the radials I'd just laid out under the vertical. He came back and said he'd used a lot of verticals and none of them had worked without radials. When we signed off, Sam came home and I told her about my contact and the radials. She said she hoped Kathy wouldn't be hanging herself on a bunch of wires in the back yard. Sam didn't properly appreciate the miracle that had just occurred.

Even though I finally had an antenna that worked, sort of, I wasn't on the air much. Getting straight A's ate up a lot of time, especially for a habitual C student.

We all had to do some sort of a "television show" for our thesis project. I knew that to get an A for my show, I needed an unusual project. Some of my classmates were adapting one-act plays for television. Most were doing what they saw on TV: a news show, a sports show, a discussion show on what they thought was some intriguing theme.

I did what I always do. Get a little help from my friends. Brad Field didn't watch television. So he didn't know what was on. Therefore he was the perfect person to write me a short skit that would qualify as original and I would get my A. Brad wrote me a fake talent show.

A teenage kid was the host of this show, and the hook was that he was a ventriloquist. Ah, that's good, you think. That's unique. But that wasn't all. This kid's dummy had a mind of his own. The dummy wasn't merely a critic, he was a pissed-off critic. The dummy's favorite word was "shit" but we never heard him say it. When everybody knew the word that was coming, the kid would make a bleeping sound. The dummy would look around, wondering where the bleep had come from.

If the kid/host thought the guy who sang "Ole Man River" was good, the dummy would say he'd heard better singing from leaking tires. Then the host and his dummy would get into an argument. The kid who played the host was a young comic wannabee. He didn't have to be a real ventriloquist, because on the dummy's lines, I'd always cut to a closeup of the dummy. This was before laugh tracks, but during my taping, the crew and some guests in the studio couldn't hold back their laughter, which of course prompted the kid to ad lib stuff not in the script and I, as the director, had to actually think on my feet, something I wasn't prepared for.

I had to keep up with the action because the faculty committee sat in the adjacent classroom watching my "thesis show" on a monitor, and of course making notes. I heard later, they too were laughing. Thank God. I mean, thank Brad. From that experience I learned that if you don't have a good script, you're not going to have a good show. That's a truism, but it's a hard one to remember—there are so many mediocre scripts around.

I got my friend Allan Hershfield to be my technical director, a crew position requiring lots of cool and unflappability. He had my script in front of him with all my shots and camera moves marked, and made sure the next shot was ready when I shouted for it. He saved my bacon on several "premature" calls I made and was able to follow the ad libbing with great calm.

When I finally called for a fade to black after I'd gone through the final credit cards on my little thesis show, I was covered in sweat though the control room was icy cold. The crew burst in and shook my hand vigorously for making it through the little comedy talent show without making a mistake (this was before the popularity of high fives).

While I was sweating out my first TV show, Sam was sweating out pediatrician visits while trying not to gain too much weight. Our second child arrived right on time and turned out to be a boy, whom we named David Lane (Sam's maiden name) Bell. Kathy called him Baby Bugger (her creative attempt at "brother") and we all started calling him Bug. Thankfully, we made a conscious effort not to call him Bug, and after only a couple of years that colorful nickname was all but forgotten.

The recent stint as an editor at the Industrial Publishing Company had improved my ability to crank out academic projects, and my streak of A's continued. The first job prospect that came along was from the fledgling ABC Television Network, which had just recently merged with what had been the DuMont Network. DuMont had started a series entitled *The Johns Hopkins Science Review*, probably the first educational series on a commercial network. After the ABC/DuMont merger, ABC kept the series, probably to keep the FCC off its back.

I went to Manhattan and met the program's Executive Producer/Host, Lynn Poole, at the New York University Club, my first, but not last visit to that elegant old institution. We chatted, not about television but about things in general and after a very casual conversation he offered me the position of Writer/Associate Producer on his show, *Johns Hopkins File 7* and I took it.

When I got back to our little home in Syracuse, I told Sam we'd be moving to Baltimore and after the excitement died down, she asked me how much we'd get paid on this new adventure of ours, and I told her that I'd forgotten to ask. A couple of days later, all of the paperwork came from Johns Hopkins and the salary, nothing to write home about, beat the publishing company and after all—my first job in television would be on a network show and as a producer/writer.

Baltimore, here we come! But not before a going away party for all of the Sequence 10 graduates where everybody ate a little and drank a lot. Or maybe only me and my buddy Les Martin drank a lot. Les had a bigger hollow leg than I did. Our wives drove us home. To say that I don't remember much about the party is an overstatement. I don't even remember the party. When we got home and relieved the babysitter, Sam and I had a nightcap to celebrate a year that ended up exactly as we'd hoped it would—with a job in television! It was another miracle.

*Our pal Brad began his Ham career with the callsign KN2GIY because he listed Hamburg, New York as his QTH (home city). The N in his prefix indicated that he was a "Novice." When he passed his General Class test, the FCC dropped the N and he was K2GIY. New York and New Jersey were in the second call area as mapped by the FCC. Most of the rest of New England was the first call area (thus the ARRL Headquarters station being W1AW since it was/is located in Newington, CT). I'm W6AQ because California is in the sixth call area. In fact, it **is** the sixth call area, all by itself. The 10 call areas begin in Maine with the ones and move clockwise around the perimeter of the United States, ending with the whole vast mid-part of the country as zero.*

My former mobile antenna in the backyard of our Syracuse house qualified as a stealth antenna because not many people noticed it. Back in the 50's, most Hams didn't have to worry much about making their antennas "stealth" because few city or county rules about such things existed. Now, however, creating stealth antennas that actually work has become a necessary art form.

My mobile antenna was of course a vertical, and the radial wires I hooked to the shield of the coaxial cable feeding it were horizontal, more or less.

Coaxial cable, incidentally, is a center wire surrounded by insulation of some kind, surrounded by a shield, usually a copper braid, surrounded by some sort of waterproof (hopefully) plastic.

END VIEW, COAX CABLE

COAX CABLE OF ANY LENGTH

SOME SORT OF WATERPROOF PLASTIC (HOPEFULLY)

BRAIDED COPPER SHIELD 95% WIRE 5% OPEN

INSULATING PLASTIC, MAYBE FOAM

STRANDED COPPER WIRE (OR SOLID IF FLEXIBLE IS NOT NEEDED)

THIS DRAWING IS SLIGHTLY LARGER DIAMETER THAN THE COAX MOST HAMS USE

I don't know why Syracuse labeled the school year in their television graduate program a "Sequence" but I was in Sequence 10. Fred Silverman was in sequence 11. He's the only person to become the programming head of each of the three (then) networks.

I know that you are thinking, how did he get the GI Bill after only 21 months in the Army? Well, the answer is: he applied for it. You may not think I was much of a soldier. Hell, I don't think I was much of a soldier. But I saved the Army lots of dollars by eliminating a fair amount of paperwork, and very possibly prevented an airplane collision because I fixed that Plan Position Indicator scope at the Army airfield in southern Germany. So whatever tuition and room and board I could scrape up from

Dave Bell, W6AQ

the GI Bill, I deserved. And during my career in television I gave the Feds way more dollars than they gave me for my Syracuse education. If I hadn't gone to Syracuse, there probably wouldn't have been a career in television.

The band switching coil in the middle of my homemade mobile antenna was just that. Moving the clip, called a Fahnestock clip, from one part of the coil to another, was like adding or removing a lot of wire to the end of the antenna, thus changing the resonant frequency. The little vertical was like half of a dipole don't you see, the ground and/or the radial wires providing the other half. Oh, you don't see? Well, take my word for it. It'll all be clear after you've been on the air for a while. And it's okay to call a Fahnestock clip an alligator clip if you're no good at German.

It's not at all unusual for a veteran Ham to give equipment to another ham who needs it, especially if he's young and poor. The BC 459 given to me by the Ham near Syracuse turned a notion into an obligation. I couldn't not build the amplifier now. You understand, don't you?

Wide Wide World was created by the legendary Sylvester L. (Pat) Weaver, who also created the Today Show and the Tonight Show. Even though Pat created numerous iconic shows, I suspect his favorite creation was his daughter, Sigourney. All of Pat's early shows were live. Why was such a complex show as Wide Wide World live? Because there was no way to record it. Videotape was just in its testing stages. Hard to believe, isn't it? Videotape today is either out or on its way out, having been made obsolete by digital technologies of one kind or another.

And why was a show whose claim to fame was little other than a bunch of different locations (around the Eastern Time Zone) such a phenomenon? Because nobody had ever done it before and high quality, unshared telephone lines had to be kept open between the source and NBC in New York. Communications satellites didn't yet exist.

Allan (Al) Hershfield, whom I talked into being the Technical Director of my little thesis production, was a perfect example of a knack that I developed—picking the right person for the right job. When I needed a unique show idea for my thesis, Brad Field came through. Throughout my long television career, my success stemmed from my ability to lean on the right talent. They all made me look good.

Al Hershfield, incidentally, followed his Syracuse MS in Television with a PhD and pursued a fascinating career that included the Feds, working for the Agency for International Development (where he was shot at in Ethiopia and Nigeria), the deanship of several universities, and the president of the Fashion Institute of Technology in New York City. He too should have been a Ham, but I didn't have time to work on him.

Chapter 17

Television—What Fun!

I'm talking about producing it of course, not viewing it. Viewing it, especially in its early days, was like attending a Ham club meeting expecting to enjoy a talk about a DXpedition to Spratley Island and instead hear from some guy prattling on about the virtues of a vertical antenna.

We may have been in Syracuse for only a year, but in addition to a dozen or so QSL Cards, we accumulated a bunch of stuff, not to mention Baby Bugger. The "stuff" included the convertible sofa with its lumpy, thin mattress and its formula stains here and there, two very comfortable but disreputable overstuffed chairs, plus my desk/shack chair, dining room set, plus kitchen junk and of course our bed and let's not forget the crib—the usual necessities for newlyweds. One thing was clear. We'd outgrown our behemoth Pontiac as our sole moving van.

My classmate Al Hershfield looked nothing like Superman, but he came to our rescue. He volunteered himself and his brother Larry (who we'd never seen before nor since) to drive all night in a U-Haul truck from Syracuse to Baltimore, following Sam and me and the two kids. Shortly after arriving at the row house we had rented but not seen before this moment, my new boss, Lynn Poole and his wife Grey, showed up with a quart of milk and a loaf of bread. Lynn and Grey picked out the row house for us and they did a good job. Al and his brother helped empty the truck and then they jumped back into the still warm cab and after an until-we-meet-again farewell, drove it back to Syracuse and returned it—all within its 24 hour rental period.

We were greeted as we moved in by our new neighbors in the row house adjoining ours. We noted that they had a 13-year-old daughter—too young to date but old enough to be responsible. i.e.: Our new babysitter. Yea!

I asked my new neighbors about the nearest lumber yard. Sam looked at me with a bit of a scowl, but didn't say anything. She knew that the lumber would support some sort of antenna. Though swamped with work, before the dust had settled on our move, I had a wooden A-frame nailed to the garage, with a 20-Meter dipole strung between it and the roof of our house with the coax feedline going into the basement through a small hole in the window frame. I borrowed my next-door neighbor's electric drill to do the deed. When we moved, I'd put a piece of chewing gum in the hole that was about the same color as the paint on the frame. Nobody'd ever notice.

We moved the day after I graduated. Before we even got the furniture where Sam thought she wanted it, and after a quick stop for basic provisions beyond what we brought from Syracuse,

I was off to Johns Hopkins to explore the campus and the area adjacent—to get the lay of the land, so to speak. I quickly learned it was an extraordinary institution plopped down in the midst of a determinedly working class city that proudly spoke its own language. Well, maybe not its own language, but an accent so dense that anyone used to hearing the King's English would be flummoxed. Bus drivers shouted out every stop, so Sam felt confident taking the bus downtown for a shopping trip. She wanted to get off at the Baltimore and Howard intersection so when the bus driver shouted out, "Bawlmer 'n Hard" she of course sat tight, only to watch her stop go by.

At 7:30 am on the day I was to report for work, I headed out to greet my new boss, Lynn Poole, whose office was in the administration building at Hopkins (as everybody called the distinguished old university). There I was met Lynn's #1 guy, Leo Geier, who walked me across campus to my new office, a desk in the old gatehouse, a stone building next to a stone bridge at a seldom-used entrance to the campus. On the walk, I asked Leo what the series' title *File 7* meant.

"It doesn't mean anything," he said. "We couldn't think of a title for a series that we wanted to cover a wider swath than the *Johns Hopkins Science Review*. I suggested *File 7* because every time Lynn couldn't think of where to file something he'd say, 'just put it in file 7,' so we decided to call the TV series *File 7*. But don't tell anybody it doesn't mean anything, just tell 'em it's a secret."

The two other writer/associate producers seemed genuinely pleased to see me. I quickly realized why. I didn't even know how to find the john and already I was behind. These guys had been working on their first few shows of the season for several weeks, and I hadn't even tried out my typewriter!

My two new colleagues, James Chimbidis and Walter Millis III, couldn't possibly have been more different. Jim was a big bear of a Greek from Mason City, Iowa with a gruff exterior and a soft, sensitive soul. Walter (never Walt) was a sophisticated New Yorker, who had grown up in a gigantic rent-controlled apartment just off Central Park. Jim was rough-hewn and Walter was smooth. I liked them both instantly.

Jim showed me around the gatehouse by standing in the middle of the room turning 360 degrees as he pointed. "That's my corner, that's Walter's corner, and that's your corner. And in that corner are the stairs down to the basement. He then took me on the great adventure, down to the basement editing room which had an editing bench, a couple of hand-crank rewinds, a 16mm film viewer and a couple of homemade film bins. Fortunately, I had learned how to splice film at Syracuse University.

The floor of the editing room was dirt packed as hard as concrete. In the summertime, it was probably the coolest room on campus. I shot a lot of film for my shows with our old Bell & Howell windup camera. When looking at my finished film in our viewer, I took care not to let any of it fall on the floor. Keeping film clean was tough under the best of circumstances, and a dirt floor hardly qualified this old gatehouse as an ideal production space.

While I couldn't appreciate it at the time, being a couple of weeks behind before I ever started was great training for a career in television, where, if you managed to stay on schedule, some executive would insist on changes (often nonsensical) and put you behind. Allegedly, to make my initial couple of programs easier, either Lynn or Leo had left me a couple of show subjects they'd pre-okayed for me to do. Somebody had done a little research and a contacts list accompanied a pile of facts. I took all of the paper home with me. One day on the job and already—homework!

I read it through, with Baby Bugger asleep in his carrier. Every time I went down the cellar stairs to my office/shack, Bug would get laid out in his car seat/recliner and accompany me. Despite his regular proximity to the Hamshack, he never did get his license! I listened around 20 Meters, didn't hear anybody, called CQ, didn't raise anybody. Called again, same result. I took Bug up to his crib in our bedroom, and went to bed. Sam was up reading. "I need to get my amplifier built," I said.

"Good luck with that," Sam said.

On that happy note, I went to sleep.

We'd been in Baltimore about six weeks when Sam announced that she was pregnant.

"How did that happen?" I said.

"Remember the party?"

"What party?" I asked.

"That one. We came home and had a nightcap?"

"If you're going to get pregnant every time we move, folks are gonna think we're Catholic."

"Maybe we should just forget about going away parties," Sam said.

153

"Maybe. Anyway, congratulations," I said, "We'll celebrate at our favorite restaurant Friday night."

"Do we have a favorite restaurant?" asked Sam.

"I'll find one by Friday."

"Great," said Sam, as she rolled over and went to sleep.

"I wonder if Lynn will give me a raise when he hears our family is expanding?"

He didn't.

My first show hit the air on November 2nd, 1958. It was, of all things, a game show which I called *Think and Answer* because it was basically a show about puzzle solving, not memory, like all of the other game shows on the air. It pitted two teams against each other, one pair engineering students and the other arts and sciences majors. I don't remember who won, but it was a unique, fun show to kick off my television-producing career.

File 7 was a perfect introduction to television producing and I really enjoyed it. Even though our budgets were miniscule, the only real limits on us were time and imagination. After I got my first two shows on the air, virtually everything else I produced came right out of my head. I did a show about Isaac Newton (as part of a "great scientist" series that Lynn wanted to do—but we got to pick our favorite scientist), cosmetic surgery for a woman who disliked her appearance so much that it thrust her into constant depression. Right on camera, she had her nose size reduced and her chin built up. That show was another *File 7* TV "first." I got a barbershop singing show past Lynn because the barbershop chorus from Baltimore suburb Dundalk won the international championship. That was a really big deal, at least according to the *Baltimore Sun,* our first-rate daily newspaper. The chorus director, Bob Johnson, was an absolute dynamo—exactly the kind of television guest producers pray for.

Of the three producer/writers on Johns Hopkins *File 7,* I was the one most often in executive producer Lynn Poole's office pitching some off-the-wall idea that was just marginally educational. Once when I went in to pitch a show about Ham Radio, Lynn said, "You're interested in things technical; how'd you like to do a show about a robot designed to operate in radioactive environments?"

Sensing a brass ring coming my way, I said, "I'd love to."

So that's how I found myself flying to Los Angeles to write and produce a show about Hughes Aircraft Company's so-called *Mobot,* which for its day was a remarkable gadget designed to stand in for a human in a toxic environment. We produced the entire show in Los Angeles (another first) and it wasn't until I flew home that I realized the show was really an opportunity for Lynn and his wife Grey to get a free, first class trip to California. (Hughes picked up the entire tab for the show.) I, of course, flew coach (writers don't get no respect), but that multi-hop prop plane trip from Baltimore to Los Angeles was great fun, and I actually saw a Boeing 707 on the tarmac in L.A. The 707 was clearly the future of commercial air travel. I realized that I was flying on a dinosaur.

The most memorable and talked about scene in my *Hot Stuff Man* was when the *Mobot* putted a golf ball into a cup. Even in 1959, frivolity was television's bread and butter. A little bit of education and a lot of entertainment was my mantra.

Hot Stuff Man reminded me that I absolutely loved Southern California. Loved it. It was magical, and I wanted to live there. Someday.

One of my shows that I most enjoyed was one I produced about the Sage of Baltimore, Henry Lewis Mencken, who was often called ". . . the great debunker." I'd heard of H. L. Mencken before I got to Baltimore, mainly from my sketchy knowledge of the so-called Monkey Trial in which evolution had been put on trial in Tennessee. A Dayton, Tennessee high school biology teacher named John Scopes taught evolution in his biology classroom and became big news around the world because his trial was really Creationists vs. Evolutionists. The Creationists won the trial but the Evolutionists won public opinion. The Creationists blamed the acerbic writing of H. L. Mencken for their PR debacle. He called the famous prosecutor, William Jennings Bryan, a buffoon—and Bryan's legal argument "theological bilge."

Mencken was the most quotable reporter at that trial. He was an elitist, a cynic and a grouch as well as an entertaining writer. In the movie about this trial, *Inherit the Wind,* Gene Kelly played Mencken, in one of the best examples of miscasting in movie history (and there are many in that competition). Ridiculous miscastings happen for many reasons, none of them good and none for artistic reasons. It's always just business.

Mencken's best friend was George Jean Nathan, the theater critic for the *New York Times* among other eminent literary credits. In my show, I used what I thought was a great poem by Berton Braley entitled "Mencken, Nathan, And God." Here's a sample:

There were three that sailed
away one night
Far from the maddening throng;
And two of the three were
always right
And everyone else was wrong
But they took another along,
these two
To bear them company
For he was the only One who
ever knew
Why the other two should be;
And so they sailed away, these
three
Mencken
Nathan
and God.
And the two they talked of the
aims of Art,
Which they alone understood;
And they quite agreed from the
start
That nothing was any good
Except some novels that Dreiser
wrote
And some plays from Germany.
When God objected they
rocked the boat
And dropped him into the sea.
"For you have no critical
facultee,"
Said Mencken
And Nathan
To God.

It's fair to say that in Mencken, I finally met an elitist of EMF fame from my days on the Showboat Majestic. I forgave Mencken being an elitist because I've always enjoyed really good writing and Mencken was a wonderful example of interesting, entertaining, and enlightening if somewhat caustic writing. Mencken also was a professional boozer. He called himself "omnibibulous" and named the dry martini the only American invention as perfect as a sonnet. You and I and most people we know would be part of Mencken's Booboisee (boob-wah-zee). From him, it didn't even seem like a put-down, just a fact.

Perhaps the most outlandishly off-topic show I did for *Johns Hopkins File 7* was, (what else?) one about Ham Radio that I called *The Ham's Wide World*, as a small homage to one of my favorite series, *Wide Wide World*. When I got a greenlight from Lynn, I immediately called the American Radio Relay League to give them the good news—a network television show about Ham Radio! I asked for their public relations director.

"We don't have a public relations director."

"Oh," I said. "Well, who deals with public information requests?"

The telephone operator paused an inordinate length of time.

"I'm producing a network television show about Ham Radio. Maybe I could speak to the QST editor," I said.

"Let me see who's available."

An assistant to somebody came on the line.

After I explained my project and asked for help, the person I was talking to said, "You'll have to write us a letter."

"I'm on a very tight deadline."

"We'll call you after we've had a chance to go over your letter."

I was really good at getting around naysayers, but I didn't get anywhere with this dame. I began to think that maybe the scuttlebutt I'd heard about ARRL headquarters being stiff-necked might be true. I sent my letter, Special Delivery, listing help I thought they could supply, and then I called the ARRL's only competition, if you could call it that, *CQ Magazine.*

When I told *CQ*'s telephone person that I was producing a network TV show about Ham Radio, she said, "Wait a minute; Wayne will want to talk to you."

Wayne of course was Wayne Green, W2NSD, the editor of *CQ,* and what passed for the hobby's number one rabble-rouser. He was constantly giving the ARRL hell for one reason or another but he usually skewered them with a lot of ironic humor. He was Ham Radio's Mencken, maybe not in terms of quality, but in tone. It's fair to say that Wayne had few friends at League Headquarters, but many Hams, me included, enjoyed his cranky editorials and breezy humor. No sacred cow was too big for Wayne to wrestle to the ground and hogtie.

When he picked up the phone, he said, "Dave, Wayne Green here, W2 Never Say Die. What can I do for you?"

Within five minutes, Wayne was ready to produce the whole show. He told me everything I'd need to squeeze into the half-hour and even volunteered to come down to Baltimore to appear on the show personally! Maybe he could host it! I told him we'd keep that suggestion in abeyance for the moment but thanked him for all of the really valuable leads, contacts, and ideas. Wayne had a bunch of short films that various Hams had shot of their activities, and two days after our conversation, a box of film arrived from Wayne, Special Delivery, at my little gatehouse office.

A couple of days later I got a call from the American Radio Relay League. Some assistant somebody or other told me that the League had considered my request and had decided that they would not be able to participate because nobody had the time to help me, but thank you anyway.

I said, "That's okay. I'm working with Wayne Green. He's already sent me a bunch of film I can use, and he may even be a guest on the show. Tell your boss thanks for considering my request."

It won't be a surprise to you, and it wasn't a surprise to me, that within an hour I got a call from the ARRL. "Hi, Dave, said a friendly voice, this is Perry Williams, W1UED, at headquarters. Your request for help ended up on my desk. What can I do for you?"

Between Perry and Wayne, I had access to almost every well-known Ham in the world. Film clips and slides and photos began to arrive by the boxful.

They would both call fairly regularly to see how things were going. In one of my conversations with Wayne, he mentioned proudly that he was a member of Mensa. I didn't show my ignorance by asking him what that was. I looked it up. It's an organization of people who have very high IQs. A friend of mine once told me that Mensa would take over the world, but they couldn't decide where to have a meeting.

Serendipitously, a front page photo and story about two teenage Hams who had bounced signals off the ionized trail of a satellite appeared in the *New York Daily News*. So I got in touch with the Maryland half of the duo, Perry Klein, K3JTE, and he readily agreed to be on the show to explain their remarkable feat, which he called "high frequency satellite scatter" because it happened at the relatively low frequency of 21 MHz (15 Meters, remember?) No less authority than John Kraus, W8JK, an antenna expert and professor at Ohio State, agreed that the satellite-signal bounce was the best explanation for their feat. As a real plus, these were a couple of young guys, thus proving to the world that not all Hams were spooky old farts.

AP Photo/Byron Rollins

Ham Radio publicity doesn't get much better than this. Amateurs beat professionals with another scientific 'first.'

I needed an average Ham to guide the home audience through the many facets of amateur radio, and I found a middle aged, popular local, Doc Kreig, W3CAY, who did a good job. In recent years I've wondered why I didn't get Wayne Green, W2NSD. I don't have a good answer to that one. I probably should have.

One of my Elmers into Ham Radio, Sam Harris, W8UKS, had moved to Massachusetts, had his callsign changed by the FCC to W1FZJ. He and some of his friends formed the Rhododendron Swamp VHF Society, which was trying to bounce signals off the moon using the amateur 1296

MHz. band. When I got Sam on the phone and told him what I'd been doing since I last saw him in Burton, Ohio, he was really pleased, and delighted that his film was going to be in my show.

The original *Ham's Wide World* went off with hardly a hiccup, partly because I prerecorded all of the conversations heard on the receivers, just to be sure that the dreaded Murphy didn't strike with one of his cursed laws, like my favorite: "Any wire cut to length will be too short."

Lynn Poole loved the show and he was, at that stage of my career, my most important audience.

It won't surprise you to learn that I also did a show about showboats which I called *The Drunkard (or the Fallen Saved)* which was one of the actual titles that we did on the Majestic until Brad Field accumulated enough original (?) melodramas to retire the old dramas to the dustbin of dramatic excess. In my show about showboats I had actors do the first act of *The Drunkard*, a barbershop quartet singing *Bird in a Gilded Cage*, film clips and stills of showboats and scenes on the rivers from Cairo (pronounced "Kayro") Illinois to Pittsburgh and towns in between so tiny that they barely existed. This show was everything you ever wanted to know about showboating and then some. And it was really educational—sort of.

Our baby sitter neighbors told us we were about 10 blocks from Orioles' stadium, and while I wasn't much of a baseball fan, I followed the Cleveland Indians casually, because my father had taken me to several Indians' games. Sam and I went to one game in two years. The Orioles vs. the Indians. Rocky Colavito played right field for the Indians. The sweaty night that we went, Rocky hit four consecutive home runs.

The day after the game, I was on 20 Meter phone (meaning voice) and I snagged a station near Cleveland. When I told him I'd been in the stadium when Rocky hit four home runs, he was envious. Actually, envious doesn't cover it. Major League jealousy is closer. To get even with me, he told me my signal was quite weak, that I was fading into the noise. I said 73 to him and doubled my resolve to get started building my pair of 1625's amplifier. All of the parts I gathered in Syracuse were in a box right under my basement shack table. Since it would take me some time to build my amp, I went over to Baltimore's Amateur Radio Center store to see if Ernie had any used amps for sale. He didn't, alas, so I had to quit procrastinating and get to work building.

I immediately pulled out a piece of blank paper and drew the basic diagram for my 1625 amplifier, as if that would spur me on to get the thing built.

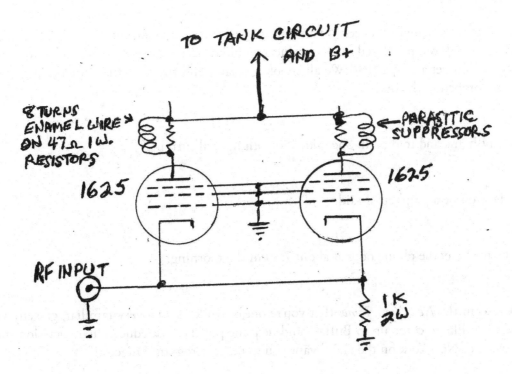

As you can plainly see if you've been paying attention, this is a grounded-grid amplifier because the grids are grounded and the output of my little 20-A transmitter is fed into the cathodes of these tubes.

At our first opportunity after Sam announced that she was expecting, the two of us went to our new favorite restaurant, Hausner's, an old seafood joint down by the harbor, to celebrate. They didn't take reservations and there was always a line and then when you got inside, a wait (at the bar for Sam and me.) It was a Baltimore institution and we enjoyed it as often as we could afford it and drank a toast to our fetus every time we went.

Sam's pediatrician at the Johns Hopkins Hospital just "knew" that our upcoming offspring was a boy because it was so large. Surprise! Our third child turned out to be a girl, 9 ¾ pounds and 23 ¾ inches long. Sam is 5' 5". It must have been the gin and tonics. In fact when I went to look at my new daughter through the viewing window I had to elbow my way between the nurses, interns and residents who wanted a look at the nearly two foot tall girl. One day old and already a celebrity! Kristine Elizabeth Bell slept through most of her debut.

Sam and I had already decided that we were having so much fun and I was learning so much that we'd spend another year with *Johns Hopkins File 7* when Lynn Poole called a meeting of the entire staff and announced that he'd cancelled the series.

"Television just isn't much fun anymore," he said. "I want to get out while we're on a high, rather than wait to be canceled."

We three Associate Producers/Writers sat in Lynn's office in a state of disbelief. I later learned that the network was perplexed that a producer would cancel a successful TV series. Lynn ended our series with yet another first! We all shook his hand and that was that. A glorious career in television nipped in the bud.

I went home and told Sam. She said, "Something will turn up."

"May you be a prophet," I said.

The next day the phone rang at about 7:30 in the morning.

"I read in the *New York Times* that you're out of work," said a very familiar, gravelly voice. "How'd you like to come up to Buffalo and help me put the first educational television station in the state of New York on the air? I want you to be my Program Director!"

"Les? What the hell are you doing at an educational television station?

"I'm running the damned thing," said Les Martin, my old pal from Syracuse Sequence 10 and good friend of Gene Hackman. "I need some help. How 'bout it?"

"I'm on my way," I said, and we were.

When I retreated to my basement office/shack with Baby Bugger and called CQ with my little 20 watt single sideband radio, I was asking for anybody, anybody at all, anywhere, to dig out my little signal and give me a call. CQ Magazine chose that name for obvious reasons—they wanted anybody, anywhere, to buy their publication—and a lot of Hams did, but not as many as joined the ARRL and got QST Magazine as a bonus with their membership.

Barbershop singing might not have much to do with Johns Hopkins and things academic, but I convinced Lynn and Leo to do the show as an homage to Hopkins' hometown, plus the fact that the subject had never before been done on television. It would be another "first" for Johns Hopkins File 7. Most important to me was that the chorus director, Bob Johnson, was a great television talent. He later became the head of SPEBSQSA, the Society for the Preservation and Encouragement of Barbershop Quartet Singing in America. That long moniker was created during Franklin Roosevelt's presidency. These barbershoppers, mostly Republicans probably, wanted an acronym longer than any of the government agencies formed during FDR's New Deal, so-called. My father called it Roosevelt's "no deal," incidentally. A "Rock-ribbed" Republican as all of the locals called him.

During the Barbershop show I set the world's record for number of cigarettes smoked in a control room in a six-hour period.

I managed to go through two entire packs of cigarettes between six AM and noon. Was I nervous about pulling off that highly complex show? Well, maybe a bit. Because of technical snafus in the studio and an extremely hungover director, we never got through a complete rehearsal so we were winging it live, on the air. The show turned out great, partly because chorus director Bob Johnson was such a showboat. When I got home, Sam congratulated me for a really entertaining show. Even Kathy burbled enthusiasm. Baby Bugger belched. I went through the house collecting cigarette packs and ashtrays and with great ceremony in front of my entire family, threw the lot in the wastebasket under the sink, and no one, however desperate, would ever take anything out of that wastebasket for reuse. I was through with cigarettes. Gradually the house began to smell less like an ashtray. Occasionally, somebody stepped in some gum.

Ham Radio was even a bigger stretch than barbershopping for Lynn Poole, but when he got to the studio and met the Hams I'd chosen as talent, he became a convert. He was so jazzed about the subject matter that he started ad-libbing during his opening comments, which of course drove our director, Ed Fryers, bananas. Like barbershop, this was the first time that Ham Radio had been the subject of a network television show. Perry Klein, K3JTE, is now W3PK and went on from his memorable performance on The Ham's Wide World *to get a Ph.D. For years he was the president of AMSAT, the Radio Amateurs Satellite Corporation. Perry proved that Hams' ages went from teenaged to antique, the same as today. The original* Hams' Wide World *show is available from Johns Hopkins or on the ARRL Film Collection DVD, which includes many of the films that my friends and I put together in cooperation with the ARRL over the years.*

When my old friend Sam Harris, W8UKS, moved to Massachusetts, he had to notify the FCC of his permanent change of address, and they soon issued him a new callsign, W1FZJ. Do you remember that the first amateur radio district is the whole northeast of the country? The Rhododendron Swamp VHF Society had the club callsign W1BU, which Sam sort of appropriated for his own use. At the time of the original Ham's Wide World program, Sam had not yet made contact with another Ham station by bouncing signals off the moon. But in July, 1960, he succeeded in making a solid contact with W6AY, the Eimac radio club in California. Eimac was a leading manufacturer of high power transmitting tubes. The company was owned by a couple of well-known Hams. Later on, Sam developed a super-low-noise amplifier which made weak-signal VHF/UHF communications much easier. Still later, he ran the Arecibo Observatory's 1000' radio telescope dish in Puerto Rico (which he occasionally used on the Ham bands.)

Ray Soifer, K2QBW, the other half of the satellite-bounce experiment is now W2RS and memorializes their successful experiment with his QSL card, a cartoon from QST drawn by the famous "Gil" to commemorate their achievement.

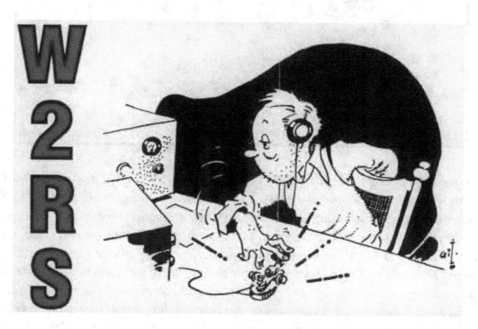

In the partial circuit diagram of the amplifier I was contemplating, the output (coming off the tubes' plates at the top of drawing) goes to the "tank circuit" so-called because it stores energy. It's more accurately called an L/C circuit, L for inductance, C for capacitance, the two elements that make up a tuned circuit that is resonant on one specific frequency. The B+ shown at the top of the diagram is the high voltage for the tubes, in this case around 600 volts DC. If you understand all this, it's time to get your license.

The ARRL, which initially didn't "have time" to help me with this show, ended up coming through big-time. Today that organization of Hams has a PR Director and a Development Director (so they can afford a PR Director and many other necessary programs)—two positions that weren't even dreamed of when I first contacted them in 1959. Today, ARRL is all Hams' best friend.

My very first network television show for File 7 *was* Think and Answer, *which I resuscitated years later as a PBS pilot which didn't get "picked up," as they say. I thought it was great fun, but PBS wasn't up for a game show, alas. Years after that, an executive friend of mine at NBC told me he had a 13 week opening in his daytime schedule, and if I could come up with a unique daytime series, he'd broadcast it. (He told a half dozen other producers the same thing, incidentally, which was okay with me. I didn't mind competition.) What I came up with was* Family Secrets, *hosted by Bob Eubanks. It was fun and marginally successful, but not a huge bump in the ratings, so 13 weeks is all we got.*

The reconstructive surgery show I did (much of it shot by me with our Bell & Howell 16 mm film camera), led in later years to a syndicated series I produced in L.A. entitled Medix *which was way ahead of its time but great fun to do.* Medix *was dedicated to cutting-edge medicine. Hypochondriacs loved it! Lucky for me, so did normal folks.*

Hausner's Restaurant in Baltimore was world famous for great food of all kinds but especially anything crab. Sam and I absolutely loved their crab cakes. We have searched the world over for crab cakes as good as Hausner's but have never found their match. This unique restaurant had a huge collection of original art, which, when the place closed in 1998, fetched over ten million dollars at auction. I hear Hausner's old building is going to become a culinary school. I hope they have somebody who knows how to make crab cakes.

When Lynn cancelled Johns Hopkins File 7, *I wrote that my career was "nipped in the bud." That of course means killing a flower before it has a chance to bloom. That's just how I felt when I heard that my career (there) was over. I loved that job.*

Incidentally, I agree with Mencken that the dry martini is the only perfect alcoholic drink, and have reminded myself of that fact on far too many occasions.

Those of you who are literary scholars or Mencken experts probably realize that I did a bit of editing on the "Mencken, Nathan and God" poem—I left off the third verse—using my critical facultee. Look at it this way: when is the last time you read poetry, even edited poetry, in a book about Ham Radio?

Chapter 18

Westward Ha!

Sam wasn't thrilled with the prospect of Buffalo.

"We've driven through Buffalo a dozen times," she said, "and I've never seen any reason to stop."

I had to agree with her. We'd driven past the city often on our trips from Syracuse to Andover and Cleveland. When I was at Hiram, now and then I visited my college roommate's home in North Tonawanda, which required working your way through Buffalo. Buffalo's attractions were Niagara Falls and steel mills and as far as I knew, that was about it. Oh, the Buffalo Bills' barbershop quartet was from there, but note that the operative word is *from*.

Like it or not, the work was in Buffalo so that's where I was headed. I told Sam putting a television station on the air would be a new adventure. I told her this job would probably be temporary. She'd heard my tales of sunshine and palm trees and she knew as well as I that Buffalo was a sorry substitute for California.

"Buffalo is west of Baltimore," I pointed out.

"Not far enough. Not nearly far enough," said Sam.

"Look at it as a rest stop on our trip westward," I said.

"Westward Ha!"

I dropped Sam and our three kids with my mother in Andover who immediately started cooking. I headed back east to Brad Field's old homestead. Brad had arranged for me to stay with his dad in Hamburg, a nice western suburb of Buffalo, while I looked for a place to rent.

Brad's father ran an unvarying routine every day. Breakfast at 7 AM while reading the paper, to work at 8 AM, home again at 6 PM, heat up a TV dinner, then eat it in front of the TV. His black & white TV set didn't have a UHF converter, so I couldn't watch WNED at "home." Practically nobody in those early days of TV had a UHF converter, so practically nobody would be watching whatever brilliant programs I managed to come up with for WNED. To receive UHF, early television sets required an external, add-on converter box which was cumbersome and expensive. Brad's father didn't care about UHF and probably didn't even know what it was.

New York State's first educational television station was in the colorful, rococo Hotel Lafayette. I glanced around the ornate lobby; then headed for the elevators and the top floor. The place was fairly deserted. I looked for a smoke-filled office and there was Les. He greeted me like a long lost relative, and a rich relative at that. He hadn't changed a bit since I'd last seen him that day about two years ago when we left Syracuse. Until I got his surprise phone call, I hadn't heard a word from him and had no idea where he'd found a job. A "position" as he would put it.

Les proudly toured me through his domain. I was most interested in the small studio and the control room, which was old but adequate. I met the chief engineer who was not a Ham, but knew all about the hobby. When he learned that I was an active Ham, he toured me proudly through his workshop, the best equipped place at the station. Les said his engineer was a genius. He kept the old junk he'd inherited from a commercial station from falling apart using "chewing gum and bailing wire."

I took one look at the metal working equipment in the engineering shop and knew exactly where I was getting the case for the pair of 1625s amplifier I'd built. I had started that project in Syracuse with a BC-459 chassis, finished the wiring in Baltimore (and Andover while on holiday) tested it (it worked) and wondered where I'd get the sheet metal case fabricated to make my little amp pretty (and safe for that matter—there were 600 plus volts floating around that tank circuit which was right on top of the chassis and easy to touch).

I discovered that Les had sold his board of directors a bill of goods when it came to my expertise. He told them that I could turn the ordinary public and parochial school teachers who appeared on Channel 17 into charismatic "master teachers." Turning teachers into television stars? Not exactly what I envisioned when I told all of the folks in Baltimore that I was going to run the programming of a TV station—an educational TV station to be sure, but a TV station nonetheless.

When I arrived the station wasn't even on the air! We'd go back on when school started in the fall. My job was to get the studio organized and the teachers prepared to present over a dozen classes a day with something like a two minute pause between them—all in that one studio.

After meeting the small staff, Les took me downstairs to the restaurant for our first "business lunch" which consisted mostly of martinis. He told me that he didn't expect either one of us to make a career out of WNED, but he thought we could get it off the ground and then move on to what he called greener pastures. We were both small town boys, so we knew that our greener pastures would only be found in big cities not noted for much green, except of course for money. I don't remember what we had to eat at that first of many lunches, but the martinis were first rate. Mencken would have approved.

During the summer break, with the station "dark," the chief engineer suggested I bring in my little amplifier so he could assess the size of the sheet metal job. Not one to miss an opportunity, I brought my entire station in, so he could see exactly what I wanted the end product to look like. The amplifier desperately needed a pretty cover, because without one it was pig ugly.

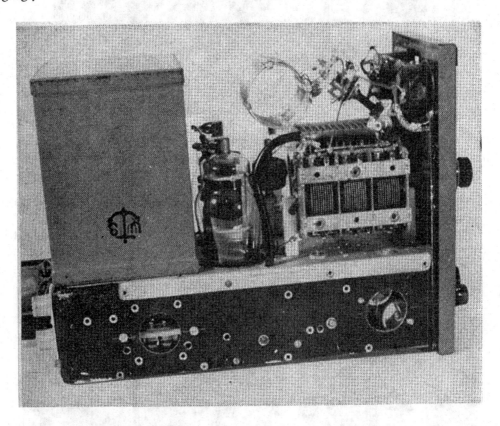

Not only was the skeleton amp not pretty, it was lethal! Touch that coil on the top and you're dead—or at least mightily impressed! (Despite the decided lack of UL approval, I made a few contacts with it in Baltimore when I finished getting it wired, and came to the conclusion that it worked just great. Signals are louder with amplifiers. Duh!)

We didn't have a dummy load in the engineering workshop so we used a hundred watt light bulb, proving to the chief engineer that a non-engineer like me could actually build an amp that works! In what seemed like no time at all, the sheet metal front panel and cover plates were fabricated, painted, put in place on the amplifier, and voila: a work of art.

My two-piece sheet metal covers hid a lot of holes and scrapes. The front panel was attached to the amplifier chassis, and the rest of the metalwork not only improved its appearance but shielded the amp against causing television interference. Allegedly.

The amp worked so well and looked so good with the 20A and the 20A's VFO that I wrote an article about it for *CQ Magazine* which appeared in the September, 1960 issue.

Is this a classy looking three-piece SSB transmitter or what? Two Hundred watts! (PEP of course, but power is power. Beats the 20 watts coming out of the 20A.)

The article for *CQ* was the first I'd written for any Ham publication and the last time I'd write about things technical. Too many Hams out there were a lot smarter about circuits and RF and formulas than I. You can be sure that before I sent the article to *CQ* I had it approved by my Elmer into Ham Radio, Jack Rodebaugh, W8LIO.

I don't remember much of my tenure in Buffalo and it wasn't just because of the martinis. I wasn't there long enough to get memories into my head. We hadn't even emptied all of the boxes in our newly rented house when I got a call from the Independent Colleges of Southern California. Lynn Poole, my old boss at *Johns Hopkins File 7*, had recommended me to produce a television series for this group of a dozen or so small private colleges in the Los Angeles area. If I was interested, could I meet with four or five of the college presidents at the University Club in New York City on a certain date? Was I interested? I didn't pause for a microsecond.

At the appointed hour I flew across the state to meet with them. They liked me and offered me the job on the spot. They even offered to pay my moving expenses. After I shook hands with my new friends the presidents, I called Sam from the lobby of the club with the good news that we were off to Lotus Land after barely half a year in Buffalo. Sam started putting stuff back in boxes the moment she hung up with me.

The two people less than delighted with our impending move were Les and my mother.

While I had regrets about abandoning WNED and appreciated the opportunity that Les had tossed my way, training teachers to have the big personalities that TV requires proved to be a frustrating experience at best and a fools' mission at worst. Some of the teachers resented my attempt to turn them into "performers," not that there was much chance of that ever happening.

Working for Les was a wild ride down paths never before traveled. Like the time I got an early morning call from him telling me I had to fill in for him at today's board of directors' meeting because he was in Puerto Rico. What the hell was he doing in Puerto Rico? He didn't know. He went out for some drinks at the Buffalo airport bar and ended up in Puerto Rico, and he was sick as a *perro*. Could I fill in for him? I told the board of directors that Les was under the weather—I just didn't tell them that the weather he was under was a lot warmer than the weather we were under.

I also represented the station in a general manager's meeting at what I think was the initial meeting of what became the Eastern Educational Network because for reasons unknown, Les didn't want to go.

After returning from that network organizing meeting (which I think was in Boston since WGBH was the 900 pound guerilla of the group), I discovered that my office had been moved from the one closest to the lobby to the room at the end of the hallway. Les had observed that the staff stopped in my office to chat (I encouraged that) and with my office back in the boonies they wouldn't be so apt to be walking by. Before Les got to work, we moved my office right back to where it had been. When Les came in, he never said a word. I never knew if he'd forgotten that he had me moved, or just chose not to stick a toe into what would be a major *mishigas*.

We parted friends, but we also parted ways. This was long before Facebook and Twitter, long before computers and the Internet, but if Les had been a Ham, we would have stayed in touch. Of that I have no doubt.

I drove to Los Angeles all by myself, heading for the greener pastures that Les had predicted at our first three-martini lunch. It was just a bit sooner than he anticipated. I found a house to rent that had room for a modest antenna, met a lot of people at the small independent colleges who had hired me, met the brass at KRCA-TV, which was at Sunset and Vine, (a legendary location for this small town boy) and got settled as best I could in a few weeks.

With the furniture scheduled to arrive the next day, at the appointed hour I headed to the airport to pick up Sam and the kids. Kathy held Dave Junior's hand as they came down the airplane steps to the tarmac just ahead of Sam holding baby Kris. It was mid-December, sunny and 70. My little family had left Buffalo early that morning during the beginnings of a snowstorm. I picked up Kathy and Dave. Sam gave me a kiss, looked at the bright sunshine, and said, "I'm home."

The phrase "chewing gum and bailing wire" of course means put together in a haphazard, slapdash way, kind of the way my little amplifier looked (before it got its sheet metal work). But Les had lucked out with his engineers. They were first rate.

To sell somebody a "bill of goods" is, these days, generally associated with some sort of scam, such as paying in advance for items listed on a piece of paper and you end up only with the paper. Back in the day, however, a bill of goods was just that—a listing of stuff someone had purchased (and received). Who knows where it went awry?

California is often called "Lotus Land" which, according to one dictionary, is "a place or state of languid contentment." I'll buy that. And so did a lot of other people, as it turned out.

"Under the weather" is a phrase meaning, of course, sick. It came from British sailing ships. When the seas were particularly rough and a sailor became ill, he was put below decks, thus he was "under the weather." One of the things I love about the English language is idioms that hang around through the centuries, such as this one, coloring our language, making it more interesting. Perhaps other languages have colorful idioms as well; they probably do, but I only know English.

The Eastern Educational Network should have included WNED from the get-go but, for whatever reason, the two founding stations were in Boston and Durham, New Hampshire, probably because they could fairly easily be linked together by microwave, whereas Buffalo was out in the boonies of Western New York and way beyond an easy connection. Also, WNED was UHF, meaning that nobody could watch unless they had a set top converter, and practically nobody had a set top box, which automatically made us second class citizens.

Besides that, having the first educational television station in the great state of New York in Buffalo, and not New York City, sort of pissed everybody off, because they were trying to make something big out of ETV. Eventually the Eastern Educational Network became American Public Television, a precursor to The Public Broadcasting System (PBS) but well before that happened I was long gone from educational television. Somehow though, I never got the notion of educating via television entirely out of my system. Three of the movies I produced much later in my career (Nadia, Do You Remember Love and The Long Walk Home) are educational as well as entertaining. Many if not most of the dozens of documentaries I produced were both entertaining and educational (I hope). Incidentally, it wasn't until 1970 or so that the FCC required TV set manufacturers to include UHF on every TV manufactured. That was back in the days when the FCC actually regulated the industry, a practice they've long since abandoned.

I mentioned Facebook and Twitter and the Internet. Some civilians are surprised that with all of the means of communicating these days that Ham Radio still survives. Well, we Hams use many of those alternative means of communications, but we still get on the air. Why is that? I think it's because Ham Radio is magic. Most Ham QSO's are between strangers who start out with only Ham Radio in common, so every conversation is a voyage of discovery. On the air conversations are not usually among old friends, but among new friends.

A so-called "dummy load" is a substitute for an antenna. Looked at from the transmitter's point of view, an antenna is the "load" and a dummy antenna is obviously a "dummy load." In our tests of my little amplifier at WNED, the dummy load was a 100 watt light bulb which we could get to be very bright when we whistled into the microphone.

I mentioned that the 200 watts out of my homebrew amplifier was PEP, or Peak Envelope Power. Somebody other than me will have to tell you what the "envelope" in PEP is. If I ever knew, I've forgotten. It probably has to do with an oscilloscope sine wave pattern. The so-called average power was closer to 100 watts. Whatever it was, the amp worked, and I was pleased.

I can't imagine why, today, anybody would want to build a pair of 1625s linear amplifier, but if you are so inclined, you can find my original article on-line in the CQ Magazine, September, 1960 issue.

When Les called from Puerto Rico and told me he was sick as a perro, *I didn't know what a* perro *was, though I suspected it was a Spanish dog. I was right, and if Les didn't get anything else out of his trip, at least he learned a little Spanish.*

Mishigas is of course a mess. It's Yiddish. Some of our most interesting, expressive words come from Yiddish. The Jews may be a small percentage of the population, but they've supplied some of our most colorful vocabulary.

WNED-TV was a very interesting blip on the timeline of my career. When we actually got on the air in the fall, I found that I could help the teachers who really wanted to master the "new" medium. I could also do any program I wanted to do as long as it didn't cost any money. For instance, the bar pianist at the Lafayette Hotel was a charming old guy who was eager to come in early and play a piano I had moved onto our rooftop patio. He entertained during what should have been our news hour, except we didn't have a budget for news. There wasn't much news in Buffalo anyway.

Incidentally, if you look at the WNED-TV website you won't find my name as the first program director. You won't even find Les Martin's name as the first general manager. You'll only find Mike Collins as a general manager in the station's formative years and for many years thereafter. Mike was my public relations director. Les actually fired him several times for misdeeds real or imagined, but I hired him back. Who knew that when writing the station's history he'd have such a selective memory of the good old days?

When the college presidents offered to pay my moving expenses, I'm not sure they realized that I had a wife and three kids, but the reimbursement check showed up without comment. And writing this, I reminded myself what a simple time it was in the early 1960's. When's the last time you could walk out to a commercial airplane and greet your family on the tarmac?

KRCA-TV was at Sunset and Vine in Hollywood. Right up Vine was the Brown Derby. I had a lot of lunches there. The food was good, the martinis were terrific, and the people watching was non-pareil! A few years after I got there, KRCA-TV moved to Burbank, where the NBC studios were. I liked being in proximity to all of the network production, but I felt about Burbank the same way Johnny Carson did. When he called it "beautiful downtown Burbank," it was far from a compliment. Very possibly the author of that colorful phrase was George Schlatter, the genius behind Laugh In *and many other successful series. Later on I worked with George for a few years and still count him as a friend. More about George later on.*

I was right not to worry about a cross-country move based on a 12 week contract. The series I produced for the Independent Colleges of Southern California went through several titles, the most enduring being College Report *and/or* On Campus *and was on the air in Los Angeles for 26 years! We won a lot of awards including more than a dozen local Emmys. That series was great fun. I personally loved hobnobbing with some of the colleges' most interesting professors and the many celebrities who regularly showed up on the campuses. More on them later too.*

Without doubt, one of the reasons I jumped at the job opportunity dangled by the college presidents I met with at the University Club in New York was that, after my first two trips out there, I really wanted to live in California. This was the brass ring I'd been looking for. I was hired on a 12-week contract. I think the presidents were surprised when I took the job on such short terms, because most of them probably wouldn't have made that leap, but I knew where I belonged, and Sam's "I'm home" said it all for both of us.

Chapter 19

At Last—Sixland

I'm beginning this chapter from my favorite summer retreat, Pier Cove, Michigan, on the far edge of the western side of the state, three miles or so south of Saugatuck, a nifty little resort town. It's late August, 2011, and Sam and I are at Brad and Mary Lee Field's big old summer house that they insist on calling a cabin. I mention this because were it not for Ham Radio, I most probably wouldn't be here. Brad, you'll remember is W8JJO, and as a consequence, we've stayed in touch over the many years since we met at Hiram College. I come in the spring and help him put up his 3-element SteppIR Yagi antenna plus a bunch of low-band dipoles, and then hang around for some on-the-air activity, conviviality, and great meals, plus now and then a round or two of bridge, a card game for people with great memories and steely concentration. I play anyway.

This morning Brad worked Heino, ES3BR in Estonia on PSK-31 (more about that fascinating mode later) while Mary Lee and I went to the farmers' market in Holland to pick up some fresh fruit and vegetables. I love farmers' markets. In addition to being an avid Ham, I'm an unrepentant foodie. You probably already figured that out.

But on with my story.

Back in Hollywood in 1960 I realized that I was taking over an existing series, but I didn't realize that the producer I was replacing was the best friend of KRCA's general manager, Tom McCray. Oooh, I thought, that might be a little dicey. But the college presidents had thought of that too, and greased the skids for my arrival with Tom and the KRCA brass. The transition was somewhat easier because the guy I was replacing didn't much like the series he was producing, maybe because it had the pretentious moniker *Foundation for Judgment*.

The first thing I did was change the series title to *College Report* which sounded considerably less pretentious and gave potential viewers a clue as to the show' content. If you saw *Foundation for Judgment* in TV Guide wouldn't you go running for the exits? I know I would. *College Report* might not have been the world's greatest title, but at least it wasn't awful. That title, incidentally, had to be cleared through NBC's title clearance department, a new experience for me.

Sam approved of the house that I'd rented in Altadena for our little family, and so did Kathy, age four, and Davey, two-and-a-half. Kris, who was one, withheld her opinion. Since the moving van wasn't due to arrive until the following day, we locked up our empty house and headed down the hill to check into a motel for the night and then out to dinner at Ernie Jr.'s Mexican

Restaurant on Colorado Boulevard. I'd been to Ernie's earlier but this was Sam and the kids' first taste of Mexican cuisine and it's fair to say that we were all instantly addicted to the refried beans, Mexican style rice, chips, salsa and guacamole, and their fresh fish slathered in butter and paprika.

The next morning I called our moving company for an ETA, only to discover that our household goods were stuck in the Donner Pass under six feet of snow and our delivery would be late. How late, nobody knew.

We couldn't afford to stay at the motel any longer, so we went to Sears and bought a couple of cots and some sleeping bags and moved in. The phone man came and installed our phone, and the electricity and gas were on, so I could start work, sort of. Our next door neighbor came over and introduced herself and, hearing of our predicament, invited us to dinner. So we met Angel and Bob Smith, who became long-time friends. Three days later, a moving van showed up in our driveway and we settled into our new adventure.

College Report was broadcast on Sunday afternoon, along with a wide variety of so-called Public Affairs or Public Service shows. Since the television stations used the public airwaves, and paid nothing to do so, the FCC decreed that every commercial TV station must do a certain amount of non-commercial, community-oriented programming as a sort of rent for the frequencies they used, and a low rent it was in my opinion.

KRCA did more than was necessary in the way of local shows, I think because the general manager, Tom McCray, was an old-school general manager, proud of his locally produced programming. Despite the fact that KRCA (later KNBC) was owned by RCA, which owned the NBC network, Tom ran the station like he owned it himself. Tom's chief engineer was John Knight, W6YY, a well-known Ham in Southern California, and one that I went out of my way to meet.

When this building was built it was called "Radio City" even though it also contained KRCA-TV. Radio was in decline, and television was beginning to boom, so within a

178

few years, KRCA (soon to be rechristened KNBC) moved to Burbank and in typical Los Angeles fashion, this terrific art deco building was torn down—only 15 years after being constructed to great fanfare. It was replaced by a bank. How ignominious!

These were those halcyon days before the professional sports mania that sucked up every second of weekend time. The FCC gradually allowed stations to do less and less Public Service programming, until stations basically stopped doing it at all. But in my heyday, stations were required to give time to worthy local organizations, and the Independent Colleges of Southern California qualified—and hired their own television producer (me) to boot.

I realized that I'd have to get some high-powered talent in order to attract an audience for a Sunday afternoon show. I was on the lookout for "Stars."

Early on, one of my colleges, Claremont Men's College (now Claremont McKenna College), a fairly conservative liberal arts college for men-only in those days, had Barry Goldwater, then a U.S. Senator from Arizona, speak to its political science faculty, government majors and others interested in politics. I asked my friend, CMC economics professor Procter Thompson, to ask the Senator to come into the KRCA studio and do a show for us. At a propitious moment, Procter asked Barry and after some hemming and hawing, he agreed, and he showed up at the KRCA Studios at Sunset and Vine, in Hollywood, right on time.

The *College Report* host in those days was Bob Wright, a local news anchor/reporter and the only conservative television talent that I'd met. He wasn't the host of my show because he was conservative. Rather, he was a good host for me because almost all of the college professors I had on our shows leaned toward liberal, so Bob didn't lob them many softball questions. Bob was obviously delighted to chat with Barry Goldwater and CMC students about politics and public affairs. Finally, a *College Report* right up Bob's alley.

I, of course, told Barry I was a Ham, gave him my QSL card, and he told me he'd send me one for our "eyeball QSO." He did it too.

In my rented house, about the only antenna opportunities were short verticals or wires out the window. When they had cleared the lot to build the three rental houses (one of which was mine), they cut down all the trees, leaving only meager antenna options.

I felt it in my bones that I was now a bona fide Californian, not only because I liked the sunshine and my job, but because Sam (and according to her the kids) liked it even better than I did. As so often happens, I had hardly settled into my new job when another job offer came in at seriously bigger bucks—in Alaska. When I told Sam about our new opportunity, she waved her hand at me and said, "Bye-bye." She was kidding, of course (I think).

That decision made, we set out looking for a house to buy (that we could afford). The criteria were good Ham location (meaning a big lot with lots of trees) and an okay neighborhood. We liked Altadena because it was like towns back east. I especially liked it because it was not incorporated but just a part of Los Angeles County, meaning that when it came time to put up a tower, I'd just put it up—without so much as a by your leave (at least that what I was told). Sam, and three little kids, inspected a lot of houses, and showed me the few that fit our specs. One that Sam really liked wasn't a great fit because it was on a really busy corner, but it was once a great house—a Greene & Greene in fact. These brothers were well known in Southern California for having designed really nifty Craftsman style homes. This one, alas, had seen some rough treatment and a couple of unimaginative modifications. And it wasn't a very big yard. It also cost more than we could afford. They wanted $23,000 for it! That was out of our price range, for sure.

Whenever I had a chance, I'd drive around areas of Altadena looking for my ideal home. On my third or fourth drive, I found the perfect place, or at least almost perfect.

You could barely see the house from the street there were so many trees and bushes ("overgrown" Sam would call it when she first saw it). It used to be the gatehouse for the mansion next door, but gatehouses had kind of gone out of fashion, even on Rubio Street in Altadena, a pretty toney street (my kind of place in other words). Sam said the house was too small. It *was* a little small, and it only had one bathroom (and an old one at that) and two smallish bedrooms, a small (old) kitchen, but a great living room with a terrific stone fireplace at the breezeway end. On the other side of the breezeway was a relatively new garage which we could divide into a master bedroom in the back and my office in the front.

One big plus for this old gatehouse: it was priced just below the top of our budget range—$18,500. This for what would easily become a three-bedroom-plus-office charming little retreat on a 100 by 300 foot lot on a quiet street. Some trips to the bank, $3,000 down, the required homeowners' insurance policy, and we were homeowners!

Yeeeeaaaaaah! Now to get the tower up, as soon as I can find a used tower!

We had barely gotten comfortable with our tight quarters, bought some new, modern furniture for the living room, and gotten my office functioning, when my mother-in-law burned our house down. She and Sam were clearing small trees and weeds out of the yard and burning them in the fireplace when suddenly we all smelled smoke, and it didn't smell like fireplace smoke either. Sam got me off the phone in my office to come investigate the strange smell. I noticed smoke on the roof in the vicinity of the fireplace that didn't seem to be coming from the chimney. Or was it?

Our fire happened on one of those smoggy Southern California days when everything hung low. The smoke from the fireplace didn't go up like it was supposed to, but gathered over our huge brick patio like some kind of cheap horror movie special effect. Sam and I stood there looking at all the smoke hovering over the patio, and then looked back toward the roof again. Sam yelled at me, "The roof is on fire!" But there were no flames! Meanwhile, Grandma was still stuffing sticks into the fireplace.

"I'll call the fire department," I said. "Get the kids out of the house."

Sam, ever the cool head, got the kids into the car, backed it up our long dog-leg driveway lickity-split and parked it on the street. The two younger kids were in the back seat, and Kathy was in the front, with firm instructions to keep the younger ones in the car, one of the times we were happy to have a two-door vehicle. By the time I found the fire department number, Sam had run back down the driveway, grabbed a garden hose and was spraying it onto the roof, which by now was really smoking. The moment that I hung up the phone I heard sirens. In less than five minutes the firemen had run into the house, covered our new furniture with tarps, and had water pouring onto our by now flaming roof. In a half-hour the firemen were wrapping it up.

Our poor little house was declared a total loss! Except for my office and our bedroom
behind it, which only smelled bad. It took weeks with the doors and windows
open for the acrid smoke-smell to dissipate from my office. Even my chain smoking
didn't mitigate the smell. (Yes, I had started again! What a nincompoop!)

A total loss. I couldn't believe it! An insurance adjustor showed up and agreed with the fire department that it was a tear-down (except for the fireplace and my office.) The policy I'd bought on our poor little house required the insurance company to put us up in temporary housing until our house was rebuilt or in our case, torn down, hauled away, and a replacement built. The adjuster told us to get going building a new house as quickly as possible.

Since I had to be near my office at the end of the driveway, instead of renting a house, we rented a 40 foot-long house trailer and parked it in the driveway's dog-leg parking area. Voila! Instant home. Probably not legal, but nobody on that street of majestic homes (mansions, really) said a word. Never having built a house, we didn't know what to do until we saw a model home we liked with a sign on it that said: "We'll build our house on your lot." It needed a little fudging to fit just right on our lot, but since Sam was sort of the general contractor, she talked the builder into modifying the house to our specs. Once the builder saw our lot, he realized his house would look great on it, so he agreed to our changes as long as he could bring future buyers to see our house. Done deal.

Our new ranch style house was "L" shaped, with four bedrooms on one wing plus two bathrooms and, on the other half of the L, a new kitchen (which we really appreciated after a year or so in the old one,) a dining area, and a huge living room with the biggest sliding glass door anybody had ever seen facing onto our old brick patio. And at the far end of the living room stood our old stone fireplace, which I still think was the culprit, but the fire chief wrote up the fire as an electrical short. How could a Ham have an electrical short? Don't answer that.

It's probably obvious to you that we really ended up smelling like a rose as a result of our little fire, and I've probably been over-insured ever since.

Since we needed a building permit for the new house, I had an Amateur Radio tower added to the original blueprints, and no inspector ever mentioned it. All I really had to do was find a cheap tower so the building permit didn't go to waste.

A good place to find a used tower was at a Ham club and LA had a lot of choices. No surprise, I decided to join the Southern California DX Club, one of the truly legendary organizations in ham radio. It was the gathering point for some of the Southern California's best known DXers, including Don Wallace, W6AM, Frank Cuevas, W6AOA, Art Enockson, W6EA, Roger Mace, W6RW, Ted Gillette, W6HX, Gordon Marshall, W6RR, Bill Orr, W6SAI, and John Knight, W6YY, to name but a few of the really old-time legends. When I got up to introduce myself, I ended by asking if anybody knew of a used tower for sale, and sure enough, I got a lead on a 72' four-section aluminum crank-up that was selling cheap because most Hams were wary of aluminum towers. Not me. I latched onto it, and in no time, with the help of a lot of local Hams, it was up on the big concrete deck right behind the house, and furthermore it tilted over into my backyard so I wouldn't have to be climbing this tower, which I didn't mind doing but for some reason climbing gave Sam a conniption fit, which is a hissy fit complete with gestures.

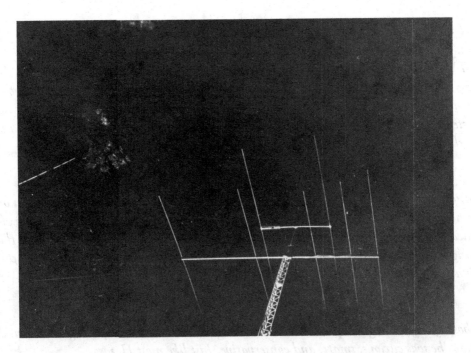

At the top of the tower was a Cushcraft two-element 40-Meter beam and the big one below it was a KLM wide-spaced 20-Meter beam. Maybe the insurance company paid for it. I sure hope so. It was connected to the house and was on the blueprints!

At one of the DX club meetings, John Griggs, W6KW, (the only station to be licensed to run 6 KW as he so often said) spoke at a meeting. He was the Southwestern Division Director of the American Radio Relay League, and he was at our meeting to relay the latest news from Headquarters and to ask for our votes—he wanted another term as our division director.

When the meeting ended, John came after me and confirmed that I had produced *The Ham's Wide World* on the ABC Television Network. He hadn't seen it but he'd heard about it, and what he'd heard he liked. John said he'd been talking to the other directors and the ARRL staff, and he thought he could talk them into funding an updated version of that film and would I be interested in producing it?

"Sure," I said.

"Let's see if I can make this happen," he said. We exchanged business cards and I told him I'd be waiting for his call.

After I'd been in California for a while, I realized that Altadena was a rather unusual place for a television producer to live. I chose it because it had the trappings of a small town, not a suburb like the San Fernando Valley which was hot and flat and to my eye at least, uninteresting. I rationalized that Altadena was sort of equidistant between the colleges of the Independent Colleges of Southern California, from Redlands to the east and Mt. St. Mary's to the west. Having met all of the presidents and my "TV Reps," so called, I was feeling pretty confident. We lived there over a decade. My big 20 Meter Yagi worked great. Except when pointed north (toward Europe). I forgot to tell you that the downside of my new home was the presence of the San Gabriel Mountains just a mile or so north of our homestead. Of course, I could work Europe "longpath," meaning around the South Pole rather than over the North Pole, and I did, with great regularity.

I mentioned that NBC was owned by RCA. It occurs to me that there may be a person or two out there who never heard of RCA. At one time it was a really big deal. The Radio Corporation of America was founded by General David Sarnoff whose claim to fame was hearing the SOS from the Titanic and alerting authorities in New York City. Sarnoff was an avid short wave listener and could easily have been a Ham, but for whatever reason, wasn't.

The host of my College Report series, Bob Wright, would have made a good Ham. He loved conversation, he was curious, smart, and conservative. Just like most Hams.

The word "moniker" has always appealed to me as a synonym for "name" which is rather bland. Hams, incidentally, have "handles" instead of names. Don't ask me where that one came from. When the Citizens' Band hoards descended on our old 11-meter band, they were all "good buddies." More about CBers and their effect on Ham Radio in a later chapter.

Procter Thompson, the Claremont Men's College professor who "hosted" Barry Goldwater during his visit to the school was a pal of mine, and a guest on numerous programs. He had tenure and was fearless. He once started a College Report show by agreeing to an extreme close-up of his mouth. On cue, he said, "Greed is good." Then the camera pulled back quickly and he said, "and I'll prove it." At his home in Claremont, Procter always had a shaker of martinis in the freezer and I had an open invitation to stop by any time. And I did too.

The "hemming and hawing" that Barry Goldwater did before agreeing to do a television program for us is an interesting phrase. Both words are depictions of noises that humans now and then make when thinking, i.e., giving your brain time to catch up with your mouth. It's from the 16ᵗʰ Century or before.

The "our house on your lot" that we bought actually had only three bedrooms, but had an attached two-car garage on the builder's plan. We didn't need a garage; we had a dogleg for the cars, so we talked the builder into turning it into a large master bedroom with a bath.

After Sam and I moved into our new master bedroom, I acquired the back room of my old garage/office for my Ham shack. I had to share it with the kids, of course, but that was okay—they didn't play with my Ham equipment and I didn't play with their toys. My shack in those early days in California was impressive—at least I thought so.

Here's what my shack looked like in the mid '60's: The Drake twins, a Henry 2K and assorted accessories (all acquired used from various southern California Hams who were "upgrading" their shacks). That Henry 2K was aptly named—a two kilowatt amplifier, with a pair of Eimac 3-400Zs in the final. It didn't run quite two kilowatts, but 1500 watts easy. QRO for sure. W8LIO would have been proud.

You of course remember what the so-called Q-signal QRO stands for, don't you? That's right, high power. You also remember I'm sure that a couple of my first construction projects were amplifiers. I loved to watch the tubes get red and the needles on those meters bounce whenever I said, "Hello radio!"

The five-element KLM 20-Meter beam on my tower was an unusual design. It had not one but two fairly close-spaced driven elements of different lengths making the frequency response broader than the common design. It was a terrific antenna.

Our two-door car in these days was a Volvo 544, a really great little car. It looked like a 2/3 size 1939 Ford. The back seat was just wide enough for three little kids to sit side by side.

From left, Kathy, Kris, and Dave. Don't they look like angels? Can't
you imagine them squeezed into the back seat of our Volvo?

*John Griggs, W6KW, the ARRL's Southwestern Division Director, looked almost exactly like
Burl Ives. You have to be an old timer, maybe an old-old timer to remember Burl Ives, a generously
proportioned, white-bearded folk singer/actor of the '60's and '70's. John had exactly the same girth
and beard and was accused of purposely grooming himself to look like the famous singer. He denied it,
of course, saying, "I looked like Burl Ives before Burl Ives did!" Burl Ives was also a Ham, incidentally,
KA6HVA, probably because he had his own boat, and got his license for possible emergencies. Ham
Radio's tag line is, "when all else fails."*

*The term "glad handing" has been around since the beginning of the twentieth century, and means
to give a friendly welcome or greeting to people in order to get their approval.*

*My poor mother-in-law got blamed for burning down our house, but that was really just in jest. She
was burning sticks in the fireplace and the house burned down. The coincidence was too much to resist.*

*Finding the phone book and then dialing the fire department phone number seemed to take forever.
Writing about it reminded me how much better 911 is (unless you get a busy signal).*

*Ernie Jr.'s Mexican Restaurant is still in the same location on Colorado Boulevard in Pasadena,
but now in a neighborhood of really fine eateries, part of the gentrification that Old Town Pasadena
welcomed in the '80s and '90s. In 1960, its area of Pasadena could charitably be called "ramshackle."*

The title of this chapter, "At Last, Sixland," will be obvious to all Hams and should be obvious to you if you've been paying attention. California is in the sixth amateur radio district (in fact, it is the sixth district all by itself) and I wanted to work in Los Angeles, thus the chapter title.

I noted at the beginning of this chapter that I was writing it at my summer retreat, Pier Cove, Michigan, in August of 2011. I'm continuing to plug away on it on a plane from Honolulu to Los Angeles in January of 2012, where Sam and I visited daughter Kathy and husband Jon to celebrate my 80th birthday. I mention this only because if I don't get focused on writing, I may end before the book does.

Chapter 20

New Ham Film, Same Old Title

Medix was a name I came up with for the second series that our little production company, Dave Bell Associates, Inc. got off the ground. This was before it became commonplace to make up new words by adding an X to the end (or the beginning for that matter). *Medix* was about medicine of course, but more particularly about medical breakthroughs and horizons.

The Los Angeles County Medical Association came up with some of the budget and "authenticated" the content. I latched onto a new, very aggressive syndication company called Syndicast and those guys steered me to the Burroughs-Wellcome Company, a drug manufacturer owned by the Brits, with US headquarters in Triangle Park, North Carolina. They were unique among drug peddlers because they were non-profit. Only the Brits would come up with a non-profit drug company. But they were a perfect sponsor. They wanted nothing to do with the content of the programs.

The originating television station for this series was the CBS O&O KNXT, whose program director, Joe Sands, chose Mario Machado to host it. Mario was a good fit. He knew nothing about medicine, but was very enthusiastic about the series, which was barter syndicated by Syndicast. It was broadcast by stations in about 60% of the country, although looked upon with great skepticism by some of them, because there was nothing like it on the air. In other words, it was way ahead of its time, a cause for suspicion among television stations. If nobody else had such a show, how could this one be any good? That's the television mentality, folks. I've had to live with it my entire life!

With all of the activity in our little company, I was thinking about producing some television specials, in addition to the *Medix* and *On Campus* series, when John Griggs, W6KW, the ARRL Southwestern Director called, all breathless.

"I can get you $12,500 for our new film—hope that's enough, because that's all I could get."

"Hey, John, that's great news!" I said. I thought for a moment. "Let's see, that means you want a half-hour TV film—that'll be 28 minutes more or less, meaning that our film pencils out to about $450 per finished-minute—not much."

"You can do it for that, can't you?" he asked, sounding a bit worried.

I immediately thought about Barry Goldwater's appearance on my College Report series; wouldn't it be a coup to shoot in his shack? Back then, every amateur radio operator in the country knew that Senator Goldwater was an active Ham, but how many had actually visited his shack and watched him do phone patches between GI's in Viet Nam and their loved ones in the States?

"If I can arrange to shoot some footage in Barry Goldwater's station, I might need some breakage," I said.

"Barry Goldwater? You think you can get Barry for our film? Headquarters will pony up more money for Barry, I'll bet." John was almost breathless.

"I'm going to try for Arthur Godfrey, too," I said.

"I love Arthur Godfrey," said John. I could almost hear him licking his lips.

I could see that $12,500 was going to be the sticker price, not including irresistible extras.

We'd been shooting a lot of film clips for *College Report* and especially *Medix*, and we were ready to tackle a full-length film, even if it didn't have a full-length budget.

Barry's office liked the idea of him being in a film about Ham Radio because they knew it was a hobby he really enjoyed. Of course we'd have to fit our filming into his schedule, which was always tight. We agreed on a date some weeks in the future, so in the meantime I outlined a possible film, got the outline approved by ARRL Headquarters, and started making arrangements to shoot. I was excited! This was going to be fun.

I had accumulated some film equipment—a 16mm converted Auricon sound movie camera, a Nagra tape recorder, a few lights, reflectors and other essential filmmaking paraphernalia.

Since my budget was tighter than the bark on a hickory tree (as my mother used to say), I'd actually have to do some planning. That's when I got my first surprise on this production.

I'd been a Ham for nearly 20 years but I had no idea there were so many facets to our hobby. I discovered that there were over 60 different ham activities that could have been filmed. Sixty! I had no idea my hobby had gotten so broad (like so many of my fellow hams!).

I wanted to start the film with what the ARRL's John Huntoon, W1RW, called the staple of Ham Radio—two guys in a QSO, hamming it up. Since I didn't have the budget to go to a far-away DX country, I decided I'd find a Ham in Baja as one end of my typical QSO. For the stateside half of the conversation I wanted a local Ham, but also a young, local Ham. W6KW told me that the West Valley Amateur Radio Club was virtually all teens and twenty-somethings. One of the leaders of the group was Matt Futterman, WB6KPN (now N6PN), who not only agreed to be the local half of my "typical" QSO, but also to narrate a portion of the film.

Our first shoot day was at the QTH of Enrique Garcia, XE2RH, in Ensenada, Baja California. He owned a wholesale grocery and was also the local Swan Electronics dealer, so of course his shack was filled with Swan gear.

During one of our many phone calls getting the shoot arranged, Enrique asked me how long he would be in the film, and I said, "Three or four minutes, probably." Later I learned that Enrique took that to mean that it would only take us a few minutes to get him on film, when in reality, it took the better part of a day.

The original plan called for us to shoot the QSO between Matt and Enrique live, not only for authenticity, but also to speed up the process. However, at the last minute, Matt had to work (he was saving up for college after all) so we'd have to fake the QSO, and put it together in the editing room. Actually, there was so much RF in Enrique's shack when he transmitted that he wiped out the recording on our Nagra tape recorder, so we couldn't have done a live contact even if Matt had been available and the band conditions were perfect. The Nagra was a terrific recorder, but get it into a big RF field and it had a brain fart.

Enrique, XE2RH, turned out to be a perfect character for our "typical" QSO to start the film. John Huntoon, the big honcho at ARRL Headquarters should have been pleased. The only thing that would have pleased him more is that the QSO had been using Morse Code, but I thought that might have been too mysterious for a typical television audience.

Dave Bell, W6AQ

The way we simulated (that's television lingo for "faked") the QSO was that I stood behind Enrique and ad-libbed what I thought Matt would say in a typical first QSO, Enrique listened and ad-libbed his half of the QSO, with the camera rolling all the while. We did exactly the opposite when we shot Matt's half of the QSO. And thus, the opening and closing conversations in *The Ham's Wide World* were faked. No one ever said, "that QSO looked phony to me." And I don't think they were being kind. Hams are quick to point out flubs in film depictions of Ham Radio. They are all purists in that regard, and proud of it!

On the trip home, with all of the camera equipment in the back of my little Chevy II station wagon, the rear bumper was almost dragging on the ground. Little did I know that the great backward tilt caused the gas gauge to report that the tank was a quarter full when in reality only a drop or two and some fumes remained.

Yes, you guessed it. We ran out of gas, right there on the main highway between Ensenada and San Diego. It may have been the main highway, but there wasn't much traffic, at least not much about to stop and help.

I raised my hood, the time honored flag of a traveler in distress. Wayne and Sam and I stood around the car looking forlorn. Oh, I forgot to tell you. Sam went on this shoot because she'd gotten our next door neighbor's daughter to baby sit, and Wayne and I decided we could use a "gofer." Sam had told me to get gas before we left Ensenada but I took a look at the gas gauge and decided we had plenty. I heard more than a few "I-told-you-so's" while we were awaiting rescue.

And rescued we were! A pickup truck with three young Mexicans in the cab stopped to see what was wrong. They didn't speak English and we didn't speak Spanish, but they quickly understood that we were out of gas. *No problema!* Hop in the back of the pickup! So I did, leaving Sam and Wayne to "guard the equipment."

The pickup truck raced up the main highway for a few miles, then pulled off onto a dirt road, bouncing through potholes and ruts only to skid to a halt at a gate with a guardhouse. The guard recognized the three young guys and opened the gate. I looked around. We were on the grounds of a giant Pemex refinery. My saviors found a five-liter gas can, filled it with gas and put it in the back of the pickup with me. Then they turned around, and headed back to my poor stranded station wagon.

They insisted on pouring the gas into my car, waited to be sure the engine started, which it did with no problem, and then gave me the empty gas can in case I was so foolish to run out of gas ever again. I tried to pay them for the gas and the ride, but they wouldn't take a cent (or a *centavo,* as the case may be.) They were happy to help and drove off in a swirl of dust—three carefree goodwill ambassadors.

So when we finally got back to L.A., after one long day of work, we had exactly one-half a QSO "in the can" (that's film lingo) plus a five-liter gas can that had *PEMEX* stenciled *on* it.

We decided to shoot the other half of the scene, at WB6KPN's shack, in one day, including a mock Field Day with the West Valley Amateur Radio Club out on a nearby hill making contacts using emergency power and "instant-up" antennas. We shot the Field Day exercise first, since that'd be the more difficult of the two.

More than a dozen kids from the club showed up at the base of the little hill, as promised, toting all manner of radio equipment, a lot of it home brew. A few parents came too, to take part in the fun and carry antennas and equipment. Somebody brought a dog. Some of the kids hooked up the equipment and a couple of others put together the prefabricated homebrew cubical quad antenna.

One of the toys that I'd picked up cheap was a very small 16mm wind-up camera. One wind was good for about 20 seconds of filming. I decided to do a shot from the antenna's point of view as it was hoisted into place. We lashed the camera to the mast right where the antenna boom connected to it. Just as the kids were ready to hoist the quad into the air, I started the camera and quickly got out of the shot.

The scene turned out exactly as I'd hoped, showing a bunch of kids pulling and pushing the mast into a vertical position. The shot ends with the camera looking straight down at a dozen or so kids looking straight up. We did the shot twice, just to be sure we got it. That meant the club members had to raise the antenna into the air three times before they could hook a radio to it, to see if it worked. (We couldn't leave the little camera there in all the shots of the antenna, could we?)

As we filmed this organized chaos, it occurred to me that really young Hams are just amazing, infected with the same mysterious enthusiasm for the hobby that I picked up when I stood at the screen door to W8LIO's shack and watched him scream "J9AAI" into his microphone over and over again. Just as we were ready to film, it started to rain. Unbelievable. It never rains in Southern California. We've all heard the song!

Tarps appeared, rickety tents were draped and hung. A Heathkit HW 100 was dropped in the mud. One kid, told to bring his rig to the site, brought everything, including his phone patch.

John Griggs had told me that this was a unique club. "Unique" is not adequate to describe this aggregation of enthusiasm. When we finally finished shooting everything that moved on that hill, including the dog, the crew left for Matt's house to finish the shoot—but the club members stayed on the hill making contacts for the rest of the afternoon.

When we got to Matt's house in Woodland Hills there was a brief respite from the rain. So we shot him putting another wood screw in the wooden mast that held up his 40 Meter dipole and then tugging on the rope to get his dipole "in place" as if he were just putting it up.

Then we went into Matt's really neat shack and filmed the last half of the Enrique/Matt QSO just like we had filmed in Baja—i.e. totally simulated.

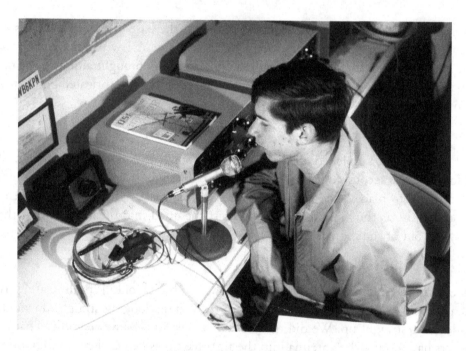

Matt turned out to be as good an actor as Enrique was. And his equipment was entirely home brew—all Heathkit.

As Arthur Godfrey mentioned in his narration (Oh, yes, I got K4LIB as one of the narrators), some of these kids aren't old enough to drive a car or buy a drink, but over half of them had the top grade of Ham Radio license, the Amateur Extra. They had passed a 20 word-per-minute code test and a fairly tough written test about electronic theory and FCC rules and regulations.

After the West Valley Amateur Radio Club obligingly demonstrated what Amateur Radio Field Day looked like, I scrounged up scenes from real Field Days shot over the years by radio clubs all over the country and strung them together showing Hams warming up for real emergencies.

For an example of a real emergency, I chose the earthquake and Tsunami (though I called it a tidal wave in the narration—who'd ever heard of a Tsunami in those days?) that hit Anchorage Alaska a couple of years earlier. Most of the footage I managed to come up with was black and white and we were making a color film.

I decided to turn the segment into a TV news report, as would be seen on B&W TV sets, which were still pretty common back then. In fact, the set we used was my office TV and I got daughter Kris and a neighbor kid to be filmed watching it. Bill Leonard, W2SKE, read the simulated breaking news narration (which wasn't hard for him to do, since before he became a VP of CBS News, he had been a newscaster at WCBS in New York City. In fact, he still had his own local show on the weekends in New York City called *Eye on New York*.)

I bought the film clips from Anchorage TV stations and local cameramen. The big wave footage came from some guy who sold big wave shots, mostly for surfing films I think. It wasn't a real Tsunami wave. If you saw a huge wave coming toward you, would you hang around and shoot it, or get the hell out of there? Exactly. Which is why I couldn't find real Tsunami footage. My stand-in Tsunami wave cost the production $30.

I had scheduled the Barry Goldwater shoot to take no more than a couple of hours, because Barry's office told me he was on a very tight timetable. My cameraman, Wayne Threm, and my sound man/editor, Dave Arnold, a still-photographer friend, Arthur Dubinski, and I decided to fly to Phoenix so we could get there in time to set up at Senator Goldwater's house before his scheduled arrival so we could make the most of a shooting day. In those carefree flying days, it wasn't a problem for four young guys to check three bags apiece into the hold of a 727, even if a couple of the bags were pushing 70 pounds each. Our rented station wagon was loaded with our "junque" as Dave Arnold always itemized it, and we headed to Scottsdale.

We knew we were at the right place when we spotted the Christmas-Tree of beams on a super tall rotating mast in the middle of Scottsdale's most exclusive neighborhood. We had a couple of hours to get set up before the Senator was scheduled to arrive. The station caretaker, Bill Eccles, K7MJC, was waiting for us as promised. First, we toured the shack, though not many people called Barry's Ham station a "shack."

It was truly a state of the art collection of top of the line Collins equipment. The filaments only went dark when the power company suffered a failure, which wasn't very often at the Senator's house on the hill.

I wanted Barry to do a typical phone patch between a GI in Vietnam and his loved ones back home. Barry and his crew did thousands of these morale-boosting phone calls every year, and every Ham knew it. To have Barry doing anything else would be screwing with tradition, and I didn't want to get on the wrong side of Senator Goldwater.

Ever the optimist, while we waited for him to appear, we filmed Barry's equipment close up (you know, meters bouncing, antennas rotating, knobs being tweaked—the kind of stuff Hams love to see). One of the regulars in Barry's shack pretended he was running phone patches, and even though Barry had the best equipment money could buy, our Nagra tape recorder went on the fritz every time Barry's big transmitter came on the air. I'd already warned the Senator that we'd probably have to fake his phone patch. He was okay with that. He understood the idiosyncrasies of electronic equipment.

As we fiddled around with our closeups, the operator on duty at AFA7UGA realized that the 20-Meter band had opened up to Southeast Asia and he of course started making phone patches. That was the scene when Barry entered the shack. I introduced him to my crew, David and Wayne and Art Dubinski. Art was busily clicking stills of everything that moved. When Barry realized that real phone patches were being run, he said that one of his rules was that when the band was open, phone patch activity was top priority.

We'd have to film his segment in the morning. He didn't have to catch a plane until 9 AM, so we could start at 6:30 or so and get it done. He couldn't do his scene tonight because he had a full evening of social engagements. My crew gave me that "what's going on here?" look, but even though I was the director, and directors were allegedly the ones in control, sometimes the talent calls the shots.

We recorded Barry's off-camera narration in his office, away from his big transmitter. We filmed his antennas. We got everything we could except what we came for—Barry doing a phone patch.

I was concerned about getting releases from the folks on the other end of the phone patch, and discussed it with Barry. He said that wouldn't be a problem. I don't know if that meant he'd get the releases or "it wouldn't be a problem." He was right. Nobody ever complained about hearing their private conversation on television. It was the only time in my career that a U.S. Senator got a release for me (or didn't, as the case may be).

Meanwhile, the operator on duty was taping his phone patches, using a cheap cassette recorder. Before we left Barry's for dinner, we listened to a couple of them. They were absolutely clean. That Radio Shack cheapie recorded both sides of the conversation just fine. Go figure. One of the patches we listened to sounded especially clear and very interesting. We chose that one to be our sample.

We left all of our equipment in place ready for the first shot in the morning, and headed down the hill for dinner and a drink. Maybe several drinks.

The following morning, practically before the sunrise, we arrived at Barry's place and were greeted by Bill Eccles. He assured me that the band was not open, so we should be able to shoot our scene. Hallelujah! It's the only time in my life that I rejoiced because the band was not open.

Barry walked in promptly at 6:30 AM, looking fresh after a late night of politicking. He listened to a phone patch recording we'd selected, approved it, put on his headset and was ready to go. His entire scene took us about 30 minutes to shoot, and Barry was pleased. "You boys work fast," he said. "I like that."

We packed up our gear and headed down the hill to the Valley Ham Shack, an independent electronics store that sold Ham Radio equipment to Hams all over Arizona. Its manager was Sharon La Traille, WA7DSW. Her job was to remind our audience that there are indeed female Hams, and good looking ones, too. She demonstrated mobile operation from her nifty little 230SL Mercedes convertible. (I loved that model Mercedes, and still do.)

Imagine, if you can, driving down a quiet Phoenix street when you spy coming toward you two cars side by side, with wires draped between them, and a cameraman on top of the station wagon filming a young woman in the Mercedes who seems to be talking into a microphone. Several cars coming toward us turned off the street before we got to them.

Another memorable scene from the new *Ham's Wide World* was Dave Atkins, W6VX, firing up his antique spark gap transmitter and calling CQ. He didn't get any takers, but my guess is that he wiped out every TV set within three blocks or maybe three miles. For a lot of the film's viewers, that was the first and only spark gap transmitter they had ever seen. It was a great reminder of Ham Radio's rough-and-tumble-try-anything early days.

I wanted to get some amateur television into our film because most civilians, and a fair number of Hams, didn't even know that there was such a thing as amateur TV. (A case could be made that, in those days, all TV was amateur, but I'm not going there.) I heard about a local Ham who was (and still is) one of the leaders of the ATV movement.

Tom O'Hara, W6ORG, built his shack in a one-car garage filled to the rafters with boxes of parts and trays full of mysterious but obviously useful junk, in addition to a loaded workbench, a smoking soldering iron, a video camera aimed at the bench, and a TV set suspended from the ceiling. His garage looked like a going-out-of-business store on Radio Row. Tom's friend WA6EPX turned up on cue, loomed large on Tom's B&W TV set, and the two of them had a short but interesting QSO. They made ATV look like a lot of fun.

All that was left was a bunch of transition shots and inserts; for instance, hands looking at QSL cards as Barry talked about their meaning and significance, which a lot of Hams consider the final courtesy of a QSO. I had stored my card collection somewhere and couldn't find them, so I asked a Ham a half mile or so down the hill from me if he had any interesting QSLs. "Sure 'nuff," said Don Lisle, K6IPV, "come on down."

In addition to QSLs, what I needed from Don was some specific over-the-air audio that sounded like it was coming out of a receiver, which of course, it was. Nothing sounds like HF (high frequency) noise and heterodynes like real HF noise and heterodynes. Dave Arnold set up to record the audio at Don's shack and I went home to supply the required sounds over the air. When I'd finished my list of noises, I went back to Don's to listen to the results and take a look at his QSL cards.

Don had pulled about a two-inch deep stack of QSLs from his drawer full of cards. Now, what follows is one of those "only in Ham Radio" moments. As I leafed through the stack of cards, what should I discover but one from DL4USA, my old club station at the former Panzer Kaserne in Sindelfingen, Germany. The handwriting on the QSL looked vaguely familiar. Closer inspection proved it to be mine! I had sent this card to Don for a contact we had made while he was operating from his mobile rig in San Diego. It was a "We've been friends longer than I thought" moment. I think our lifelong friendship was cemented then and there while we recalled that memorable contact as my non-Ham soundman watched in wonderment.

I always swore that I'd never start my own business because even my laggard consciousness was tweaked by the hours my mother put in at Bell's Store. Even my father had to burn the midnight oil sometimes when he got behind writing insurance policies. So what is the first thing I did the moment I had a couple of employees? I started Dave Bell Associates Inc. What else could I do? I had too much work! That phrase "burn the midnight oil" means of course work late by the light of an oil lamp. Even Andover had electricity when I arrived there in the mid 1930's from my birth city of Omaha, Nebraska by way of Denver. Oh, yes, I started life in Omaha. Johnny Carson's hometown too. Did I tell you that Johnny's second wife Joanne worked for me for five or six years? Later.

When I came up with the name Medix *for our television series, it was the only use of that made-up word that anybody could find. Google it now and there are hundreds, maybe thousands of references. I should have registered it.*

Barter Syndication was popular in the '60s and '70s. The word "barter" of course means a trade of one thing for another. Syndicast gave Medix *free to television stations and the stations took the series complete with two minutes of Burroughs Wellcome commercials plus a couple of minutes of somebody else's commercials owned by Syndicast. The station then put three minutes of their own commercials in the other commercial slots: thus a barter.*

The term O&O is archaic radio and television broadcast lingo for stations that are "Owned and Operated" by a broadcast network, such as the "big three" network stations in Los Angeles.

I hope it's obvious to you that On Campus *was the new and improved* College Report.

Arthur Godfrey, K4LIB, was one of the country's most popular radio personalities in the 1960's and '70's. His voice was unmistakable. He agreed to narrate our film, probably because Barry Goldwater was the star. I never met Arthur. I sent him the script and he recorded it. He sent it back to me with a handwritten note that said, "if you want me to redo something, I will." No retakes were necessary.

Our first shoot day was at XE2RH's QTH. Surely you remember the "Q" signals Hams have used as shortcuts since time immemorial. QTH is of course, "location."

The RF in Enrique's shack that destroyed our audio recording is short for Radio Frequency, which Hams use loosely to note strong radio signals and a lot of other things.

The "soundman" on The Ham's Wide World *was my old pal from college, Dave Arnold, who should have become a Ham but for reasons unknown, never did. Even though Dave had been around Ham Radio since the Showboat Majestic, the coincidence of the DL4USA QSL card impressed him.*

I mentioned the word "breakage" regarding the new Ham's Wide World *budget. You try to get it when you're asked to do something not in the original budget. Barry wasn't in the original budget. I like breakage*

The Auricon camera was a popular 16mm movie camera because it was quiet. Most 16mm cameras sounded like paper shredders. The original Auricon only held 100 feet of film, enough for about two and a half minutes. My Auricon had the popular 400 foot film magazine conversion that some bright guy dreamed up, meaning we had a 10 minute film capacity before we ran out. By comparison, today you can shoot two-hours of high definition video complete with audio using a camera about the size of an iPhone.

My wife Sam went along to Enrique's house in Ensenada as a "gofer," a common film term referring to a person who goes for things.

I suspect that Barry Goldwater never asked anybody for a release for his phone patch. I knew from personal experience that the Senator was not a big fan of releases. When he appeared on my College Report *show, I handed him a talent release from NBC. He took one quick look at it and handed it back unsigned. "I'm not holding NBC harmless," he said. "They've got more money than I do." I told the general manager of KNBC that the Senator wouldn't hold NBC harmless, and Tom McCray said, "Hell, neither would I," and threw the release in his wastebasket as he muttered, "God damn lawyers."*

John Huntoon, W1RW (at the time W1LVQ), was the editor of QST *and a very influential Ham at ARRL Headquarters. His reputation was that of a tough guy, but he approved my film outline with nary a change. I mentioned that John wanted to start the film with a typical QSO, which you'll remember is one of the "Q" signals, this one meaning "conversation."*

Swan Electronics was one of the small Ham equipment companies that started in a garage and quickly outgrew several manufacturing facilities because their SSB (Single Sideband) voice transceivers were so popular, durable, and relatively inexpensive. Their many transceivers used the phasing method of generating single sideband, the same as my first sideband rig, the Central Electronics 20A. Hams liked Swan transceivers because they had lots of audio. They seemed to sound louder than their actual signal strength.

I noted that one of the West Valley Amateur Radio Club kids brought all of his equipment, including his phone patch. As you've deduced by now, that's a gadget that transfers signals from a radio to the telephone lines. Of course there was no phone on the hill, but if AT&T had come by and installed one, that young ham would have been ready to make a phone patch, just like Barry Goldwater's station!

I mentioned that Matt Futterman's equipment was all "home brew." It was all Heathkit, the great kit creator of the era. They had terrific step-by-step instruction books so anybody who could read (and solder) could build a Heathkit. True home-brewers looked down their noses at kit builders, because they didn't have to scrounge through boxes of resistors and condensers and chokes and all the rest of the paraphernalia that went into radios of the day. And they had instructions! *What kind of a real Ham would stoop to reading instructions? The nice thing about Heathkits compared to many other home-brew projects is that the Heathkits worked!*

The acknowledged top-of-the-line ham equipment of that era was Collins—and that of course is what Senator Goldwater had. It's appropriate that the Senator have the best equipment—and besides, Art Collins, W0CXX, was a friend of his.

Senator Goldwater's callsign was K7UGA, but for his phone patching he used his Air Force MARS (Military Amateur Radio Service) call, AFA7UGA. The armed services in those days had frequencies adjacent to the Ham bands, so they would have "clear" frequencies for their communications.

The term "heterodyne" has various meanings. The heterodynes I'd recorded and played over the air to be recorded at K6IPV's place were squeals or tones caused by two amplitude modulated Ham stations being on adjacent frequencies. Understand? Squeals are one example of heterodynes.

I puzzled about my expensive Nagra tape recorder wiping out in strong RF Fields when a cheapie Radio Shack cassette recorder worked fine. My friend Bill Pasternak, WA6ITF, explained it to me. I understood what he said, but the explanation goes beyond the scope of this book. If you really need to know why the cheapie worked and the top-of-the-line didn't, contact WA6ITF. He'll explain it to a fare-thee-well.

Every large city had its "radio row." The biggest and most compact was in New York City's lower Manhattan in the vicinity of Cortlandt Street. From the dawning of radio this was home to dozens of stores that catered to the needs of radio experimenters. It was three or four times the size of the radio row that I discovered in Cleveland. This great New York ham haven was condemned so they could build the World Trade Center.

Everybody including me was impressed that Barry Goldwater so willingly participated in this film about Ham Radio. He certainly shared my love of the hobby. I celebrated our shoot in Barry's shack with my own QSL card to mark the occasion.

The guy on the left is me, holding the slate (normally used to mark the scene number on the film and show a sync point between the film and the audiotape by clacking the "sticks" attached to it.) In this case it's being used as a "flag" to keep light out of the camera lens. The cameraman is my old cinematographer/pal Wayne Threm, and the guy in the center is Barry, going through a stack of QSL cards.

The reason I called this new film The Ham's Wide World, *exactly the title I used for the* Johns Hopkins File 7 *episode was, simply, I couldn't come up with a title I liked better. Besides, the original HWW was a live television show, and the thing about live television shows was, it was live. If you weren't watching television at that moment in history, you missed it.*

But miracles sometime happen. Johns Hopkins kept kinescopes of most of the File 7 *episodes and I got a copy of that old black-and-white film, which the University gave me permission to include in* The ARRL Film Collection—*a bunch of the Ham Radio films that I produced—all on one DVD. So that DVD starts with the "new"* Ham's Wide World *and ends with the original* Ham's Wide World. *You can get it from the ARRL. Taken together, this film collection is a history of Ham Radio in the 20th Century. It's worth having in your library.*

Chapter 21

DR. STRANGETONE:
Or How I Learned to Stop Worrying and Love the Code (the confessions of a phone man)

My happy little family and I drove our fire-engine red Volvo 544 up to Yellowstone one summer in the early 1960's, hauling our primitive tent-trailer behind. The park ranger told us not to store any food in the kid's tent or in the tent trailer, or we'd be rudely awakened by a hungry bear or two. "Keep your food in the trunk of your car," he told us. We did what we were told. The only other thing in the trunk was an impedance matching network I'd built to help match the base of my big vertical antenna to the output of my Multi-Elmac AF 67 Transciter.

In the middle of the night, I woke up because Sam was poking me.

"Something is banging in the car," she whispered loudly. I listened, and sure enough, there was a rhythmic pounding from the back of the car. I cautiously peered around the edge of our tent and discovered that the passenger side door was open and the dome light revealed a huge bear in the back seat of our Volvo. The rear seat-back cushion was out on the ground and the bear was tugging on our ice chest, which was in the trunk. The bear knew there was food in that chest and he wanted it. His problem was that the hole from the back seat into the trunk was too small for the ice chest to pass through.

That bear wasn't too smart or he would have known that. Frustrated, he continued his rhythmic tugging of the ice chest. Then the bear heard the familiar sound of a park ranger truck rattling up the road and he instantly leaped from our car and ran off down the road with the ranger's truck banging him in the ass at every opportunity. Finally Mr. Bear wised up and ran into the woods. The next morning we put the car back together as best we could and headed for the nearest gas station so we could buy a can of air freshener. I don't know if you've been close to a bear, but let's just say that their hygiene is not the best.

I share this story with you because that bear and I had something in common. He knew there was food in that ice chest and he wanted it.

Before I get to what Mr. Bear and I had in common, I need to digress to set the stage.

Several months after I got my first license in the mail in early 1951, the FCC came out with a "Report and Order" that changed the old Class A, B, and C licenses to Extra, Advanced, General and Novice. Everybody called this new brainfart of the FCC's "Incentive Licensing," but I called it Insensitive Licensing because the FCC had upset my tender sensibilities. I had just spent the better part of three years trying to get my code speed up to 13 words-per-minute and now the FCC decided that 13 wpm was cruel and unusual punishment. They dreamed up the Novice license, with a code speed of five words-per-minute! The Novices had a lot of restrictions on their operations, but *they were on the air!* Had the FCC come up with this inspiration in 1946 I would have been on the air in 1947 or '48 instead of '51!

I did what most Hams did with the FCC's "Report & Order"—I ignored it. For twenty-some years I was happy living with the knowledge that I'd never again have to shed any sweat in an FCC office. We all blithely ignored the Extra Class license "opportunity" with its 20 word-per-minute Morse code proficiency requirement.

All of the incentives the FCC could dream up were as carrots dangled over the wrong end of a horse. *Except one.* Hams who'd had their tickets 25 years or more (like me), if they had their Extra Class license, could apply for what Hams all refer to as "two-letter" calls, meaning two-letter suffixes. And not only distinctive calls, but *calls of your choice*—subject to availability, of course. I could swap my W6BVN for who-knows-what. Maybe my initials, or even better!

The only problem was that I didn't have an Extra Class license because I didn't know the Morse code 20 words-per-minute.

You've heard of in one ear and out the other? That was me and Morse.

In 1975, my code speed was in the three to five words-per-minute range because I hadn't used CW since I passed my general class license test in 1950.

Now here comes the justification for telling you my bear story: The difference between me and Mr. Bear was that the hole he was trying to get the ice chest through would never get bigger. However, I knew that my handling of the accursed code could improve if only I set aside a lot of time and applied myself, at least that's what it says here in small print.

What the hell. I learned it once, and I could learn it again. I discovered the West Coast equivalent of W1AW. W6QIE sent code practice five nights a week at 8:00 PM, starting at five wpm—just my speed! (Well, maybe a little fast).

This time I wasn't going to fool around! This time I was going to apply myself! I made a vow to listen to Morse code every night for 20 minutes minimum. I managed to do that five nights a week for a year. On the weekends, I'd listen to CW QSOs on the Ham bands. I learned to copy bad fists. Actually, W6QIE's code practice was sent "live," so there were sometimes mistakes in his sending, plus a little lilt from enjoying his Bug too much.

A Bug is a very clever contraption, combining an axle on pivots with springs and weights, all attached to paddles. Push the lever to the left and the Bug makes dashes one after another until the spring becomes unsprung, and pushing the lever to the right makes dots. Your timing has to be good to send just the right number of dits and dahs. Hams sending with Bugs developed "fists" as distinctive as phone operator's voices.

Dave Bell, W6AQ

I went from almost solid copy four wpm to more than 20 wpm in that year. See, I *was* smarter than that bear!

Just for fun, with some regularity I got on the Novice bands with my Kilowatt and shocked all the newcomers with my big signal and my decrepitude. They knew I was an "old timer" from my callsign, and I knew they were novices because they had an "N" in their prefixes. These guys sent anywhere from five to ten wpm—just my speed.

Now and then I would drop my pulsating kilowatt onto a CW DX pileup and ask the DX station to QRS (slow down) amid cat-calls from the CW aficionados on the frequency. And you haven't heard a cat-call until you've heard one on CW.

I built an electronic keyer and bought the best paddle I could find. I had to practice using this modern version of the old mechanical Bug.

This device is a paddle. Compared to a Bug, it's simplicity itself. Instead of weights and springs, the dots and dashes are made electronically (and perfectly) in the keyer, a clever electronic device.

I retired the old hand key (the J-38 that W8LIO had given me many years before). It was just as well; that J-38 never worked very well anyway.

206

For some reason, Hams call these things "straight keys." I don't even know why they're called keys, much less straight keys. To make a dot you push the lever down and let it up immediately. To make a dash, you push the lever down for three times as long as you pushed it to make a dot. Push it down for longer than that and you run the risk of blowing something up.

While I was relearning the Morse code, in 1975, Sam and I found a terrific old house in the Hollywood Hills that was a 10 minute drive to my office. In those days, I thought that our expanding little company needed an office in Hollywood—in the center of the action. We had made enough money to put a down payment on a building (the old FotoKem property, for those of you who know Hollywood, near the corner of Barham and Cahuenga.) I was really tired of the half-hour to hour-and-a-half drive from Altadena to Hollywood every day. So we sold our home in Altadena, took down my aluminum crank-up tower and sold it to my friend Jay, W6EJJ, because at that time the City of Los Angeles frowned on aluminum as a structural material. We moved into our "new" 1926 Spanish style house in the Hollywood Hills, with a view of the Pacific Ocean about 10 miles to the southwest, and a view of the Hollywood Sign and the Griffith Observatory from the backside of the house.

Ted Gillette, W6HX, was the legendary tower installer in Los Angeles and he happened to know the whereabouts of a steel Tri-Ex LM-470 (the 470 meaning four section with a total height when cranked up of 70'). The price was right, so I bought it, and Ted arranged to have it delivered to my front yard, which caused the neighbors no little apprehension. It was the first "improvement" to our new abode.

How many Hams does it take to pick up and move an LM-470? Well, I had 26 and it was none too many. Back in those days, Sam allowed me on the roof. No more.

I may have missed a day or two of code practice during the move and the erection, but it was worth it. That tower is my "big one" even today, over 35 years later.

5700 HILL OAK DRIVE   HOLLYWOOD, CA. 90068

W6AQ   DAVE BELL
EX - W6BVN

I celebrated my view to the ocean with this QSL Card. That's Hollywood in the foreground and Century City beyond. My antenna is a so-called "Quad" which you'll read about later.

I spent three solid weeks of my 1976 vacation listening to code cassettes and boning up on the radio theory I'd need to know in addition to the Morse code. Since my first test in 1950, all the radio circuits had gone from tubes to solid state (i.e. transistors and printed circuits.) Getting solid state into my solid head took dedication.

In August of 1976, slightly over 25 years since I passed my first licensing exam, I nervously drove down the Harbor Freeway and the 405, and eventually got to the FCC offices in Long Beach, about an hour ahead of schedule. I sat around being nervous. Why had I quit smoking? The FCC examiner beckoned the small hallway crowd into the examining room. He tried to look stern and no-nonsense, but he wasn't old enough to pull it off.

I sat down determined to copy the 20 words-per-minute solid. "Be on the lookout for commas," I said to myself, remembering my first code exam.

We were given pads and pencils and the code tape began. It sounded slow to me. Maybe the examiner was playing it at 16 wpm in deference to my age. I took a moment to read what I was copying. I could actually read it! It made sense! And then came a comma and threw me off. Concentrate, I told myself.

When the Morse stopped, we handed in our papers and the examiner began checking them. When my name was called, all young bureaucrat said was, "Pass."

"*Pass*?" A pass in the TV world means they're *not* going to buy it. Is that what he meant? He wasn't buying my interpretation of the Morse code?

I couldn't resist asking: "I *passed* the code test?"

"Yes, you did," he said with a trace of a smile. "Congratulations."

"Thank you, thank you, thank you," I said. I think he was worried about being kissed.

Then he really smiled and said, "Maybe you'd like to go out into the anteroom and relax a bit before the sending test." He obviously didn't want a coronary right there on government property.

I shakily got up from my chair and wobbled into the anteroom. I'd done it! Hot damn! I wondered once again whether the fact that I only hear out of one ear had anything to do with my difficulty with the code. My monaural hearing was a good excuse, even if irrelevant.

Now all I'd have to do was send CW for a minute with no mistakes. Omigod! Would I be the only Ham in history to pass the receiving test but flunk the sending? I got nervous all over again.

Most of the Hams who came out of the testing room told me, "Congratulations," and slumped out of the anteroom to continue their code practice sessions.

When I got called back into the testing room, I plugged in my keyer, my paddle, and a little speaker that I'd brought. I sent a couple of Vs and my friend the examiner gave me a paragraph to send. I didn't get a good start; in fact my fist was uncopyable, even to me. I paused, and started again. I sent about six words perfectly and the examiner said, "That's enough. You pass." He obviously couldn't stand the punishment that my fist was creating.

The radio theory and rules test was anticlimactic and actually pretty easy. Maybe I'd over prepared. "No," I said to myself, "you did good."

In late September, my Extra Class license arrived in the mail, to be returned to the FCC immediately with my current license, along with my carefully thought out list of two-letter calls in order of preference.

In mid-November, while I was shooting a documentary in upstate New York, Sam called and said, "You have an envelope from the FCC."

"What's my new callsign?"

"I haven't opened it."

"Well open it," I shouted into the phone. "I'm peeing my pants here!"

Finally, Sam said, "You're W6AQ."

The phonetics "African Queen" flashed across the marquee of my mind, and I tried talking out of the corner of my mouth. I called my assistant, "doll." He looked at me strangely.

W6AQ. How about that? It was the last A-something suffix on the FCC's availability list and I was delighted with it. I still am. Dit-dah Dah-dah-dit-dah. Now that it's behind me, the year of constant spare-time work to get W6AQ really hadn't been much of a hill for a climber.

A strange thing happened on my way to an Extra Class license. I actually learned to like the code. I'm still not particularly good at it, but I enjoy it. Many Hams view Morse as the Hams' secret language. After getting my Extra Class License, so do I.

Of course not all Hams know CW, since the FCC dropped the last code test requirement in 2007 or so. You can become an Extra Class ham these days without knowing dit-dah from dah-dah-dit-dit. But an interesting thing is happening. Now that Morse is no longer a licensing requirement, more Hams are learning it. Novices are long gone, but you can find Hams calling CQ at five or 10 wpm with some regularity.

It's for sure that Hams are an extraordinary bunch. And the *crème de la crème* are the brass pounders! Dit-dit-dit dah-dit-dah!

Way back up the log, I wrote an article for QST *about my adventures with Morse and gave it the same title that I gave this chapter. The article was published while* Dr. Strangelove *(the movie) was uppermost in many people's minds—since it was such a stem-winder. I loved that movie.*

The Multi-Elmac AF-67 Transciter (a made-up word) was fairly old when I put it in the Volvo, and it was AM, not SSB, but it worked, and getting on the air now and then kept the kids quiet for a few blessed moments. Why Elmac called it a "Transciter" (a combination of Transmitter and Exciter) is anybody's guess. An "Exciter" is just a transmitter designed to send a transmission to a bigger amplifier (which I didn't have one of in the Volvo).

The impedance matching network I built for the trunk of the Volvo was in its own aluminum box at the base of the antenna. The impedance at the base of the antenna was six or eight ohms and the AF-67 liked looking at 50 or so ohms, so I tried to match them up. Wikipedia has a good definition of "impedance" if you're curious.

How did the bear get into our car? The Volvo not only looked like a 1939 Ford, the door handles were the old-fashioned kind that you grabbed and twisted down to open the door. Bears might not have been able to manipulate push-button doors, but I'll bet they were on the lookout for Volvos. Somebody forgot to lock the rider's side door before we sacked out.

When the kids got a smell of the post-bear Volvo, and saw all of the bear grease on the headliner, they rebelled, refusing to get in the car. They suggested that we let the car air out for a few weeks and that we extend our vacation for a like amount. Barring that, they suggested that we buy a new car. You know how you get used to smells after a while? We never got used to that one. And my insurance agent didn't believe me when I told him why I needed new upholstery.

Some Hams call their FCC licenses "tickets;" perhaps because they are permission to take the world's most fabulous ride.

Incentive licensing was widely blamed on the ARRL and indeed, possibly some of the brass there had a hand in it, but it was the FCC's doing: their attempt to improve the quality of amateur radio operators (though I hadn't noticed they needed improving). The younger guys, like Matt Futterman, WB6KPN (now N6PN), the star of The Hams Wide World film, sailed through all of the tests without breaking a sweat. But old farts (like me) had a tougher time with the whole thing because we lost privileges and had to take tests to get them back. Y'might say we were pissed.

Jay, W6EJJ, who bought my aluminum tower from the Altadena house, stored it for a while beside his driveway. A decade or so later I asked him how he liked it, and he said it was still prone beside his driveway. But someday he'd get it up. That's the way Hams are.

W6QIE, the west coast, over-the-air code practice equivalent of W1AW, really made his Bug sing. Some of his dashes were five or six times as long as his dots. I tried using a Bug now and then, but I never got the hang of it. Then electronic keyers came along and saved my ass. Every dot and every dash was perfect. Now if I could just send the right one at the right time . . . .

Remember cassettes? They were sheer genius in a reel-to-reel world. And the portable machine that played them passed in those days for small. Then solid state came along, and I graduated to an MFJ digital code reader, which was in my pocket every morning for my without-fail jog, long after I'd passed my Extra exam. MFJ Enterprises, incidentally, was started with one line of popular gadgets built by a Ham in a hotel room in Mississippi, and now it is the largest manufacturer of Ham accessories in the world—by far.

I generally use the term "solid state" to mean no tubes. Remember tubes? They glowed in the dark and were replaceable. By and large, dead solid state is only throw-awayable.

After I hooked up my electronic keyer in the license testing room, I sent a series of "Vs" because the letter "V" sent by itself is, to hams, the same as t-e-s-t. Another nifty short-cut.

The word "fist" in Ham Radio parlance refers to the quality of the Morse you send. "He has a great fist," is often heard at Ham get-togethers. There's an organization called "FISTS" which celebrates the joys of CW with on-the-air contests and get-togethers and a nifty publication for all of those like-minds. CW stands for Continuous Wave, or Morse. But you, of course, already knew that.

Dit-dit-dit Dah-dit-dah are the letters S and K and when they're sort of run together, they indicate that this is the end of our Morse code conversation. It also stands for "Silent Key," indicating a Ham who has shuffled off to that big DXpedition in the sky.

Hams even have shorthand for their pals who have croaked!

Chapter 22

Plus a DXpedition

I've always believed that serendipity visits those who stuff their schedules so full that only with a lot of good luck will everything get done. That's me. Everybody tells me that I overschedule myself, and perhaps I do, but it never seems so at the time. Only later, when I find myself busier than a cat covering up sheeeut on a marble floor.

Like when I found myself at LAX (when it was just the Los Angeles International Airport) juggling two carry-on bags with a transceiver in each, along with a 16mm movie camera, twenty rolls of 16mm color film and various necessary accessories such as power supplies for the transceivers. The power supplies were the heaviest items. Two big suitcases were going into the hold of Pan Am flight 3 from LAX to Tokyo, then on to Hong Kong. My wife, Sam, carried the tickets and passports. She figured that was an equitable division of labor. She said she saved on my labor when she insisted that we only take two suitcases, not four as I'd originally planned.

We were heading to Japan, our first trip there, in the fall of 1977. The excuse for going was to film a bunch of MDs from the Los Angeles County Medical Association meeting some of their counterparts in Hiroshima. They were going to learn firsthand about the effects of radiation poisoning from survivors of the first atomic bomb blast. The film I shot would be part of a *Medix* TV Special.

I had also committed to film some activities at JARL, the Japan Amateur Radio League, in Tokyo, for an upcoming film about Ham radio, which I was doing for the ARRL.

And our friends Mary Lee and Brad (W8JJO) Field were expecting us to visit them in Matsue, where Mary Lee was a Visiting Expert teaching English as a second language. Brad, in addition to being the fancy man, was busy writing novels, plays, and articles when he wasn't visiting local Hams.

But before any of that happened, we were heading to Macao, that little Portuguese island south of Hong Kong that even then had gambling casinos and a nightlife that kept the colony's priests sweating. We, or rather I, had been invited to operate CR9AJ's station in the CQ Worldwide DX Phone Contest. This insanity had begun innocently enough about eight-months earlier when I mentioned to my friend Bernie, W6PJX, that I was itching to go on a DXpedition.

"Great; let's go to China," said Bernie, picking the one country where we had zero chance of getting a license, what with the cold war and all. As far as I could tell, the whole country had only one or two licensed Hams, and, with few exceptions, they only talked to Hams in other communist countries. I hadn't even *heard* a Chinese station in, well, ages.

This is Bernie's QSL card; John Wayne with his arm around Bernie's neck. That QSL will tell you a lot of what you might need to know about Bernie. Anytime you wanted a creative suggestion, however absurd, have a chat with Bernie.

When I suggested to Bernie that China was out, he said, "Great! Let's go to Hong Kong!" That at least was a British colony with several active Hams. Bernie's suggestions, however off the cuff, got me thinking of that part of the world. When I learned that the Los Angeles County Medical Association brass wanted me to film their excursion to Hiroshima, which took place the week after the CQ Worldwide DX Phone Contest, it was settled. My first DXpedition would be to Asia. Somewhere. But not Japan, which had more Hams per square inch than any country in the world.

I ran into a DXpedition veteran, Dick Norton, who, at the time, was either W6DGH or the much niftier callsign N6AA. We were both at SAROC, a raucous Ham convention at the Sahara Hotel in Las Vegas. Why the Sahara? On the front yard of the hotel (yes, in those days some Strip hotels actually had front yards and grass) was a big tower and a beam. An influential Ham talked the owner of that hotel into putting it up! Dick was just back from a DXpedition to the Caribbean, where he had "borrowed" a shack from a local Ham (but he took his top-of-the-line transceiver, the legendary Signal One CX7, with him). He convinced me that borrowing a working shack was the only way to go. No struggling with antennas, no fish-eyes from hotel clerks, no last-minute shortages, denials, or reneges. He also suggested I hand-carry whatever equipment I'd be taking since his Signal One was dropped on the tarmac by baggage handlers somewhere on his flight home, which did it very little good.

The CX7 cost almost $2,500 in 1970 dollars!

Another reality descended on me on March 21ˢᵗ of 1977 as I finished operating in the ARRL CW DX Contest. I may have passed the Extra Class 20 wpm code test, but I was not a CW operator. Luckily, I was aiming for a phone contest for my first DXpedition. I'd leave the CW maelstroms to those ambidextrous folks with the glassy-eyed stares.

Taking N6AA's advice, I searched through my QSL card collection looking for stations I'd worked in the Macao/Hong Kong area with the thought of "borrowing" a station for the contest. The two best prospects were Torres, CR9AJ, in Macao, and Phil, VS6DR, in Hong Kong. Torres and Phil became my #1 and #2 "innocents abroad". I dispatched an air mail letter to Torres, since I'd worked him most often, wondering about getting a license in Macao or discretely hinting that maybe I could borrow his shack (and his callsign) for the last weekend in October. It was a little cheeky, but, as my mother used to say, "Faint heart ne'er won fair maiden." My mother claimed that was the only Shakespeare she knew. The quote turned out to be Cervantes but she was in the right neighborhood.

I called the ARRL for advice, talked to Bruce Johnson, WA6IDN, their DXpert, if I may coin such a word, who told me that Macao might be difficult, but that we had a reciprocal agreement with Hong Kong. Try Hong Kong. And if that didn't work, there were lots of little islands in the Pacific.

I figured anyone with this nice a QSL card must be an okay guy.

In April of '77, having heard nothing from Torres, I attended the International DX Convention in Fresno, California, hoping to find some DX station from the Pacific there, but only located a couple of KH6's (Hawaiians). I discovered that most of the grizzled old DXers at that convention didn't need any countries reachable by anything more comfortable than a burro.

When I got home from the DX Convention, I wrote another letter to CR9AJ, enclosing a copy of my original letter, and trying not to sound as if I was begging, which of course I was. Anyone who knows me can tell you that subtlety is not my long suit. A sledgehammer was about to drop on Torres.

At the next Southern California DX Club meeting I was told to forget about Macao. Maybe their postal delivery is slow! Or even nonexistent! What about Tibet? Mongolia? The suggestions got more and more absurd, depending on what country the speaker might need a QSL card from. Each suggestion got farther and farther from Japan.

When I got home, I wrote Phil, VS6DR, the same sort of pleading, help with reciprocal license/borrow your shack kind of letter I had sent Torres. At least I knew that the Brits had a good postal service, and I assumed that tradition carried over into their colonies!

In the middle of July, the International Amateur Radio Union contest convinced me that I couldn't let a business-paid trip to Japan go to waste without adding a DXpedition to the itinerary. The prospect of the CQ Worldwide DX Phone contest somehow managed to focus my frustration. I needed to make the inscrutable East scrutable.

At ARRL's suggestion, I wrote to David, 9V1RH, for advice and assistance, since "he knows everything that's going on in his part of the world." I thought to myself, "the Ham radio world is really vast, since Singapore is not all that close to Macao, at least on a map." I sent David a copy of my letters to Torres, since I had zeroed in on him as my principal target. I had many contacts with Torres and I really wanted to go to Macao. I imagined it as an island of foreboding and intrigue, a place that was foggy and damp and dark, even in the daytime. I envisioned bumping into Humphrey Bogart and Sidney Greenstreet and Peter Lorre. In my mind's eye, Macao was that kind of place. And in Ham Radio circles, it was moderately rare.

In exactly one week I heard from David in Singapore, proving that it was possible to send and receive trans-Pacific mail in less than an eternity. His first paragraph said, "Concerning a license in Macao—frankly, I don't like your chances." If that weren't enough, he let me know that in Singapore, one had to have a permanent address in order to obtain a 9V1 call, and he suspected the same would be true for Hong Kong, even with the U.S./Hong Kong reciprocal agreement.

Shortly thereafter, I got a letter from Phil in Hong Kong. He apologized for the tardy answer, but he had been traveling. While he would love to host me at his station, his antennas were down and they wouldn't be up again until the next year.

So VS6DR was QRT and didn't have any suggestions except to say that the top floor of a couple of Hong Kong hotels should be good locations and that a bribe would do wonders getting some antennas put up.

I sent a letter to the Hong Kong version of our FCC with all of the required information, requesting a reciprocal license. All of the licensing was handled by the Post Office. At least I knew that particular governmental agency was in working order.

And then, a Eureka moment! A day after Labor Day, a little less than two months before the CQ Worldwide DX Phone Contest was to begin, a letter arrived from Torres. It had taken him a little over four months to learn that I could *not* get a reciprocal license in Macao, but it *was* okay for me to use his station and his callsign, and he was inviting me to do so! It was like a sea breeze on a smoggy day. He described his QTH (110 Meters above sea level), his equipment (not very strong) and his home (at your service).

Torres' letter was generous and welcoming. While I didn't know it at the time, the letter was a shadow of the hospitality that awaited us. I would have to reciprocate. But how?

I called my friend Les Johnson, K6PUR, at Atlas Radio in Solana Beach, California, only about 110 miles south of Hollywood. I'd bought numerous Swan (predecessor to Atlas) radios over the years, and in fact had a Swan 400 in my car at that moment. Wouldn't Les like to donate an Atlas 210X to the only Ham on Macao? Les, a DXer at heart, thought about it for a moment and decided that Torres ought to have a dependable radio. As a bonus, he sold me one at cost to leave with Brad, W8JJO, in Japan.

I made plans to spend the following weekend at our beach house in Encinitas, and on the way down, stopped at Atlas Radio to pick up my two 210X's before Les had a chance to change his mind. I also got a tour of the factory where the little rigs were being put together.

When I got back to Hollywood, an airmail letter from the Hong Kong Post Office awaited me. I could certainly get a reciprocal license right after I'd been in residence there for three months. However, like Macao, they had no problem with me using an existing station if it was okay with the licensee.

Then I heard from Bernie, W6PJX, who I'd kept apprised of every step of my negotiations because he was going to accompany me, remember? Well, he'd gotten an offer to be director of photography on a movie-of-the-week and he'd taken it.

"What about our DXpedition?" I wanted to know.

"That'll have to wait," said Bernie.

"This DX contest isn't going to wait! That's like expecting the Rose Parade to wait," I said. This trip is all set!"

"Sorry, David," he said. "This was too good a script to turn down."

"Who's going to carry all of this equipment?" I pleaded.

"You won't have a problem with it," Bernie predicted, ever the optimist.

"Thanks for the vote of confidence," I said, and hung up.

You'd never guess from looking at Bernie that he was a victim of the Puritan Work Ethic.

So that's how I found myself at LAX juggling carry-ons meant for two people. I could feel myself getting round-shouldered.

Somehow I managed to get my carry-ons into the overhead bins and we were off for Tokyo on Pan Am Flight 3, a 747 SP. (The SP might have meant Small People, because there wasn't a lot of leg room in the back of that plane.)

We arrived in Tokyo 12 hours and one day later, whereupon we were herded into a customs-less "holding area" where we cooled it for a few hours while we awaited our flight to Hong Kong on Pan Am #1. The biggest problem with our holding cell was the lack of coffee. How can I sit around for two hours without a cup of coffee? I managed it, but I was a nervous wreck.

Landing in Hong Kong was great fun. The 747 came in low, heading right toward a humongous hill, then suddenly the plane flipped what seemed like 90 degrees in a hard right turn, put its wheels down, and we were on the tarmac. After getting some instructions from a passing Brit on how to use a pay phone, I called Torres and spoke to his daughter Magdalena. They would wait for us to arrive on the five P.M. hydrofoil from Hong Kong, tomorrow. Great! Sam and I headed to a hotel to get some much-needed shut-eye. After touring around Hong Kong for a few hours the next day, we piled all our stuff into a taxi and headed for the hydrofoil dock. We got there just in time to see the three P.M. hydrofoil take off for Macao. We bought tickets on the five P.M. hydrofoil and found a bench so we could relax and people-watch.

As the five o'clock hour approached, we heard an announcement in Chinese, or if it wasn't Chinese it might as well have been, and suddenly all of the passengers waiting for the hydrofoil jumped up and headed down the dock. "What the hell," I thought. "What's happening?

What was happening, Sam discovered, was that the five P.M. hydrofoil had been cancelled and everybody was rushing to get a place on the slow-as-molasses steamship, also headed for Macao, but at a much more leisurely pace and, we discovered, the last transportation of the day.

If I'd had roller-skates on, all I would have needed to do was stand up with my two big carry-on bags and two big suitcases and the force of humanity would have propelled me to the big steamship. As it was, I was trotting along with the crowd, mumbling apologies for banging into other passengers and attempting not to be run over. Sam ran to get us tickets for the big steamship.

About eight P.M., the lights from Macao's casinos came into view and shortly thereafter we found ourselves on a huge dock as the other ferry passengers raced to their destinations. They at least knew where they were going. It looked to be about a quarter-mile to public transportation and not a porter in sight. This contest may not get me a trophy, but I could see a bad back in the near term.

After paying an entry tax of about five dollars to get off the pier and onto dry land, I borrowed a phone from a souvenir shop and I called Torres. Again I talked to Magdelena. Torres would be right down to pick us up. As I struggled to get the bags to the street entrance, a cherubic policeman came toward me pointing his finger, as if I'd just sneaked around Customs. What Customs? I hadn't opened a bag in Japan, Hong Kong, or Macao. "Bella?" he questioned.

My hair-trigger mind reacted instantly. "Bell," I said.

"Torres," he said, pointing to a hill in the distance. Communications had been established.

I was the overdue visitor.

He dashed off toward an official looking phone before I could tell him that Torres was on his way down to pick us up, not that he'd understand what I was saying anyway. Portuguese is a weird sounding language.

I got a warm feeling about Macao. Even the cops were looking for me. I was expected. Recognized. "Bella," I said.

My wife thought I had lost what few marbles I had left.

After getting to Torres' home on the big hill, we spent the next couple of hours hooking up the Atlas 210X, socializing and eating. Torres' wife, also named Magdelena, viewed cooking as an artistic endeavor. During dinner, I realized that when I asked Torres a question, his daughter Magdelena would often answer. Magdelena, who spoke beautiful English, was translating for her father, and mother as well, in as unobtrusive a way as possible.

Torres, CR9AJ, and his young daughter/translator, Magdalena.

Even after all of the times I'd spoken with Torres on the air, I didn't realize that he spoke very little English, probably only about 100 words or so. i.e. he spoke "Ham" English. He could get by with the usual on-air dialogue, but if you strayed off into something not "Ham," Torres would have to get Magdelena into the shack.

At about 11 P.M., after a magnificent meal, I asked to be excused to get ready for tomorrow's contest, which started at eight A.M. local time. I quickly tuned around all of the bands, and discovered that 40 meters was blanketed with an especially raucous jamming, coming from due north. Let's see; that'd be China or Asiatic Russia. Torres told me that 75 Meters was also jammed, and had been for quite a while, so when his 75 Meter antenna fell down, he didn't bother to put it back up. So that left me with 20, 15 and 10 Meters for the contest. Not awful. At least I had that big log periodic antenna on Macao's highest hill. It could be seen from anywhere in Macao.

The next morning at five A.M, standing on Guia Hill under the big antenna, I watched the ancient junks sailing out to sea as they had done for centuries, provided a beautiful picture that's still in my memory. I sat down in front of a big Portuguese breakfast, and after wading through a delicious plateful of eggs and sausage, I managed to excuse myself from the table before seconds were handed out.

An hour or so before the contest, I made sure the logbook and dupe sheets were ready and that I had a couple of extra pencils. Then I tuned around 20 Meters to see how busy the band was. There were a few JAs and an Australian, and a few others, and the band was quiet. My plan was to establish a frequency just before the contest and then start CQing the moment the contest started. At about 7:50 A.M. local time, I called CQ and was immediately answered by a JA. I gave him a five by nine and told him I'd see him in the contest. I worked half a dozen others just prior to the start of the contest. I had established my frequency!

At eight A.M. the band lighted up wall to wall with Japanese stations, every one of them over S9. I called CQ several times on "my" frequency before I finally snagged a JA. By the time I logged the contact and wrote his suffix in my dupe sheet, a 9V1 in Singapore had moved onto my frequency and was calling CQ. He was 40db over S9 off the back of my beam. I called him and he came back to a JA. I called him again. Again a JA. I swung the big log periodic around and he didn't seem to be any louder. I called him again. No luck. This guy couldn't hear me. I wanted to tell him this was "my" frequency and I couldn't even get him to hear me!

I finally bagged him, and before I could tell him he had stolen my frequency, he was shouting "QRZ Contest" into his microphone. I gave up and tuned to look for a clear spot. I found one, called CQ, and nobody heard me. Again. Same. I wasn't getting out! So I tried search and pounce. I worked half a dozen JAs. I moved up to 15 Meters. The band was loaded with JAs. I called one. Nothing. I called him again. Nothing. Even the JAs couldn't hear me!

And that's the way it went.

I switched antennas from the log periodic to the three-element triband beam that was only 20 feet or so off the ground. Signals were louder on the tribander. I called a few stations. I got some of them on the first call. The tribander seemed to work better, even though it was just about directly underneath the log periodic!

I learned many things from my first DXpedition contest experience. First, one hour's prep is inadequate. Duh! Second, if vertical antennas radiate equally poorly in all directions, as the old cliché goes, then log periodics radiate equally poorly in one direction.

Nearly 500,000 points later I had learned that the Japanese operators are very polite, but they have to hear you in order to demonstrate *how* polite. I learned what it was like to be "behind"

JA while I tried to work Stateside and European stations. I learned the impossibility of creating a pileup of any kind, anywhere, with an S5 signal. Therefore, for most of the contest I was Search & Pounce, not a good situation for one of the rarest callsigns on the planet.

I learned that good operators, while running JAs, could hear a different voice through the pileup. These ops would always say, "JAs stand by please. Who was that other station in there?" After working me, they'd often say, "Any other non-JAs calling me?" If they heard nothing, they went back to running JAs.

Not every big signal had a savvy operator behind the microphone. One of the loudest Stateside signals was working JAs one after another, and I called him. He said, "Is there a JA7?"

"CR9AJ," I said.

"JA7 what?" he said.

"CR9AJ," I said again.

"CR9 stand by. Who was the JA7?" he said.

I was flabbergasted. Here I was, a multiplier, and he told me to stand by? Sayonara, putz. I spun the dial on the Atlas 210X. There's a certain amount of arrogance that comes with knowing you're the only station in your country and if they don't work you, they don't get the multiplier. At least one Stateside Ham didn't seem to grasp the difference between multiplication and addition.

But there were a few bright spots. After working W9LT, I told him I couldn't hold a calling frequency and he said, "You can have this one. I'll find another." Who says the good guys are all gone?

After the contest, we had one day for sightseeing. The only thing I remember is the front wall of St. Paul's, a huge church built by the Jesuits around the turn of the 17th Century. It burned down during a typhoon in 1835. I guess the Jesuits didn't have insurance. They've always been risk takers.

Sam and I were driven to the ferry terminal by Torres, accompanied by the two Magdelenas. After hugs all around, the hydrofoil whisked us off for our return to Hong Kong and then Pan Am back to Tokyo for our trip to Hiroshima by train.

Sam served as my official, paid, camera assistant in Hiroshima, so I insisted that she carry some of the load in addition to the airplane tickets and passports. I met the delegation of doctors at the appointed hour, filmed the meeting with their Japanese counterparts and then their very poignant meeting with some A-Bomb survivors. The doctors were given a guided tour of the part of the city that had not been rebuilt and was a memorial to the victims. The word to describe that tour is "somber."

I said goodbye to my doctor friends and grabbed another train back to Tokyo. There we boarded a Bullet Train (a trip I had been looking forward to) and as the second hand on the clock in our passenger car ticked to the appointed hour, the Bullet Train started its quiet departure on its way to 200 kilometers per hour.

We were headed toward Matsue for a quick visit with our old pal Brad Field, W8JJO, and his wife Mary Lee, acting as a "Foreign Expert" at Shimane University. They had just barely arrived and were making their little apartment into a home when Sam and I showed up, like bad pennies. They would have far preferred us to arrive in the spring, after they had settled into their new digs, but we were in Japan in November, so November was when we appeared.

I immediately gave Brad the remaining Atlas 210X and a power supply, thus lightening my load considerably. That little radio had a lot of miles on it. Every time I picked it up, it felt heavier. The Fields' apartment was on the second floor of a four-level building, and the antenna situation looked bleak. Besides, Brad had told himself that he was going to spend the year writing novels and plays, and this was going to be a sabbatical from Ham radio. Not long after we left, Brad sold the 210X to a Japanese Ham. For whatever reason, Japanese Hams wanted to own American equipment (even though Japan was at that time the world's biggest manufacturer of Ham radio receivers, transmitters, and transceivers and probably still is).

Before heading back to Tokyo, Brad and I visited the shack of JA4CX, Atsumi Kawaguchi; a splendid shack for sure, with a huge homemade tower and beam on the roof of his house.

Atsumi's shack is full of American equipment—the Drake transmitter and receiver and a big Heathkit amplifier. No wonder he was loud.

Another Bullet Train ride to Tokyo and some down-time (one day, big deal). Sam took a tour to Mt. Fuji while I headed for Akihabara, radio row for this part of the world. When Sam's bus got to Fuji, it was totally socked in. She couldn't see a thing. Oh, well; it was an interesting bus ride, so she said, although I'm not sure there is any such thing.

I, on the other hand, was in Ham-hog-heaven at Akihabara. Never, never in my life had I seen so many radio stores selling Ham equipment or parts stores selling, well, parts.

The next day I took a taxi to JARL headquarters where I filmed anything that moved. I found the QSL Bureau the most interesting because of the huge number of cards and envelopes that were stacked around and the frenzied activity of the mostly women sorters. My friend Kan, JA1BK showed up to take me to lunch. We drove over to the Playboy Club where we joined some other of his JA friends. After a great and interesting lunch, complete with Japanese Bunnies, Kan took me back to Headquarters, and I continued filming. When I finished up, I got specific instructions on how to get a subway back to my hotel so I didn't have to waste my money on a taxi.

When the subway surfaced and the scenery looked definitely rural, I knew I was on the wrong train, but had no idea what to do. I looked around for an American but my train car was full of Japanese of all ages so I said in my best voice, "Does anybody here speak English?"

Everybody looked my way for an instant, then went back to what they were doing. I noticed a very small boy, maybe five or six, at the other end of the car looking at me. He said something to a man who must have been his grandfather or great grandfather. The man stood up, and he and the little boy came up to where I was sitting. The little boy said, "I have some English."

I said to him, "I need to get to downtown Tokyo."

The little boy translated for his grandfather, who looked at me and held up a finger, indicating that he understood. At the next stop, we three got off our train and crossed over a bridge to the other side. The old man went to the ticket kiosk and bought a ticket. Then we all sat on a bench, waiting. One train came, and the old man shook his head and waggled his finger. The little boy said, "No you train."

The next train came and we all stood up. The old man and the boy bowed and the little boy gave me a ticket and indicated that this was my train. I offered to give them some money for my ticket and the ones they'd have to buy for the remainder of their trip, but the old man would have none of it. I waved goodbye, boarded my train, and settled in for my ride to Tokyo.

I told Sam that story on the flight home. It gave us a nice, warm feeling about Japan. We decided we'd have to come back again, and actually see something next time.

It was many years later before we got back to Japan, once again to visit our friends the Fields. This time we managed to do a little sightseeing. We weren't even deterred by the six point something earthquake that rattled our hotel (and us) our first night there. The facades of several buildings had fallen into the street, so when I went for my morning jog, I had to jump around some serious pieces of concrete.

The scatological phrase involving the cat attempting an impossible chore was an artifact from my Showboat Majestic days—one of Bud the deckhand's favorite expressions. I tried to spell the word the way Bud said it. If it upset your tender sensibilities, I apologize.

It's hard to believe today, but the only sure way to correspond back in 1977 was by airmail, which could take anywhere from a week to an eternity. Some people now get annoyed with me if I don't respond to their emails in a day. I remind them that I'm of an era used to waiting weeks for a response, and if there is none, blaming it on the Post Office.

Early in my Ham career, I attended as many Ham conventions as I could. SAROC, the Sahara Amateur Radio Operators Convention where I got DXpedition advice from N6AA, was one of my favorites. Unlike virtually all other Ham conventions, this one was privately run and, for all I know, profitable. Most conventions are fronted by Ham radio clubs or ARRL and are non-profit (but a few of them make potsful of money).

   My favorite Ham convention is the International DX Convention, in Fresno in the 70's but in Visalia now (because it's halfway between LA and San Francisco). You have to really want to go to a convention to go to Visalia (although there are several terrific restaurants in that little city). The other big convention is the Dayton (Ohio) Hamvention, which regularly draws 25,000 Hams to a city that can comfortably hold, maybe, 5,000.

   I changed my callsign in 1976 (after I passed the Extra Class licensing exam) from W6BVN to W6AQ; in my opinion a huge improvement. By now, you've figured out that the operator's callsign is really important to him (or her). Dick Norton, W6DGH, was waiting to get his two-letter suffix callsign until the FCC released the letter N as a prefix. His timing was perfect. He got N6AA. Just the one he wanted.

   You might be wondering how I, a producer of documentaries and things educational (neither occupation, as we all know, pays bupkis*) could acquire a beach house in Encinitas. It was actually across the street from the beach, but what the hell, a beach house is a beach house. Anyway, I knew that the Summer of 1971was going to be very busy for me at work, and I also knew that if I didn't take a summer vacation, four little kids and my wife would divorce me.*

   So, clever me, what I did was rent the penthouse of a big Santa Monica across-Ocean-Avenue-from-the-beach condominium, and put down $2,000 to hold the apartment. A couple of weeks before our anticipated holiday, I needed to sign the lease, sign insurance papers, and pay the rest of the rent. I took all four kids with me so they could see where we were going to have a great time this summer.

   When the building superintendent saw my brood, he said something like, "Oh, I'm sorry. We no longer allow children in our rentals." They allowed them in March but they didn't allow them in July? I argued, I swore, I told the kids to cover their ears, but even with my most colorful vocabulary, that guy wouldn't budge. So that weekend we went down to Encinitas to visit friends who had a summer house there. We looked around for a house to buy and discovered that we couldn't afford even the least expensive one.

   But we could afford an empty lot and found a great one for sale across the street from the ocean. We got a loan and Sam became the "owner-builder," supervising a bunch of roughnecks who put together an A-Frame house that was easy to finance because it came as a kit. Sam finally got it built, it looked great, and had a terrific view of the ocean. So that's how I ended up with a beach house. Sam did it.

   Dick, N6AA, was one of a dozen or so Hams in southern California who owned a Signal One CX7 transceiver. It was a magnificent piece of equipment—when it worked. In those days I drove an old Jaguar. I told Dick the Jag was my Signal One.

My friend Dick McKay, K6VGP, who was a 747 pilot for United, told me that Hong Kong was his favorite airport because it was so much fun landing there. He said, "You flew an ILS (an instrument glide slope they called an IGS) which if you kept going would run you into a hill. At 680 feet you made a visual 47-degree right turn and trued to line up and land. It was really a lot of fun and kept you awake." He told his passengers to get a right hand window seat on that trip, because during that sharp right turn you could see people eating dinner as the big 747 roared past their condos toward the air strip. But the Hong Kong authorities ruined it by building a new airport—safer but not as much fun.

The term "Search and Pounce" is probably obvious. If you can't hold a frequency while you call CQ, you have to search for other stations who are calling CQ and pounce on them. That's the flip side of "running JAs," which you do when you "hold a frequency," CQing and nailing one calling station after another, sometimes 30 or more in a minute.

The only other log periodic antenna I've used, other than the one that didn't work at Torres' place, was a "standby" antenna at W6EEN's contest station. While Don thought his worked okay, to me it seemed like just another dummy load in the sky. I'd describe how it works for you, but in my experience, it doesn't, so why explain it?

Kan Miziguchi, JA1BK, is a very well-known Ham worldwide. He asked me how many times I'd been to Playboy Clubs. I said, "never before." I don't think he believed me. To this day, that's the only one I've ever been in.

JA4CX, whom I had visited with Brad in Matsue, showed up rather unexpectedly
in Hollywood with his girlfriend, Nao, who is JA1OWP. They visited
Sam and me at our place in the Hollywood Hills, where Sam snapped this
picture after Atsumi had properly admired my tower and antennas.

JA1OWP is waiting for me to hook up with somebody in Japan, which normally wouldn't have been very difficult. Incidentally, I didn't know these Japanese friends planned to visit Hollywood. One day I got a call saying they were in town, and asking if they could they come up for a visit. For the most part, Hams always feel welcome and always are welcome.

My DXpedition, while hardly a success from the standpoint of score, was a lot of fun and a great adventure. And I made what for its day was a zinger of a QSL card.

CQ WW DX Phone Contest, October 29 & 30, 1977

CR9AJ

OP: W6AQ

As we flew home, I vowed to quit assuming serendipity would save my ass every time.

Chapter 23

Getting Very High with Ham Radio

As they say in those obnoxious television commercials, "But wait! There's more!" Perhaps the most populated Ham band is Two-Meters and I've barely mentioned it.

Since I've spent most of my air time on the "low-bands," that's what I've been writing about. But there's a huge world out there home to many, maybe *most,* Hams.

Unlike television and broadcast radio stations, Hams aren't assigned one frequency on which to transmit, but a so-called "band" of frequencies. The Twenty-Meter band, for instance, covers all of the frequencies between 14 and 14.350 megahertz, and during contests every one of those 350 kilohertz get used.

The low bands are ten segments between 1.8 MHz and 30 MHz. The Very High Frequency bands are Six Meters, Two Meters, and One and One-Quarter Meters, more commonly called 220-MegaHertz. The Ultra-High Frequencies are the vast spectrum above 440-MHz, divided into bands up toward the frequency of light. Somewhere way up there, where the wavelengths are measured in millimeters, are the Super High Frequencies, but you'll excuse me if I don't dwell on those. Just knowing that they're up there is more than enough knowledge and about all most Hams know about them.

The Ultra-High and Super-High frequencies attract the true techies of Ham Radio—folks who'd rather build and tinker than chat. Their definition of DX is 100 miles, or depending on how high the frequency, even one mile, unless you're bouncing signals off the moon. That's a whole different story and one you're not going to hear about here, except to remind you that my Elmer into the hobby, W8LIO, was doing Moonbounce back in the mid-Fifties with my other pal, Sam Harris, W8UKS. Sam moved to Massachusetts and became W1FZJ, and was a stalwart in the Rhododendron Swamp VHF Society with their station, W1BU. It was world renowned for its groundbreaking activities in the very short wavelengths.

My forays into the shorter and shorter wavelength world beyond the High Frequencies started in late 1972 when I bought a used Jaguar XJ6, which was just like new. (A friend of mine said it was just like new because it had spent so much time in the shop. I loved that car, but eventually put a Chevy V8 under its hood. I surprised a few hotshots at traffic lights.)

Anyway, I didn't want to transfer my Swan 400 and big low-band antenna to the Jag, so I bought a used VHF Two-Meter FM radio.

This Icom IC-22 was my first Two-Meter FM radio. It was crystal controlled, so you never had to worry if you were on the wrong frequency, and it was indestructible. In fact, I gave this one to Bill, WA6ITF, about 20 years ago and it still works!

The FM transceiver itself had limited range, just a few miles on a good day, but years earlier a Ham named Art Gentry, W6MEP, is credited with inventing a clever, fully automated relay device called a "repeater." The first repeater was Art's own, K6MYK. Since Art was a broadcast engineer, he had access to a small building on Mt. Lee, just up behind the famous "Hollywood" sign.

Every year millions of tourists aim their cameras at the Hollywood sign. Up Mt. Lee behind the sign is the old broadcast tower which held the K6MYK repeater antennas (as well as dozens of commercial ones) and the house near the bottom of the tower housed Art's remarkable creation. (This photo, incidentally, was taken from my back patio using a fairly long lens.)

As repeaters grew popular, many were placed on high places like hilltops and received the little transceiver's signals and re-transmitted them at higher power for all the world to hear. Well, maybe not all the world, but all the surrounding area up to probably 100 miles or so. Many clubs had repeaters, including the Southern California DX Club, the one I used first since I was a dues-paying member of that popular club. I was on that repeater not only to make contacts, but to listen for announcements of low-band DX, which appeared regularly. "9M6AAC is on 14 point 205," was a typical DX alert. This was the one repeater in town occupied by a bunch of low-banders, so I felt right at home there.

Many of my High-Frequency friends predicted that I would not last on VHF. But the idea of Two-Meter FM repeaters intrigued me. Oh, I forgot to mention: Two-Meters is virtually all Frequency Modulation. I was used to Single-Sideband on the low bands. SSB (and AM) modulate the *amplitude* of your signal while FM modulates the *frequency* of the signal. Now you know. You'll never have to ask again.

Being cautious by nature, I decided to listen to some repeaters other than the DX Club's for a few days before trying a contact.

At first it seemed that all of the crystals that came with my used transceiver were on the wrong frequencies, because every channel sounded as if I'd tuned into the audio portion of an old *Highway Patrol* television show.

A voice would come on and say his station was "ten-eight."

When conversations were in progress, you'd hear "ten-four," which I remember *Highway Patrol's* Broderick Crawford growling into the microphone when he understood what he had just heard on his radio. But *I* didn't understand.

Now and then I'd hear "ten-ten" coming out of the speaker of what some Two-Meter aficionados would call my "J.A.Pan." (As I discovered on my day at Tokyo's Akihabara, most Two-Meter transceivers were made in Japan. The prefix for Japanese stations was JA. Many of the transceivers were about the size of a small cake pan. There you have it.) Some folks on Two called radios like my ICOM IC-22 "rice boxes" but I refused to stoop to that one.

"Ten-Seven" was also heard and to this day I have no idea what that one means. It does, however, remind me of my dice sequence the few times I'd play craps at the Sahara in Las Vegas, and therefore conjures unpleasant memories. Many Hams attributed the "Ten" phenomenon to the great influx of Citizens' Band operators who moved up to Ham Radio. CB at the time was a cesspool of foul language and "Breaker-Breaker" shouting. For the more civilized of the ex-CBers,

Two-Meters was a sanctuary from chaos. Some "real" Hams decried the invasion of the CBers, but I thought it was a good thing, despite the annoying "Ten" artifact.

Back in the 70's, I gave a lot of speeches about aspects of Ham Radio and I always made light of Ten signals. After my talk, some VHFer would point out that I didn't have to use them. I'd counter with, "No, but I have to understand them or I won't know if the guy on frequency is standing by for a call or signing off." Excuse me, going "ten-ten." Or is it "ten-eight"?

The novelty of the "tens" gradually faded into Ham Radio oblivion, but since I didn't use them, I certainly didn't miss them.

Being a low-band rag-chewer by nature, one aspect of Two-Meter repeaters caused me no end of grief. There were few sins more egregious than "timing out." The magnitude of your transgression is made clear to you by everyone else on the repeater. Back in the day, more than one Los Angeles repeater timed out after a mere thirty seconds, requiring you to have your verbal wits about you at all times. (A lot to ask, in my opinion.) If you have a multi-syllable name, half of your time is up by just telling your contact your name and location. Of course you don't have to give your name at all. Repeater veterans often never volunteer their names, assuming their notoriety precedes them, or perhaps preferring the mystery of anonymity. At least on Two-Meters, the Hams gave their *real* names (often called *handles)*, not CB monikers like Tadpole and Big'un.

I noticed while listening to mobile stations that while they invariably mumbled their callsign they'd always follow that with "mobile six" very distinctly. It seems that the FCC had gotten fussy about knowing what call area the station was operating from as if someone from Alabama or Afghanistan could be heard by a Southern California repeater. Citations had actually been sent for saying "mobile Los Angeles" or "mobile on the Hollywood Freeway" instead of "mobile six." Perhaps the FCC's slavish devotion to this bureaucracy-run-amok was a result of their total inability to clean up the mess on the Hams' former Eleven-Meter band, now home to millions of Citizens Band operators. Hams obeyed the rules. CBers created a game with no rules. i.e. *chaos*.

I clearly remember my first conversation on one of the "open" Two-Meter repeaters. After listening for a couple of minutes and hearing nothing, I keyed my microphone and said, "Is anyone around this morning?"

A voice of practiced boredom said, "There's always somebody around."

I'd apparently committed my first VHF faux pas. Only a Newby would not have known that "there's always somebody around."

Charging right ahead, I said, "Hi—this is W6BVN." Then I added, hastily and clearly, "mobile six. Handle is Dave. How copy?"

"Full quieting," came the laconic response.

After a silence of ten seconds or so I said, "Wanna have a QSO?"

After another long pause, the bored voice said, "I'm listening."

Allowing a similar pause, I said, "To what?"

After a few seconds, the voice said, "Aaah, y'got a point there."

We had a nice little QSO after that, although much of it consisted of apologizing to unseen listeners for using up so much repeater time.

And in those early days of Two-Meter repeaters, you didn't have to listen too long to know that a few of the low-band fruitcakes joined their ex-CB counterparts to take joy in jamming Two-Meter repeaters—meaning transmitting some kind of interference and holding open the repeater until it timed out. One of the repeaters regularly had a dog barking. I wondered if the Technician test was really so easy that dogs could pass it. The dog wasn't all that smart though. He timed out the repeater every time he came on the air.

Some few Hams considered jamming repeaters a sport. One nitwit decided to jam the Southern California DX Club repeater. He was good at it, but we discovered his identity, and badgered the FCC to reprimand him. But they looked at such miscreants as the Hams' problem. A lawyer in our club was an absolute bulldog chasing DX. Joe Merdler Esq., N6AHU, took personal offense at the jamming. When the nitwit thumbed his nose at the FCC and continued to muck up our frequency, Joe contacted his friend the Congressman, who invited Joe to Washington. Joe went, played audio tapes of the jamming, and the Congressman pressured the FCC to go after the bad guy. The nitwit was tried in Federal Court and lost. He went to prison. He lost his Ham license and his equipment. The jamming stopped. When the nitwit got out of prison, the jamming started up again, but not to the Southern California DX Club's repeater. He was off our repeater frequency, but there were lots of others to annoy. He went back to prison a couple of more times. For a guy smart enough to get a license, he never got the message.

At the behest of Bernie Abramson, W6PJX, my pal in Hollywood just down the hill from my new house, I was introduced to the Bel Air Repeater Association, basically a bunch of low-banders in "The Industry"—meaning the entertainment biz. I was impressed that the Oscar-winning writer/producer Ernie Lehman, K6DXK, was a member. Ernie wrote one of my favorite movies, *North by Northwest*. He also did *West Side Story* and *The Sound of Music* to name only a few. Another member was Mel Shavelson, W6VLH, who started his career writing for Bob Hope and went on to become president of the Writers' Guild and get two Oscar nominations.

Mel's Ham radio career was highlighted in a film made by my friends, Bill Pasternak, WA6ITF, and Roy Neal, K6DUE, entitled *The New World of Amateur Radio*. Another repeater group member was Byron Paul, WA6RNG, Dick Van Dyke's manager, which is how I got the comic-actor to host one of my Ham radio films. It was a fun repeater, known for its great phone patch. That device turned repeaters into cell phones, twenty years or so before cell phones. I even bought a handi-talkie to take advantage of the Bel Air repeater's phone patch.

My HT was tiny compared to all others in use at the time. I attached the touchtone pad so I could dial the phone after the repeater gave me a dial tone. I gave two Tempo Ones courtesy the ARRL to King Hussein of Jordan, JY1, when I filmed him for The World of Amateur Radio. *That adventure, one of the highlights of my Ham career, is described in the next chapter (no skipping ahead!)*

When the phone companies came to their senses, realizing that Ham Radio repeaters were nifty gadgets (but only for Hams), they began putting up their own repeaters (which they called cell towers) on high buildings and hills. The phones they came up with were about the same size as small Ham handi-talkies (or HTs) and basically did the same thing; transmitting a small signal to a cell tower where it was amplified and sent to the person on the other end of your call.

The big three phone manufacturers in those early days were Nokia, Eriksson, and of course Motorola. When cell phones came along, I pretty much gave up repeater phone patches, mainly because, as you'll remember, Ham Radio is a totally non-commercial service and I wasn't allowed to call any of my business associates, not even to see if they wanted to go to lunch.

Ham Radio is often called a "service." And in emergencies, it always provides one. The Ham Radio slogan is, "When All Else Fails." Why are Hams so reliable in emergencies? First of all, each Ham owns his own equipment, uses it often, and knows how it works. Second, the repeaters are owned by Hams and they know how to fix them. Many repeaters have alternative power sources if the power company fails during the emergency (count on it). Most Hams who participate in emergency communications have taken the emergency preparedness classes created by the ARRL. All of these Ham responders, in other words, are trained, and know what they're doing. For some, probably many, the chance to help out in emergencies is the reason they got their tickets. VHF/UHF frequencies are the mainstays in local emergencies.

Wait! What about Field Day—that one weekend a year when all Hams move out of the comfort of their shacks into the great outdoors? Isn't that practice for emergencies? Yes, of course it is, but given my background and orientation, I consider Field Day a contest, and have decided to put it into the contests chapter. Arbitrary, I'll admit.

If emergency preparedness is such an important part of Amateur Radio, and it is, why have I waited so long to mention it? The reason is that I've only been involved in it peripherally. For all of my early years in Amateur Radio, emergency preparedness was rather informally organized, and by the time it really got humming and became an invaluable service, I was otherwise occupied. Now I rationalize my dereliction by considering emergencies being a young man's (and woman's) game.

That said, I'm an active member of a VHF/UHF repeater system called the Disaster Amateur Radio Network, or DARN. Los Angeles ARES uses DARN as its communications system, and the system owner, Dick McKay, K6VGP, regularly loans the network to other worthy groups. There's a members' net on Sunday mornings that I check into fairly often. There's a monthly brunch at a local restaurant, and I try to put in an appearance at those as well. And I contribute to the upkeep of the system. So I figure I'm doing my bit.

An entire book could be written about Hams and emergencies, but not by me.

While most activity on Two-Meters and above is FM, another group of so-called "Weak Signal Operators" use Single Sideband and now and then CW plus various digital modes to communicate directly, not through repeaters. I was curious about VHF and UHF SSB and CW operations when serendipity once again came my way. I used to go to the TRW swap meet one Saturday a month, just like hundreds of other Southern California Hams. It was an opportunity to paw through lots of used equipment and bins full of nifty parts that, who knows, might be invaluable someday. Most vendors at Ham Radio swap meets sell dozens or hundreds of pieces of junk—excuse me, *equipment).* One Saturday I spotted a Ham with just one item for sale, displayed on the hood of his pickup. It was a brand new Yaesu FT736R, the very rig I'd been imagining in my shack. This one covered four of the VHF/UHF bands, had all of the options, and was a bargain. Like one of Oscar Wilde's characters, I can resist all but temptation.

The FT 736 R is now nearly an antique, but it still gets the job done on VHF and UHF. Those four little boxes that are stacked up behind my paddle control mast-mounted amplifiers up on my towers adjacent to the VHF/UHF antennas. They boost the signals right at the source, the antenna, because one-hundred feet of coaxial cable considerably diminishes the Very High Frequency signals.

The FT 736 R offered one big problem: getting it into my shack without Sam seeing it. I waited for a propitious moment; then sneaked it down the stairs to the shack, like a reverse cat burglar.

I discovered a group called The Western States Weak Signal Society, so I joined. They sponsored "nets' which met on a different VHF/UHF band every night of the week. So for a while, at the appointed hour, I'd head for the shack and check in (on Single Sideband). I confirmed my suspicion that my hilltop location was a good one for VHF. I got into some VHF contests. They were fun, but somehow for a veteran low-bander like me, making a contact with San Diego wasn't the same as making a contact with Swaziland.

The Western States Weak Signal Society had annual conventions during its heyday, and at one of these conventions Sam and I met a couple destined to become life-long friends; Robert (K6YR) and Gini Griffin. Robert and I discovered we were a couple of Low-Banders at a VHF convention, but that wasn't all we had in common—both of our wives were artists, Sam a quilter, and Gini a painter. That chance meeting illustrates one of the hallmarks of Amateur Radio—you never know who you're going to meet on the air or at an electronics swap meet, or a convention of like-minds. It's all part of the magic of Ham Radio.

VHF and UHF repeaters are characterized as "open" and "closed." The open repeaters may be used by anyone and the closed ones were for repeater group members only and often required certain sub-audible tones to make the repeater "open up," meaning turn its receiver on. For some Hams, being allowed to operate on a closed repeater was akin to getting the keys to the Holy Grail. Some of the "closed repeaters" were super-closed to the point that members did not admit that the repeater existed. A case can be made that some Hams are a bit weird.

Many Hams on repeaters were Technician Class licensees because the FCC restricted Techs' activities to the VHF and UHF bands which was okay with most of them—that's all they were interested in anyway. Novices lost their voice privileges on VHF, probably as another FCC "incentive" for them to upgrade to Tech. A lot of them did. Some of them, pissed, dropped the whole hobby. In Ham Radio, incentives often have unintended consequences, and rarely make anyone happy.

My first QSO on an "open" repeater got me a signal report not of S9 or some variant thereof, but "full-quieting." That means your little signal is strong enough that when the repeater "opens up" to receive your transmission, you're not accompanied by any noise, which of course would be retransmitted with your signal.

The FCC has not always been as ineffective as during the period of the repeater jamming. A Ham named Riley Hollingsworth, K4ZDH, took over the FCC Enforcement branch and became all Hams' hero. The bad guys didn't want to get a phone call and hear the voice on the other end say, "Hi, this is Riley." He retired from the FCC and now writes a common sense column for CQ Magazine *labeled "Riley's Ramblings." Reason enough to subscribe to* CQ.

I mentioned digital as an alternative to SSB, CW, and of course FM. Digital is fascinating because it relies on computers as a key link in the radio chain. One of Ham Radio's two Nobel Prize winners, Joe Taylor, K1JT, has created numerous digital modes, which can "hear" weak signals that are inaudible to the human ear. Consequently, JT-65 and other digital modes are great for moon-bounce.

I mentioned that I was a rag-chewer, someone who could and would carry on at great length about topics of overwhelming interest (to me). I'm not sure it still exists, but in the early days the ARRL sponsored a Rag-Chewers Club, complete with a certificate suitable for framing, to add to your "wallpaper."

The phone dial thingy (that's a technical term) on Walkie Talkies was known as a "Touchtone pad" or if a smallish one, perhaps a "Pipo Pad." Pipos were the miniature pads made by my friend

Joe, WB6BJM in Los Angeles. "Pipo" was Joe's dog. The Tempo One HT was imported from Japan and sold by Henry Radio; the "candy store" to all Hams in Southern California.

My film-making Ham friends and I were somewhat responsible for the surge of Citizens' Band operators into the Ham Radio ranks, because we made a film for the ARRL entitled Moving Up to Amateur Radio. *The title alone indicates the inferior ranking of CB to Ham Radio, though CBers didn't seem to notice. This film is also part of the ARRL Film Collection for sale by that organization at a bargain price.*

You may consider me a name-dropper and your consideration is correct. In my television producing career, I understood star power, so the Bel Air Repeater Association was right up my alley. I found that the bigger the name, the nicer the person, with few exceptions.

Sam and I were introduced to Robert and Gini Griffin by mutual friends, Fried and Sandy Heyn, WA6WZO and WA6WZN. Fried was a longtime Southwestern Division Director of the ARRL, a really time-consuming job. I asserted, in the many speeches I made in those days, that while Fried was the director, Sandy did all of the work. Fried never denied it; he just shrugged.

I mentioned my disdain for 10-codes to my friend Bill Pasternak, WA6ITF, and he told me about the 12 codes in use on a few repeaters in the 70's. He said that "12-4" meant that you are full quieting and I hear you fine, but I am ignoring you. According to Bill, whom I consider an authority on VHF/UHF operation, "12-7" meant I'm at lunch but these burgers are giving me indigestion. I think somebody's leg is being pulled.

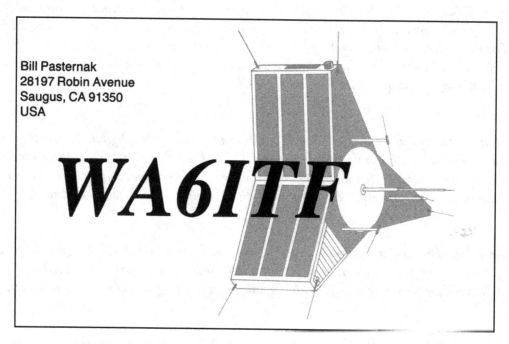

Bill Pasternak
28197 Robin Avenue
Saugus, CA 91350
USA

WA6ITF

Here's Bill's QSL Card. He's obviously a fan of satellite operation.

Chapter 24

The King and I

In 1979 I was working on another film for ARRL called *The World of Amateur Radio,* which was a sequel to the original *Ham's Wide World.* I tried for the better part of three years to get His Majesty King Hussein of Jordan, JY1, to commit to being filmed. I tried every means of communications except e-mail. Of course there was no e-mail in '79. (Hard to believe, isn't it? A world without e-mail. How did we ever manage before that whiny little computer voice said, "you've got mail.")

I was in contact with JY9BB, a genuine gentleman from Virginia named Blackie Blackburn, who was his majesty's Communications Advisor. As the completion date of the film drew nearer and nearer, my calls to Blackie became more and more frequent and more and more frantic.

The final deadline came and went so I finished the film and sent it to the lab.

Sending it to the lab was the charm. I got a call from Blackie saying that His Majesty wanted to be in my film. I think to myself, "Now? The film is done! It's too late!" To Blackie I said, "Great! I'll get back to you!"

I called the ARRL and I told them that King Hussein wanted to be in our film, but the film is *done!* After what had to have been one of the quickest meetings in League history, I got a call from headquarters saying, "let's put the King in our film."

I said, "I'm out of money. I spent the entire budget!"

You know what they said? "Oh, Oh!" Which rhymes with "No mo." I made it clear to the skinflints at the League that if they wanted the King in our film; that was *breakage!* ARRL reluctantly coughed up a couple of more bucks for my cameraman, some film stock, and processing. By this time my little company owned cameras and post-production equipment, so these were free in the view of ARRL.

But the ARRL's largesse didn't get me to Amman, so I called Blackie to tell him that the ARRL desperately wanted King Hussein in our film, but "We don't have any budget left! I've spent all of the money!"

Blackie said that His Majesty would fly me to Jordan and put me up while I was there. In the immortal words of Don Corleone, he made me an offer I couldn't refuse. All I'd be out was my salary and since I wasn't paying myself anyway, It was a done deal!

Alia is the official airline of Jordan, named after King Hussein's wife. When the King wanted free tickets on Alia, he got them. He even got me free tickets on TWA, who flew me to New York to catch my Alia flight to Jordan. Blackie told me that another Ham was also booked on the Alia flight, a Texan, who was a pilot for Alia returning to Jordan from a stateside vacation.

Wayne Threm, my long time associate and ace cameraman and I were the last two people into the first class section of the Alia 747. I looked around. Who here looks like a ham? At the same time another guy was also looking around. He was wearing a pilot's uniform, which was a clue. We locked gazes as I'm sure Stanley and Livingston did; kindred spirits for sure. "Are you Dave?" he asked. That was my introduction to Clyde Huddleston, 5B4DI, a short but bigger-than-life Texan, the first of many, many memorable characters to come in the next week.

The big jet lifted off and as soon as the wheels were up, so was Clyde. "Let's go upstairs," he said as he headed up the stairs with me right behind. The upstairs on most 747s is filled with passengers, but in those days of trouble and strife in the Middle East, the upstairs was a security area, housing four shifty-looking guys with mean-looking guns. Maybe AK47s. What did I know? Clyde breezed right past them before they had a chance to stub out their cigarettes, much less pick up their weapons. So much for security. Into the cockpit we went.

The pilot turned around and recognized Clyde at the same moment that the understandably annoyed security guys jerked open the cockpit door. The pilot greeted Clyde and blew off the confused guards with a dismissive wave of his hand.

Clyde introduced me to the cabin crew, all of whom turned around and greeted me and chatted with Clyde as we were coming up on Boston off to the left. No one was flying the plane! It reminded me of a WPA project!

Years later I learned from my friend Dick McKay, K6VGP, a 747 pilot for United Airlines on some of the fabled Pacific runs, that once the wheels are up on a 747, the crew doesn't really have much to do until it's time to put them down again. For this they get $150,000 per year?

Clyde said to me, "Wanna get on the air?" And before I had a chance to answer, Clyde told the co-pilot I'd like to operate a little Ham Radio. What frequency did I want to operate on?

"14.205," I said, and the navigator punched in 14.205 on a panel, offered me a seat, a mike and earphones, showed me the audio gain control, and I was on the air, W6AQ aeronautical mobile from the cockpit of a 747 over the North Atlantic.

As I held the microphone and listened to the familiar band noise of 20 Meters, a thought came to me. I worked very hard for my license to begin with and extra hard for my Extra-Class upgrade. Would the FCC approve of me operating out of the cockpit of a Jordanian 747? Clyde assured me that it was okay. After all, the boss did it all the time.

I don't know how many Hams believed I was in the cockpit of a 747, but only one commented that he wanted some of what I was smoking.

Finally, when the 20 Meter band began to fade away, I hung up the mike, thanked the crew for the good time, and went back to my seat for a nap.

A few hours later, the sun coming through the windows woke me up. After breakfast, Clyde and I headed back up to the cockpit for some more Hamming. As we flew over central Europe heading straight for Amman I asked the co-pilot where we were. He said a word that in those days, in DX circles, was magic. He said, "Albania."

So I got on 14.205, pushed the mike button and said, "Anybody using this frequency? This is W6AQ aeronautical mobile over Albania." It caused a mini-pileup. The Italians really turned on the afterburners. Just their fan noise was 40 db over nine and when they spoke, the S-Meter was in danger of breaking off.

I went QRT for lunch and by then we were on our approach to Amman.

My cameraman and I deplaned and looked around for our 16 bags that came off the plane and were whisked into the terminal. What happened to our camera equipment, film and other junk that we brought to get Hussein on film? Those of you who have seen *The World of Amateur Radio* know that the JY1 segment is only about one minute long. It took seven days, 16 bags, two carry-ons, and a journey of nearly 20,000 miles to get that minute. Before we got to customs we were greeted by Blackie, JY9BB, and a grinning little guy named Mohammad Balbisi, JY4MB, who would be my constant companion for the next seven days. A couple of tough-looking security guys appeared out of nowhere with all 16 cases of equipment and helped us out to Mohammad's illegally parked vehicle.

Pretty soon we got to our home for the next week, what else but the Amman Holiday Inn? It was the second best hotel in Amman, the best being the Intercontinental. According to Mohammad, the Intercontinental was full.

Mohammad was a civil engineer for the government, but His Majesty asked him to shepherd me around during my stay, probably because his other job was Secretary of the Royal Jordanian Radio Amateurs Society. He and I went to lunch together five of the seven days I was there. After about the third day of togetherness, I called him "Mo" once and he looked at me kind of funny so I said, "Does anyone call you Mo?" He said, "No Mo,' and then smiled. He added, "but you can call me Mo if you like." So Mo it was for the rest of the trip.

(IMAGE SOURCE: http://uksmg.org/news.php)
I thought Mohammad looked like Jerry Colonna, but I never mentioned it to him.

When Mo and I were out at lunchtime, we'd go into some restaurant that looked good to us, and it didn't matter how many people were waiting, we somehow always got a table immediately. And when the check came, well, actually, the check never came. I couldn't have bought Mo lunch if my life depended on it. We never saw a check. I wonder if His Majesty was ever billed? If I had to guess, I'd say, "no." You've heard the expression, "There's no such thing as a free lunch?" In Amman there is. I guess it's good to be King!

Mohammad was in charge of our shooting schedule and our first full day in Amman was a day off. Why? So I could get over my jet lag. "But I don't get jet lag," I told Mo. "Of course you do," he said, "everybody gets jet lag." And that was that. In those days I was a jogger, so Monday I jogged around Amman, soaking up the local color and worrying. Worrying because Mo had let slip that HM (that's what the inner circle called His Majesty) might be going to London on Wednesday for a week because his wife, JY2, was having some minor surgery done in a London hospital. What this told me was that the local clinic wasn't very local and if I didn't get HM on film on Tuesday, we might have traveled nearly ten thousand miles for naught.

But sure enough, Mohammad called and said we were filming HM on Tuesday, and to load up our gear and get ready to go at the crack of dawn. His Majesty will be filmed at 8 AM.

Tuesday morning, Mohammad arrived at our hotel at 6 AM. A half-hour later we were at the palace gates, which in those days was 10 miles or so outside of Amman. We arrived at the guard station. All 16 cases were opened and inspected. Once inside the palace we arrived at guess what—another guard station. All 16 bags were opened and reinspected. (I once made a documentary at Stateville Prison in Joliet, Illinois. The security at the palace was tougher.)

Finally, two hours after we arrived at the front gate, we got shown into His Majesty's Ham shack. The Palace shack is what the architect for the place thought was going to be a closet. It was about twenty feet long and eight feet wide. I know numerous shacks in the states that are more, well, palatial than HM's. It was a borderline impossible place for filming. But such is the lot of the documentary filmmaker—constantly making chicken salad out of chicken you-know-what.

Since it was already past the appointed hour of 8 AM, we quickly set up the lights and camera and in record time were ready to go. Nine o'clock. Nothing. Ten o'clock came and went. Every time a door opened, everybody jumped up, but HM did not appear. Every other hanger-on in the Palace appeared, and each was dutifully introduced. Most of them had call signs. I concluded that in Jordan, it's politically correct to be a Ham.

Finally, at about two o'clock in the afternoon, one of the doors opened and His Majesty finally appeared. He was not tall, but stood tall, and exuded a formality that I've seen surround other politicians. His English was as precise as in a British prep-school. After introductions were completed, His Majesty said to me, "What would you like me to do?" And I said, "I'd like you to have an ordinary QSO, an ordinary conversation with any station you find on the air, and then I'll ask you a few question about Ham Radio and that'll be it."

"Okay," he said, "That'll be fine."

He sat down at the Drake TR 7 transceiver (I know what you're thinking: "What, he can't afford a Collins?") The rig had already been turned on and tuned up several times by the ever-present Blackie Blackburn, who is, as I mentioned, His Majesty's communications advisor.

The King said, "You want me to call CQ?"

And I told him, "That'll be fine, Your Majesty."

Wayne fires up the camera and His Majesty fires up the transmitter on cue.

HM's CQ goes like this: "Hello CQ, CQ, CQ. This is JY1 calling CQ. Hello CQ, CQ, CQ. This is JY1, Japan Yankee number One calling CQ and listening."

What did he get? Nothing. Nothing but band-noise.

HM raised his eyebrows and tried again. Exactly the same result as the first time.

More band-noise.

*HM changes frequency. Maybe some other clear frequency
will be better than this clear frequency.*

HM looked at Blackie with his eyebrows raised as if to say, "Is this damn thing working?"

Blackie smiled sheepishly and shruged.

His Majesty heard a Russian calling CQ so he called him and Eureka! He got him. Blackie heaved a sigh of relief. His prayer was answered. The Russian sounded like Akim Tamiroff who had already had one screwdriver too many.

The Russian said, "JY1, uuh, JY1 question mark, this is UA3ZZA near Moscow. My name is Ivan, Italy Victor Alpha November, Ivan, and you're 5 by 9, but I missed your call. All I got is JY1. What is the rest of your call please? Break."

The King thanked Ivan, gave him his report and says, "The handle here is Hussein, Hotel United Sierra Sierra England Italy November, and my callsign is JY1. There is no more. That's all there is. JY1. So back to you, Ivan." As he turned it over to the Russian, he repeated very clearly, "JY1."

After a long pause, Ivan came back, "Sorry, I do not understand your call sign! JY1 question mark, question mark, this is UA3ZZA. JY1, what is the rest of your call sign?"

Hussein replied, "My call sign is JY1, that's all there is, just Japan Yankee number 1. There is no more. That's all there is. Just JY1."

It took a small eternity for Ivan to get it through his head that "JY1" was it. I wondered how many QSO's of HM's were merely convincing some Ham that, "that's all there is, just a J, a Y, and the number 1."

We'd been rolling film for five minutes, getting no answers to CQs and finally we got a ham in Russia who was certain he was talking to a bootlegger.

As soon as HM wrapped up that bizarre QSO a small pileup appeared on the frequency, including several Italians yelling their heads off, there were a couple of water-cooled Russians, all of whom got buried by DK2OC, who said merely, "JY1, this is DK2OC, Delta Kilo Two Oscar Charley in Berlin. How copy your Majesty?"

Imagine what Ivan thought as he listened on the frequency, as we all do after a QSO. Your Majesty? What means Your Majesty? I'm sure the poor fellow was more confused than ever.

His Majesty had a nice QSO with Uli in Berlin, and when he signed off, everybody on 20 Meters was calling. JY1 said to the calling throng that he had to QRT because he was helping make a movie about Ham Radio. Oh, swell, make me the heavy. Hussein turned down the gain and the noise went away. But I couldn't help but notice that the S-meter stayed up against the pin.

HM turned to me and said, "Now, what questions do you have? I asked my questions, he answered them, and after a three-hour wait, it was all over in fifteen minutes. His Majesty stood up, thanked me, thanked my cameraman, apologized for keeping us waiting, and was out the door.

Mohammad said that His Majesty had invited all of us to lunch. Wait a minute! I was there the whole time. When had His Majesty invited us to lunch? Nobody had said anything to Mo, but there it was, another delightful mystery. Checks never came and telepathy seemed commonplace.

So at about two-thirty in the afternoon, we headed to another part of the palace for lunch.

I had everything I came for in the can, and it was only the second day of a seven-day trip.

Incidentally, when my oldest son heard that I was going to Amman, I got a frantic call from him. "Don't you know that the Middle East is blowing up? You're nuts to go over there now!" What son David was upset about was the Egyptian-Israeli Peace Treaty that got so many Arab noses seriously out of joint. It had been signed only a week prior to my arrival. That's why I wasn't at the Intercontinental Hotel. It was full of diplomats. And guards with AK47s.

Zbigniew Brzezinski had been to Amman just a few days before I arrived. Brzezinski, you of course remember, was Jimmy Carter's National Security advisor. Brzezinski was trying to talk Hussein into giving his blessing to the peace treaty, something Hussein could not do since he was sandwiched between Syria and Iran, to say nothing of Israel. In fact, you could stand on the balcony of the palace, look west through a good set of binoculars, and see jet fighters taking off from their airfield in Israel. Talk about being between a rock and a hard place.

In the dining room, the table was elegantly laid out for exactly the number of people who had crowded into the Ham shack. Eleven men stood behind their chairs, each place marked by a call sign. We stood there, waiting for the head of the table to arrive, which Hussein did momentarily, nodded and sat, and we all sat down to a typical Arab meal—ten thousand teeny little bowls filled with chopped up this and that and you'd better not ask. It was like Hussein had the Cuisinart franchise for that part of the world.

The luncheon conversation started out with Ham Radio, how much HM liked the Drake TR7 transceiver, then it went to new Ham Radio equipment, such as one of the first synthesized, miniature FM handy talkies, the Tempo S1.

I gave two Tempo S1's to His Majesty as a thank you from ARRL for his

hospitality. He was really delighted with the gift. I got the feeling that nobody

ever gave the King anything but plaques and problems. He was especially

delighted that he could talk on all of his military's secret frequencies, just

adjacent to the Two Meter band.

There was only one Two Meter repeater in Amman, which then *73 Magazine* editor and publisher Wayne Green, W2NSD, takes credit for—perhaps correctly. HM regularly showed up on the repeater as did his cousin, Prince Raad, JY2RZ, along with several dozen other Hams. It's an open repeater, but it's never been jammed.

At lunch, after a half-hour or so of Ham Radio talk, the Egypt/Israeli peace treaty, and the problem with Palestinians (who in the King's view should have been over in Israel or in Syria or Egypt—anyplace but Jordan). HM again apologized for keeping us waiting that morning, noting that the peace treaty had not brought *him* any peace, whatever it might have done for Egypt and Israel. He mentioned that he would have put me up in the Intercontinental Hotel (which he said was better than the Holiday Inn and near the American Embassy), but it was full of diplomats and he wanted to keep me out of the line of fire, just in case. I told him I appreciated that.

As we finished eating, one of HM's aides came in, a guy wearing a grey pin-stripe mourning coat, whispered in His Majesty's ear, and lunch was over. His Majesty was gone, off to tend to some other world crisis. We headed back to the shack to finish wrapping our equipment. As I was leaving the dining room, I dawdled for a moment to look around. The mourning coat guy who had whispered in Hussein's ear to end the lunch came over to me. "I don't know who you are," he said, "but you got twice as much time with His Majesty as Mr. Brzezinski did."

I'm convinced that getting more time with His Majesty than Brzezinski did was simply a matter of being a Ham. If Jimmy Carter had realized the importance of Ham Radio in the

Hashemite Kingdom of Jordan and had sent a Ham to negotiate with Hussein, the Ham might not have gotten any farther than Brzezinski did with diplomacy, but he would have had a much longer and more pleasant lunch.

When I got back to the shack, Mohammad told me that HM had invited me to use his station. Really? I hadn't seen anybody say anything to anybody. It must be that telepathy thing again. What call do I use? Mo had already told me I was officially JY8AQ, all without so much as signing an application form. "You can use JY1," he said.

I ask you: Would you like to operate using one of the rarest and best-known calls in the Ham Radio world?

So while Wayne, my long-suffering associate, packed up all 16 bags, I did the important stuff. I got on the air. By now it was after 4 o'clock in Amman, coming up dawn in California, so I aimed the mighty TH3 toward the West Coast of the USA. You read that right; the King of Jordan used a tiny TH3 Yagi at about 40 feet—I swung it long-path to listen for the deserving ones in Six-Land. Incidentally, even though HM lived in a gated community not at all unlike some of the places around California, there were no antenna ordinances or CC&Rs.

Blackie had the rig fired up and at about 14.215 I hear my old pals in L.A., K6YRA and W6RTN, talking cross-town, complaining about the lack of DX on the bands. I decide to surprise them. As they pass it back and forth, I shout, "Break, JY1!" Nothing. They didn't hear me. On the next over I did the same thing. Nothing. They were twenty over nine and I couldn't break their damn cross-town QSO. They of course had their amplifiers on.

So I QSY'd to 14.205 and said, "Is anybody using this frequency?" A familiar voice came on and said, "David, is that you?" It was my friend Bernie, W6PJX. He figured I'd get on my favorite frequency and was just waiting for me there at 14.205, hoping for the best. So W6PJX became the first Southern Californian in ages to work JY1. Bernie obligingly phoned my wife, Sam, woke her up, and we chatted on the phone patch for 10 minutes while the deserving waited, grinding their teeth. I signed off with Bernie and said, "JY1 listening for Southern California."

When I worked everybody I could hear in the Southland, I stood by for 6's and 7's and had a massive pileup, and that was before DX packets. And so it went from JY1, much to the chagrin of dozens of Italians and Russians anxiously standing by.

As our departure neared, two parties were thrown in my honor. The formal one was hosted by Prince Raad, JY2RZ, and virtually every Ham in Jordan was there, including my pilot friend,

Clyde Huddleston, 5B4DI. At that lunch I was presented with a Longines watch with the King's Crest on the face. I still have it, though it quit running years ago.

I of course had given HM two S1 handy talkies, which I suspect ran longer than the watch. Even so, I think I got the better end of the deal. The jeweler I took this watch to said the works were rusty and consequently unrepairable. Rusty? Out here in the desert? How could it possibly have been rusty? Another mystery.

Hussein came to the U.S. a couple of months after my visit. I saw a photograph of him in Washington, using the S1 on a local repeater.

The other party for me was an elaborate luncheon at his home thrown by JY5US, the Surgeon General of Jordan. (Like I said, it paid to be a Ham.) The ceremonial part of this get-together was Mohammad presenting me with my Jordanian Amateur Radio license.

License No. 125	رقم الرخصة ١٢٥
The Royal Jordanian Radio Amateurs Society Certifies that.	تشهد الجمعية الملكية الاردنية لهواة الراديو في المملكة الاردنية العالمية بان
Mr. DAVE BELL	السيد ديفبيل
Place of birth. U.S.A.	من مواليد الولايات المتحده الامريكيه
home call sign. W6AQ class.	ذو النداء الدرجة
has been offered a visitor license and callsign (jy8AQ) according to the rules of the society.	قد منح رخصة زائر لهواة الراديو واعطي النداء (jy8AQ) حسب انظمة الجمعية.
This license is valid	تعتبر هذه الرخصة سارية المفعول
from 27 March 1979 to 9 April 1979 Date. 27 March 1979	من ١٩٧٩ / ٣ / ٢٧ الى ١٩٧٩ / ٤ / ٩ التاريخ ٢٧ / ٣ / ١٩٧٩.
Chairman RJRAS. RAAD IBN ZEID JY2RZ	رئيس الجمعية الملكية الاردنية لهواة الراديو رعـــد بن زيـــد

Here it is. Good for ten days. The shortest term license I've ever gotten.

No women guests appeared at this luncheon, but some were audible in the kitchen. Young boys, obviously used to doing it, served the meal.

At this party I met the second best known Jordanian Ham, JY3ZH, Zedan Hussein. He ran the Arabian Knights net on 14.252 for years and had a booming signal. He was not related to the king, although you'd never get that bit of intelligence from him. Zedan was the Maytag dealer in Amman. He had a lot of time for Ham Radio, of course, because he never had to repair anything. (If you don't know what that reference means, your memory of old television commercials has faded.) Zedan missed Prince Raad's party because he was in Germany at a washing machine convention.

Zedan was holding forth across the room from me. Mohammad was standing behind him, looking a little pained that he was subjected to Zedan's BS—again. Then Zedan shouted across the room at me, "Where have you been in Jordan?" I told him I'd jogged all over Amman, saw the old Grecian Theatre, which was a big surprise—Greeks in the Middle East? Who knew? I told Zedan that I'd been down to Petra, the fortress carved into the rocks where Lawrence of Arabia holed up, and . . . .

"Have you been to the Dead Sea?" he interrupted.

"No," I said.

"We will go," said Zedan. "When are you going home?"

255

"I said, "Tomorrow.""

"We will go this afternoon!" That wasn't a question, it was a fact.

Mohammed was not happy. He was very deliberately shaking his head, "No."

So I said to Zedan, "Well, I think Mohammad has something planned for me."

Zedan didn't even look around for Mohammad. He just said, "He has nothing planned for you." And that was that.

He said, "I will pick you up at 3 o'clock."

So at three o'clock I'm standing in front of the Holiday Inn and in comes this grey Mercedes 450 SEL. I get into the car. It may have been the only time I've ever gone 60 miles an hour in a parking lot. Without even pausing at the exit, Zedan made a left turn into a six-lane boulevard and we were off. I look around for my seatbelt and Zedan said, "What are you doing?" "I'm looking for my seatbelt!" Zedan laughed and laughed.

Had I said something funny?

No belt and this guy doesn't know any speed but wide open. If you ever heard him on the air, you know that. All of the gain knobs on his radio were fully clockwise all of the time.

The six-lane highway very shortly becomes a fairly narrow, two-lane road with lots of trucks. So Zedan speeds up. He passes trucks. Beep beep! He passes them on the right. Beep beep! I look over at the speedometer, which is about like Zedan's signal, almost up against the pin. Mercedes are magnificent machines, but the engine on this car was going eeeeeeeeeeeee!

As we came over the crest of a hill, in the distance I see something that looks like snow, but it can't be snow, it's 80-degrees outside! It's a gigantic herd of sheep trying to get from one side of the road to the other. There are sheep-dogs barking, shepherds wrapped head to toe in cloth, as they have been for thousands of years, waving their carved wooden staffs. Fast approaching the sea of white, what does Zedan do? Beep beep! But does he slow down? We're going downhill. He speeds up!

The dogs are running back and forth, the shepherds are pushing the sheep off of the road, and we are going beep beep! I can see hitting those sheep and the big Mercedes shooting into orbit!

At the last possible second, as if by divine intervention (we are in the right part of the world for that sort of thing after all), the sheep part as the Dead Sea once did, and Moses—I mean Zedan—zooms through the flock without a care in a carload.

I looked out the rear window through the swirling dust and saw those Arab shepherds trying to get their cloth coverings down out of the air! Obviously, Zedan knew what he was doing. After that experience, the Dead Sea was a real anti-climax. Zedan pointed across the water toward Israel and said, "4X4—I never work any of them." And then he gave me a big wink.

He said, "Put your hand in the water." I put my hand in the water. He said, "What does it feel like." I said, "Glycerin." He said, "Right. Back in the car." That was it for the Dead Sea.

We got into the big Mercedes, fishtail 180 degrees, and streaked off toward Amman. The shepherds were gone. No fools they. That road went to the Dead Sea and back. Those shepherds knew that if Zedan managed to get his car stopped before it plunged into the sea that he would be back, so they were nowhere to be seen. Zedan got me back to the hotel and I immediately had a martini. Actually, I had several. I spilled most of the first one getting the glass to my lips.

The next day we loaded our 16 cases and two carry-ons with our clothes and toiletries and left for the airport. Mohammad had arranged with the Palace for an official representative to meet us at the airport and see us through security. But when we get there, no one from the Palace was around. And as good as Mohammad is at restaurants, he didn't seem to have any clout with airport security, and I could see missing our flight as they picked through 16 bags.

As if in answer to a prayer, I heard a voice echoing through the marble terminal. "Hey, Dave!" It was Clyde Huddleston, decked out in his Alia pilot's uniform. I told him the Palace had failed to show up, Mohammad was off somewhere calling for help, and these guys want to inspect every piece of equipment and we have a plane to catch.

Never before in my career had I fully appreciated what an airline Captain can do in an airport.

Our 16 bags were piled high on a huge cart in front of the security guy. Clyde moved between the cart and the security guy and said, "Follow me."

Clyde pulled the cart forward and the security guy reached over to take a bag off the cart. Clyde hit his hand as he says, "These boys have been filming His Majesty. They're official palace visitors. These bags are not to be opened." Clyde said to me, "Show the guy your watch, Dave." I show him the watch. The guy's impressed. But he doesn't know what to do.

Clyde reached over for the stickers that say, "OK." These are the ones for bags *after* they've been searched. He started slapping the stickers on our bags. The poor security guy was clearly confused but he saw Clyde sticking stickers on our bags, so he reached over and started sticking them on too. In a moment, every bag was okayed and headed toward our plane. My cameraman and I each have a carry-on briefcase and as we get to the metal detector, that guard reached out for my briefcase and Clyde hits his hand too. We go breezing right through the metal detector that dutifully makes a racket and in a moment we were on the tarmac.

Just then, Mohammad catches up with us, out of breath, and says, "See, it's all taken care of."

He looked at Clyde and they both laughed. In this part of the world when officialdom fails, a greater power intervenes. In this case, the greater power had four stripes on his sleeve.

Mohammad gave me a hug and says, "73, see you again, I hope."

"Me too," I managed to say. "Me too."

Clyde escorted us onto a waiting bus, which takes passengers out to the planes parked on the tarmac. A crowd of people waited for the doors to open on the bus. Clyde went right through the crowd, with us in tow, knocked on the bus door, which opened, and we got on.

Clyde closed the door and told the driver to take us out to the plane. The driver protested that he is supposed to fill the bus before he goes, but he doesn't get three words out when Clyde pointed to the stripes on his sleeve, pointed to the 747 and says, "Drive." Other passengers were waving for the departing bus to return, but Clyde was on a mission.

When we got onto the plane we immediately went up to the cockpit, where I saw a couple of familiar faces. We went through all of the introductions again and the co-pilot said to me, "What frequency do you want to operate on?"

So, on the return trip I spent about six hours in the cockpit operating JY8AQ aeronautical mobile before I went down the stairs to my seat in first-class and sacked out.

It had been a perfect trip until we got to US Customs. They decided to look in every one of the sixteen cases, and practically dismember our briefcases. When they opened the ammo box and saw the tape-wrapped cans of exposed film, the meanest of the dumb bunch of Customs Agents said that they'd have to hold the film, get it processed, and look at it before they could let it into the country. I'd brought exposed film into the country before and never had anyone demand to look at the images.

I grabbed a nearby chair and sat down at the Custom's guy's inspection table and said, "We're not going to do that. Get your supervisor."

"He's not here right now."

"I'll wait," I said, and made myself as comfortable as possible. We were blocking one entire line of incoming passengers, but I didn't give a damn. This guy wasn't keeping my film, he wasn't processing it, and that was that.

My buddy Wayne, ever the conciliator, said to the Customs Guy, "Why do you want to look at our film?"

"It might be pornographic," said the knucklehead.

That set me off. "What! You think we went to Jordan to shoot pornography? Jordan? And it doesn't matter, because you guys have no jurisdiction over pornography or any other film images," I shouted. And then as loud as I could, with a long line of pissed-off passengers behind me, I said, "You must like pornography."

I was just getting warmed up when dipshit's supervisor appeared. "What's the problem here?"

"This guy won't let us keep his film so we can inspect it."

The supervisor turned to me and said, "That's right, we've been looking at suspect films coming into the country."

"This is film taken of King Hussein of Jordan." I stuck my watch under his nose. "You read Arabic? That's the King's Crest and those Arabic letters under there say *Al Hussein ibn Talal.*

That's King Hussein to you. You seize this film and you have an international incident on your hands! I'll see to it. You want that?"

The supervisor said to the troublesome lackey, "Let 'em through."

That was my one and only problem with U.S. Customs.

The World of Amateur Radio, like The Ham's Wide World before it, was shot on 16mm film, because small videotape cameras had not yet appeared on the television scene, and I liked the look of film better than tape anyway.

The Jordanian airline Alia was named after King Hussein's third wife, who died in a helicopter crash in Amman in 1977.

Clyde Huddleston lived on Cyprus when he wasn't in the cockpit of an Alia 747, thus his Cypriot callsign: 5B4DI. Cyprus is a mostly Greek island with a long history. It is the birthplace of Aphrodite. See what I mean? The Turks occupy the north one-third of the island as a result of the latest of dozens of wars fought over this pile of rocks in the Mediterranean.

You must be really old if you recognize "WPA"—short for Works Progress Administration, one of FDR's government-sponsored boondoggles (according to my father) that gave shiftless people jobs (again, according to my father). In my later life I came to appreciate some of the great artworks and classic buildings put together by the WPA—like Union Station in downtown Los Angeles. My father's friends referred to him as a "rock-ribbed Republican." I never figured out exactly what that meant, but he sure didn't like Franklin Delano Roosevelt one bit.

At the time I flew over Albania, that country had not allowed any form of Ham Radio in years, and thus was near the top of Ham Radio's "most-wanted list." That's why, when I gave my location, I attracted so many stations—each hoping that I would "count" as Albania. Some Italian Hams have the reputation of running very high power; thus the reference to their "afterburners." The term "db" stands for decibel; a world of logarithmic measurement too complicated for this treatise, but 40 db over S 9 is known by Hams everywhere as really loud.

Mohammad, JY4MB, became my "go-to" guy in the Middle East. When DXer friends of mine from Southern California wanted to use the RJRAS club station for a contest, I got on the phone to Mohammad, who made all of the arrangements. They had a great time (and left the station in better shape than they found it).

A "bootlegger" in Ham-Speak is a person on the air without a license.

When I referred to "water-cooled Russians," I'm implying that their amplifiers use water-cooled tubes—meaning they're really high powered.

"CC&Rs" are Conditions, Covenants and Restrictions, the holy grail of homeowners' associations, which among other things prevent Hams from putting up antennas, for fear that the antennas will look ugly to some homeowner. If "ugly" concerned the homeowner, he never would have bought in some of the monotonous, treeless tracts I've seen. Many homeowners' associations would have been right at home in Hitler's Germany. Amman had no CC&Rs.

Which reminds me: When we moved to Hollywood in 1975, I checked to see if the house we were buying had any CC&Rs. Since our house was built in 1926, I doubted it. I was wrong. The development that included our old house indeed had CC&Rs. You could not sell to Catholics, Jews, Orientals, or Negroes. It must've been a pretty dull neighborhood back in the roaring 20's. Nothing about antennas, though, so I was okay.

You of course remember that QRT is one of the most used of Ham Radio's "Q" signals—meaning "I'm shutting down."

Akim Tamiroff was a well known actor from the thirties through the sixties. Throughout his career he kept his thick Russian accent. A malaprop-spouting character he played in one movie was the inspiration for Boris Badenov, famous from the Rocky *and* Bullwinkle Show.

The Two Meter repeater in Amman was "open." You'll remember that "open" means anyone within range with a handy talkie or mobile radio can use it. When I asked Mo if the repeater ever had a problem with jamming, he just gave me a look that said, "You're kidding, right?"

"DX-Packets" are announcements of DX stations in digital form broadcast on VHF or UHF stations, usually sponsored and maintained by the local DX club. The over-the-air packet announcements have mostly been replaced by "Packet-Clusters" on the Internet.

I was in Amman (the first time) in the immediate aftermath of the Egypt-Israel peace treaty. About fifteen years later, Jordan became the second Arab country to recognize Israel.

When I mentioned "the deserving ones in Six-Land," I am of course talking about my Ham friends in California, which is a long way from Amman. Most of the King's contacts with U.S. stations were with the eastern half of the country. JY1 was rare everywhere, of course, but especially in the bottom corner of California.

The only thing Zedan gave me time to do at the Dead Sea, other than to feel the density of the water, was to pick up a small rock by the shore. It made it all the way back to California with me where it sat on the kitchen windowsill in its own little bowl. It started to shed almost immediately, and in twenty years or so disintegrated entirely into a small pile of rust. It's time for me to go back to the Dead Sea.

That would have been the end of my adventures with the King of Jordan, except for the call I got in 1983 from my friend Roy Neal, K6DUE, the science editor-reporter for NBC Network News. He and our mutual pal Bill Pasternak, WA6ITF, were putting together a video for ARRL entitled Amateur Radio's Newest Frontier. *And what was that "newest frontier?" It was Amateur Radio on board the space shuttle. (In Ham Radio there's always a newest frontier). Roy, with all of his science bona-fides, pulled a few strings and got Mission Specialist Owen Garriott, W5LFL, to schedule a chat with JY1 on one of his passes over Amman from the space shuttle Columbia. Would I be interested in videotaping the conversation?*

Would I? You bet!

This flyover would happen sometime in October, 1983. I was scheduled to be in Yugoslavia at that time, overseeing the filming of Nadia, *a movie we were making about the first "perfect-10" gymnast,* Nadia Comaneci. *I planned to get back to Los Angeles in the middle of the shoot to see how our other television projects were going, so I'd make a detour to Amman on my way home.*

Because of a faulty valve or some other "dime store" device (according to Roy), the Columbia schedule got pushed back a month. Fortunately, the new fly-by now coincided, more or less, with the completion of the Nadia shoot.

I arrived in Amman on the evening of Monday, November 28th and after I was "found" by the palace security person, I was driven to the Amman Marriott, a splendid new hotel. The moment I walked into my room, the phone rang, and it was my old friend, Mo, JY4MB.

For the next three days I remade old acquaintances and spent as much time on the air as possible, 90% of it on CW. (I had taken my own paddle, keyer, and headphones this time, incidentally, since the first time I went to Amman, a casual search of various shacks failed to turn up any device that was designed for making Morse code.)

I made about five-hundred contacts in the relatively few hours I had to operate. Getting through the Russian QRM and the Italians with their afterburners to make some Qs with the deserving in the States was not exactly a walk in the park, but it was fun. While I worked one station after another on Morse, a few Israelis called, knowing I was not allowed to talk to them. I sent the dots and dashes that said, "no prefixes." If all I heard were callsign suffixes, how was I to know what country the caller was in? Besides, there weren't many Hams in that part of the world who knew CW.

The contact between JY1 and W5LFL was set for Sunday morning at 8:00 AM, local time, so my video cameraman, Duane Dahlberg, WB6WMA, who had joined me in Amman the day before, got all of our equipment to the Royal Ham Shack on Saturday, so we wouldn't get stuck in bag-inspection hell. Besides, when shooting video, we only had four cases, not the 16 we needed for film. Duane, incidentally was the chief engineer of our homemade editing suites and the mobile unit we built to record our daily morning show on USA Network, Alive & Well, the first "health, wellness, and beauty series for women," sponsored by Bristol-Myers. One of the hosts of that series, incidentally, was Kathy Smith, who was an exercise guru and later on made beaucoup bux selling VHS tapes to women who wanted to look like her. Another host was Joanne Carson, Johnny's second wife. Joanne was what's known in the TV biz as a "piece of work." You could diligently prepare questions for her to ask, but likely as not she wouldn't ask them—she'd make up her own—which were usually better, and certainly more out of left field than the ones we prepared for her.

In the King's shack, Blackie Blackburn, JY9BB, not only had one Two-Meter station set up and ready to go, but also a backup station just in case. His Majesty was not going to miss this QSO.

A few minutes before 8:00 AM, His Majesty appeared in the shack, was reintroduced to me and introduced to Duane, sat down, keyed the Two-Meter transmitter and said, "Hello, test!" He leaned back in his chair to await the fly-over of the Columbia.

Duane rolled the tape about five minutes before we expected the contact, and we all stood around nervously awaiting Owen, W5LFL to call HM. The appointed hour came and went. Time passed slowly. Should HM call Owen? As we weighed this, Owen's voice came booming out of the Two-Meter transceiver.

HM wanted to know about life on a space shuttle and Owen wanted to know about life at the Palace. They had a good QSO going when Owen went over the horizon and so did the short QSO. Hussein sat back with a satisfied little smile, nodded to Blackie, "Good job."

I presented HM with an honorary

Northern California DX Foundation

membership plaque.

For some reason long forgotten, I booked the Sunday Alia flight to New York, which departed at 11:00 AM, meaning that after the shoot, ceremony, good-byes, etc., I had about an hour to make it from the palace to my plane. Since Amman is a high desert climate, weather around the airport is almost always perfect for flying and as a consequence, the New York 747 generally left on the dot.

On December 4th, however, the flight left an hour and fifteen minutes late because some person "from the palace" had to get to New York with a videotape of His Majesty. Fortunately, I still jogged every morning so running through the airport was easier for me than for most of the airport security people. The most difficult part of the journey involved facing three hundred passengers sitting in an airplane waiting for "someone from the palace" to show up. I tried to pretend that I was not that person, a difficult task since the door immediately closed behind me and we started to move before I'd even found my seat.

While my experiences with the kind of influence necessary to hold a 747 on the ground have been relatively few, I have an appreciation of power and a special appreciation for the people who have that power and don't allow it to corrupt them. I was impressed with King Hussein of Jordan. It's too bad there aren't more like him.

And now for what I think is an interesting aside: My friend, the writer/director Keva Rosenfeld, was going to Jordan and wondered what to say to King Hussein if he met him. After assuring Keva that he would not meet King Hussein, I said, "But if you do, tell him that W6AQ says hello." Keva wrote "W6AQ" into a little notebook, which he stuck in his pocket.

Well, wouldn't you know that Keva's plane was the one millionth (or some such number) to land at the Amman International Airport and there at the bottom of the stairway was His Majesty, welcoming everyone to Jordan. Keva checked his notebook and when he got to HM, said, "I bring you greetings from Dave Bell, W6AQ." Keva said the King looked startled, then smiled and thanked Keva for relaying the message as the two shook hands. What are the odds?

And finally, in case you're wondering what King Hussein's QSL card looked like, here's mine:

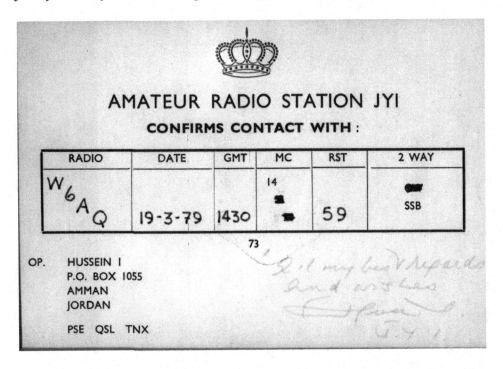

His Majesty signed the card but the ink has faded so that his signature is subliminal.

Chapter 25 (The Last)

Contests and Movies

I describe myself as a casual contester. That's actually a borderline oxymoron, because contesting by definition is a sporting event that requires all-out participation! My favorite is the IARU (International Amateur Radio Union) contest which takes place the second full weekend in July for one 24-hour period. That's another thing I like about this contest: it's short (at least compared to most other Ham Radio contests) and the rules state that you can use Voice, CW or Digital (radioteletype or PSK) or a combination of two or three.

Every four years, more or less, superimposed on the IARU Contest, is the World Radiosport Team Championships. During WRTC, about fifty, two-person teams of the world's best contesters compete against each other and all the rest of us ordinary Hams who operate in the IARU contest. So it's really a contest within a contest.

The WRTC took place in San Francisco in 1996. I happened to be in Vancouver, BC Canada at that time producing a television movie for NBC. I had sold them an intriguing script called *The Traveler* and NBC decided to produce this *noir* movie, which should have been shot entirely at night, in Vancouver in the middle of July. Problem: There is no night in Vancouver in July. It's sunny from four AM to ten PM. And the city of Vancouver wouldn't permit you to shoot film in residential neighborhoods after eight PM. We were screwed and I was grumpy.

Furthermore, the director NBC absolutely insisted that I hire had never directed a film before, and the line producer that NBC hired was a personal friend of the head of movies for NBC and they talked every day. This effectively left the Executive Producer (me) out of the loop.

The novice director had this idea that if you arbitrarily cut the first few lines of dialogue and the last few lines of dialogue from each scene, the movie would move faster. I told him it would be shorter for sure, but not faster. He didn't argue with me. In fact, he didn't talk to me. I, who had an Emmy for one of my movies, was saddled with a director who wouldn't talk to me!

To complicate matters, as if they needed complicating, my contact at NBC decided to take a three-week holiday to somewhere in the Middle East and was totally unavailable. So I was stuck dealing with the head of NBC movies who wasn't my favorite person in the biz. Once when I actually managed to get her on the phone, I told her that with all the random cutting the director was doing, our movie would not only come in too short, it wouldn't make any sense. She told me the "dailies" looked great and she had to take another call.

Since I was contractually required to deliver a 92-minute movie, I sent her a letter (with a copy to my agent) disclaiming all responsibility for the length and continuity of the film, to prepare for that inevitable moment when the doo-doo would hit the fan. The big boss at NBC didn't respond to my letter, so I figured I was off the hook.

The plot of my movie required a dead "alien" which we designed to look like no other alien. I arranged for it to be built in Los Angeles and shipped Fed-Ex to Vancouver. As further proof that my movie was jinxed, Fed-Ex lost my alien. It just disappeared. (It occurred to me that maybe my alien didn't like the way the picture was going and fled back to its own planet.) We had to rent a standard alien from a prop house in Vancouver. It broke my heart to have to use a big-headed, small-bodied, bug-eyed alien, when we had designed such a unique one. Our alien was anorexic in the extreme and had an exceptionally craggy (ugly) head. I wanted to sue Fed-Ex but NBC wouldn't hear of it. After all, they were a client! I did manage to get word of Fed-Ex's dereliction into the trade papers—*Variety* and *The Hollywood Reporter*. Small satisfaction.

I could do nothing about the ineptitude all around me—even Fed-Ex was against me—so I decided I was just going to have a good time. NBC was renting me a penthouse suite in a nice downtown Vancouver hotel, so I set up an antenna on my big outdoor patio and made some contacts. The World Radiosport Team Championship was that weekend so rather than spend all day on the set watching the director massacre my movie, I got ready for the contest.

I ran QRP (five watts) so I for sure wouldn't interfere with any of the electronics in the hotel (since I hadn't asked their permission to set up the antennas on the deck). With an antenna as high above ground as mine was, I did okay, and for the first time on this trip, had fun. At that moment, the mid-summer IARU contest became my favorite—and I don't think I've missed one since.

While an IARU contest takes place every year, the next WRTC competition was scheduled for Slovenia in 2000. I decided that I'd make a video of it since most civilians and many Hams didn't know how this contest combination worked. I had the notion of trying to make the World Radiosport Team Championships into a real Olympic event. The summer Olympics in 2000 was happening in Australia and when I looked over the competing events, I was convinced that the World Radiosport Team Championships would fit right in.

I ask you: Isn't a worldwide contest with thousands of participants a bigger deal than rowing, badminton, or luge? Is luge huge? Or for that matter, *Taekwondo*, fencing or archery? Or curling? If hairdressers can qualify for the Olympics, why can't we?

In early July, 2000, the picture-postcard country of Slovenia hosted 53 teams of competitors, 106 of the world's best contesters, plus 53 referees, one chief referee, Dave Sumner, K1ZZ and a chief scorekeeper, Dick Norton, N6AA. You might say that Tine Brajnik, S50A, the head honcho of this affair, had covered his bets from AA to ZZ. Dozens of hangers-on like me, XYL's, kids, girlfriends, and curious Hams from all over the world, gathered in the resort town of Bled, Slovenia, "on the sunny side of the Alps" as the Slovenians like to say. We all actually flew into Ljubljana (pronounced *Lubleeana)* airport and were whisked off to Bled in waiting army jeeps driven by real Slovenian GIs.

Slovenia is a mountainous country, and on top of every mountain is a mountain top. Host-country Hams had put together Ham shacks on 53 mountaintop locations, so the competitors would start with a level playing field if you can call a bunch of mountain tops "level."

Each pair of contestants brought their favorite transceivers, plus boxes and bags of interconnecting cables, paddles, headsets, footswitches, Velcro (yes, at least one contestant brought Velcro so his paddle and other small accessories wouldn't be moving around on the operating table), special microphones, lucky charms, etc. They were given 24 hours to set up their stations.

The contest started on Saturday at 2 PM local time. Before that, we had a brunch at Hotel Bled and an elaborate and suspenseful ceremony, the highpoint of which was the sealed-envelope-callsign-selection by the competitors. They weren't allowed to know their contest callsign until five minutes before the contest started—so each sealed envelope was entrusted to that team's referee. All the teams knew that their callsign would begin with an "S" followed by three numbers (everyday callsigns never have more than two numbers) and then one final letter, such as S576M. With that callsign, every Ham in the world would know he's talking to one of the WRTC competitors. And, I noted, the competitors would only have five minutes to program their computers and get used to sending their callsign.

On the big day, I decided to follow an Army jeep full of VIPs to the mountaintop locations nearest Bled. Let me assure you that my rented Opel wasn't as good climbing up steep dirt roads, creekbeds, and logging trails as the Jeep, but with more than a little wheel-spinning, I got several locations on film. After that, I filmed the aftermath, banquets, announcing of the winners, and the closing ceremony, etc., etc., etc.

"Etcetera, etcetera, etcetera," said the King of Siam in the wonderful musical, *The King and I.* Everytime he found himself at a loss for words, he'd say, "Etcetera, etcetera, etcetera." I understand his dilemma. While I'm not at a loss for words, I fear you may be approaching a loss of patience with the length of this memoir, so as one of Shakespeare's characters so famously said, "I shall be brief." I've been having so much fun recounting my experiences that I've neglected many of the facets of the hobby that some Hams would consider their favorites. Like Field Day, for instance.

Field Day, always the fourth full weekend of June, is the most publicized activity in the broad spectrum of Ham radio events, when thousands of amateurs all over North America set up "in the field" or in parking lots, or on school yards, mountaintops, or anyplace they can put up their antennas, run their generators, and contact as many other Hams as they can hear. Virtually all Ham clubs organize Field Day sites and most of the members participate. The two Ham clubs that I belong to, The Southern California DX Club and The Southern California Contest Club, being organizations with very specific interests, usually did *not* organize Field Days.

But 1978 was an unusual year. The SCCC had been on a tower-trailer building binge, and decided to show the world how Field Day should be done. Only contesters, and serious contesters, would announce in advance, "We're going to win!"

Marty Wohl, N6VI, and Wayne Overbeck, N6NB, were two of the ringleaders of this assault on long-existing records. Each of the club's new tower trailers held a crank-up tower which would be winched from its horizontal resting position to the vertical operating position and then cranked up to either 55 or 70 feet.

The parade of tower trailers leaving N6NB's house would fill any Ham's heart with joy.

On top of each tower was a multi-element Yagi antenna with lots of forward gain. They needed that gain because their strategy was to run QRP (5 watts maximum) because it got them the biggest power multiplier, five-points per contact.

There were too many towers to fit into the photograph!

During those few years when the SCCC had all of the towers on trailers and antennas to go with them, they got into Field Day three years running, winning the first and third year and coming in second to an East Coast station, W2RQ/2, the second year. W2RQ had 25 operators and five stations going simultaneously. That 1979 loss surprised and maybe annoyed us a bit, so we went from five operators manning two stations to a dozen or so operators manning seven stations. I say "us" because while I didn't operate, I shot video of the SCCC operation, ran back to the office, rough edited it, wrote a script, and got it on the evening news. The operators were happy to hear they got on television.

Wayne, N6NB, designed and built the tower trailers with a lot of help from his friends. Wayne is an antenna expert and a Ham with boundless enthusiasm for the hobby. It's probably time for the SCCC to mount another killer Field Day effort. Obviously, for a bunch of contesters, Field Day is a contest first and a "test your emergency equipment in the field" second.

I'm often at my friend Brad, W8JJO, and XYL Mary Lee's summer "cabin" at Pier Cove, Michigan over the last weekend in June.

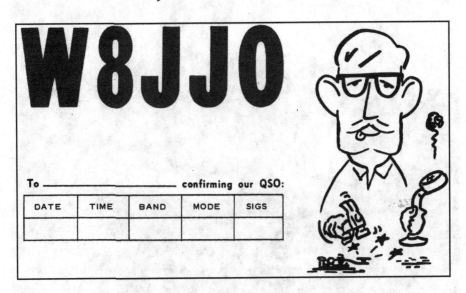

*Brad's QSL card is distinctive because of the caricature, which
Brad himself drew. Not a bad likeness either.*

At his summer home, Brad doesn't belong to a local club so I'm on my own for Field Day. In 2012 I took my little Elecraft KX1 transceiver across the street near the shores of Lake Michigan, set up my card table, threw a wire up into a handy tree for an antenna, put up my usual sign, *Ham Radio information, 1 cent,* and made a few contacts running two-watts. One old boy walking his dog stopped by, gave me a penny and said, "I know all about Ham Radio, but how much power does that little thing run?"

"About two watts," I answered.

"And what's your most distant contact?" he wondered.

"Florida," I said.

"It's amazing, isn't it?" he said as his big dog, showing no patience for Ham Radio at all, pulled him away,

"Have fun!" he said.

Then it started to rain, so I put up my umbrella.

It always rains on Field Day. And I try to publicize my alma mater however I can.

Another Field Day I wasn't at Brad's place because I was making a movie in Salt Lake City entitled *Just a Dream* which was being directed by Danny Glover.

Most movies shoot six days a week, but Danny would only agree to shoot five days a week. That was how I managed to have Field Day weekend off.

Our movie was about what happens to the ordinary citizens of a small town when the cast and crew of the feature film *The Misfits* descends on their town to shoot that fairly notorious film. *The Misfits* starred Marilyn Monroe and was Clark Gable's last film. It's said that working with Marilyn killed him. *Just A Dream* was about the influence this dramatic spectacle had on a 12-year-old local boy. The script was by Ken Topolsky and Melanie Wilson, and I loved it.

Just because I had a really good script didn't mean that I'd be able to get a film made. Then my partner at the time, Ted Weiant, heard that Showtime was looking for a script for Danny Glover to direct. Bingo! We got the script to Danny, he liked it, we took the "package" to Showtime, and they bought it.

On the Saturday morning of Field Day, I took my little transceiver on the cable car to the top of the nearest Wasatch Range mountain, a tourist attraction right on the edge of Salt Lake City. I set up my Ham Radio "demonstration." I taped my sign to the edge of the table I'd chosen as an operating desk. As usual, it said, *"Ham Radio information, 1 cent."* I duct-taped what was really a mobile antenna to a railing, hooked a couple of radials to the braid of the coax feeding the antenna, and stretched them out along the ground. At the appointed hour, I started making contacts.

It's not much of an antenna, but it's hard to beat the location.

A Park Ranger ambled over and I thought, "Uh, oh." Because, as usual, I hadn't asked anybody's permission to set up my little Ham station. He said, "How you doin?"

273

I said, "Great. This is a terrific Ham Radio location."

"Doesn't surprise me," he said, and went on his way looking for miscreants.

Later on a kid came over, looked at my sign and watched me make a couple of contacts. After a while he said, "Whatcha doin?" Then quickly he added, "I don't have any money."

"Are you over 21?" I asked him.

"I'm going on eight," he said.

"The one-cent charge is for 21 years old and older. Kids get their questions answered free."

"Whatcha doin?" he repeated.

So I told him. He listened to the Morse Code from the headphones and nodded his head. He sent a few dots and dashes and listened to those. He nodded.

"Pretty neat," he said as he saw his father coming, looking a bit frantic. "Thanks."

I collected four or five cents and made thirty or forty contacts between the interruptions, and as the park was about to close, I folded up my antenna, unplugged my little radio from the battery, headphones, paddle and antenna, and headed for the cable car and reality.

The *Just A Dream* script called for a look-alike stand-in for Clark Gable. We had a local casting call but nobody looked the least bit like that silver screen icon. My partner whispered something into Danny's ear. Danny looked at me and said, "Dave, *you* look like Clark Gable. Have makeup put on a mustache and let's have a look. Oh, and have them darken your hair."

Danny Glover and yours truly as Clark Gable's stand-in.

That summer I got my moment in the limelight and my KX1 survived its first major contest (although for most Hams, Field Day is not really a contest, but a demonstration of emergency preparedness).

There are as many different styles of Field Day as there are Ham clubs.

Some far-away Field Days are called DXpeditions. There are also as many styles of DXpeditions as DXpeditioners. I've already told you of my first DXpedition, to Macao, which avid contesters would have considered a total failure, but it was a success to me, because I had a blast!

Many DXpeditions take to the air during major contest weekends. In fact, contests are probably the main motivator for DXpeditions, unless you're going to some frozen flyspeck like Heard Island in the Antarctic. For that rare an entity, a contest would just get in the way of making as many contacts as possible with as many stations as possible.

You know that I'm a believer in serendipity. My friend Don Lisle, K6IPV, told me he was planning a trip to visit a good pal of his, "Sweet Billy" Taylor, VK6XA, in Perth, Australia. On his way home, he planned on stopping at a Ham Radio resort (yes, Virginia, there are such things) in East Malaysia. Don knew I was planning a trip to Japan to visit my friends Brad (W8JJO) and

Mary Lee Field. Mary Lee was once again teaching English as a second language to a bunch of Japanese educators and Brad went along as the fancy man.

I checked my calendar and discovered that I could make a stop in East Malaysia on my way to Japan, but I had one problem. Don was suggesting we meet there the second week of February, but the ARRL DX CW Contest always takes place the third full weekend of February. In those days, Don was not much of a contester. Now that I think about it, he still isn't.

I told Don I'd meet him in East Malaysia on my way to Japan, but it'd have to be a time-frame that included the ARRL DX CW Contest. After some hemming and hawing, Don agreed to push his trip up one week so we could meet at the Hillview Gardens Resort. This well-known Ham Radio resort was on a plain overlooking Keningau and has lots of antennas all in place and ready to go. Whoopee! Another adventure on the horizon.

Malaysia Airlines had the best fare to Malaysia (no surprise there) so I booked an exit-aisle seat and had lots of leg room on the big 747. After a brief stop in Taiwan for fuel, we proceeded to our final destination, Kuala Lumpur.

Another Malaysia Air flight delivered me to Kota Kinabalu, where I was picked up by Phil Weaver, 9M6CT who had moved to East Malaysia from Hong Kong. You'll remember that Phil was formerly VS6CT, the guy in Hong Kong whose antennas were down when I was looking for a borrow-a-shack in the Pacific or I might have operated my first DXpedition from Hong Kong rather than Macao.

Phil and I knew each other as many Hams know one another, from a chat or two at the International DX Convention, and from on-the-air QSOs. He was heading over to Hillview Gardens the next day for a birthday party (his), so he told the Hillview proprietors that he'd deliver me to their doorstep.

After I dropped my bag at my overnight hotel in Kota Kinabalu, Phil drove me over to his place for a couple of drinks and to check into the SEAnet on-the-air net, a dozen or so Hams who met weekly on a specific frequency, to chew over events of the past week and announce upcoming items of interest. This was my first opportunity to try out my newly minted Malaysia call-sign, 9M6AQT, which got a warm greeting from Hassan, V85HG, the "net-control" station in Brunei, a small, sovereign nation on the north coast of Borneo. East Malaysia covers 25% of that big, rain-forest-covered island and Indonesia has the lion's share. See; DXpeditions can be educational as well as fun.

When Phil and I got to Hillview the morning after my arrival, we were greeted by the resort's creators, Alfons and Doris Undan, 9M6MU and 9M6DU respectively. When I wondered aloud where my pal Don was, Doris told me he was getting his nails done. Nails done? Was it going to be *that* kind of DXpedition?

Don, K6IPV, as I'll always remember him.

Neither Don nor I was a genuine CW operator—Morse didn't come naturally to either of us. So why had we picked a CW contest for this DXpedition? Because that's the contest that was going on when we could meet in Malaysia and believe me, that's the only reason.

The first thing we did was check out the station. Just to make sure we had a rig we could depend on, I brought my nearly new Yaesu transceiver with me all the way from Hollywood (nuts, I know, but that's how Hams are). After all of those miles, the radio worked great, but the big 20 Meter Yagi wouldn't rotate, and it wasn't pointed toward the States, the only direction we were interested in for this contest. Alfons' antenna-guy couldn't come to fix the antenna until next month and Doris wouldn't let Alfons climb the tower. Don and I flipped a coin to see who would put on Alfons' old safety belt and climb the big tower to fix the antenna. Don lost the toss. Then, disaster!

I won't say that Don was a bit porky; let's just say that the safety belt was sized for someone considerably more svelte. Don pointed out that *I* was a bit more svelte, so up I went. What choice did I have?

The gear that turned the big beam had lost some teeth, so it was unfixable (by me). However, I did manage to point the thing toward the States.

Look closely and you'll see me up there 100 feet in the air, where I don't want to be—Still crazy after all these years.

When the contest began, we could only hear a few stateside stations, so we got off to a leisurely start. As the radio propagation to the States warmed the ionosphere, our station was "spotted." Don was operating, and all of a sudden he pulled the headphones plug and the speaker burst forth with an enormous pileup of stations calling us. He handed me the headset and said, "Your turn."

I bumbled my way through one callsign after another, with Don listening and pushing notes in front of me whenever he copied a caller in the maelstrom. I don't know how many hours I sat there working one Stateside station after another before the band conditions changed and the callers were fewer and weaker and I could finally take a break. What a relief. What fun!

The banner that greeted us on our arrival became our QSL card for this unique DXpedition.

Not every DXpedition gets a greeting like this.

Our DXpedition to East Malaysia was an easy one. Some Hams, like those in the Voodoo Contest Group, get to a different country in Africa for the CQ Worldwide CW Contest (the world's most popular contest), and they do it year after year after year. These Voodudes, so-called, and others like them are professional in their dedication to the sport. Don and I were just having fun.

A few years after our Hillview Gardens Resort adventure, Don and I met in the South Cook Islands, this time with our XYLs, got a condo on the beach, put up an antenna, and did it all over again—only this time it was a phone (voice) contest. We were logging lots of contacts until we were visited by a spectacular lightning storm. We quickly disconnected our antenna cables and threw them outside. Mother Nature forced us to sleep through the first night of the contest.

One of the local Hams we met on that trip was Victor Rivera, ZK1CG. Partly because my XYL Sam loved the South Cooks, and in those days it was easy to fly there, I went back and "borrowed" Victor's shack for yet another contest. Of course, as at Hillview Gardens, when I arrived, Victor's antenna was not rotating, so this was my QSL Card for that mini DXpedition:

ZK1AQT

Rarotonga, South Cook Islands
Operated by Dave Bell, W6AQ
and Victor Rivera, ZK1CG

*Victor and his pal replaced his dead rotator just before the contest with one I had
schlepped all the way from Los Angeles. (Incidentally, if it weren't for my QSL
Cards, I'd have a much tougher time remembering where I've been!)*

One last note on my contesting escapades: I heard that a Northern California Ham had sold
his bank (not all Hams are in the electronics game) and retired to the Palm Springs area in the
great "low desert" of Southern California. A mutual friend told each of us that we'd hit it off.
Don Doughty, W6EEN, and I met at the International DX Convention in Visalia, California,
had a couple of martinis and were fast friends from then on.

Don had put together his dream contest station in the desert, with five one-hundred foot
towers and four complete operating positions, each with a kilowatt amplifier. Don invited
me to be one of the team of operators, since he was planning multi-multi operations. I spent
many enjoyable phone contests at Don's place, and W6EEN made it into the top-five scoring
multioperator stations with some regularity. Neither Don nor I did the CW contests. Some
unbelievably serious CW ops headed to the desert for those contests. One even brought his
own chair. For a number of years, W6EEN was a station to be reckoned with, before Don
got tired of towers falling and the endless equipment maintenance. His was a complex but
beautiful station.

Don holding a T—shirt with our simple philosophy. In front of Don is Norm, W6ORD, Ron, K6XC (wearing headphones), Mark, KI7WX, and me.

I will admit that contesting at Don's was unique. For a few of the phone operators, including me, one of the attractions was the cocktail hour and Don's famous Tanqueray (gin) martini. No serious contester would ever admit to drinking during a contest, but I'm an old-time truth teller. I can have one martini and operate a voice contest. I can't even walk near the bar and operate a CW contest.

At W6EEN's shack, there were always lots of phone operators around, allowing me time to socialize at the bar, which I probably enjoyed as much as making contacts. In the movie business, the "martini shot" was the last shot of the day and at Don's, my martini signaled bedtime. I'd hit the sack early, set my alarm for sometime in the middle of the night, and get up and spell some bleary-eyed operator.

So here we are, at the end of my tale. I fully expected to end with my comments about PSK 31, a unique teletype-style mode that my friend Brad, W8JJO, uses almost exclusively. He talks all over the world using 30 watts, a modest amount of power indeed. But I haven't gotten around to configuring my station for PSK or any of the newer, more robust digital modes, so you'll have to discover those ingenious modes on your own. I'm looking forward to them because they look like fun to me. I may even do a digital mode DXpedition.

So, 73, and I'll see you down the log.

I mentioned that I'd won an Emmy for a movie I'd produced (Do You Remember Love with Joanne Woodward and Richard Kiley) but it sure didn't get me any respect from that bunch of bozos in Vancouver. They weren't even impressed with my Peabody!

Actually, early in my career when I was producing a lot of local shows and syndicated shows, my company won a boatload of "local Emmys" but those don't count in the network business.

Often, when it's discovered that I'm a television producer, I'm asked what *I've done. I generally say that I've done a few movies and that my company originated* Unsolved Mysteries, *starting with a few specials on NBC. If that's before their time, I mention that I did* LAPD—Life on the Beat *for MGM in syndication. If those two series don't register, I mention* World's Most Dangerous Animals *on CBS and* Missing-Reward *in syndication hosted by Stacy Keach. If those shows get a blank look, I mention that I've done a number of docs for HBO including* Skinheads *and* Asylum, *which premiered at the Sundance Film Festival. I might mention* Angel Death *hosted by Paul Newman. They've usually heard of Paul Newman. Then I say something like there are a lot more (true) but you're too young to remember them. Whether they're too young or not, the flattery usually manages to change the subject. The truth is, when you've been in business for fifty years or more, you'd better have done a lot or you'll be broke.*

Motion picture "dailies" are quick film prints of yesterday's shooting. Generally, all of the scenes at a certain location are shot on the same day, to avoid the expense of duplicate setups. That means there's very little continuity to dailies, and thus no sense of story. Dailies invariably look good, and first cuts of the movie invariably look bad.

Incidentally, the first "cut" of a movie is contractually the "Director's Cut" which is supposed to run ten or fifteen minutes longer than the "Final Cut" (so the executives can make suggestions for cuts, scene swaps, alternate takes, and all manner of meddling). The director's cut for The Traveler *came in short, and even worse, parts of it didn't make any sense, as I'd predicted in my letter to the programming boss at NBC. There wasn't any footage to make it longer because the director made so many cuts before he shot each scene. I got my pal the writer, Brent Mote, to try to edit the picture so it made sense. The network executives were looking for scenes that were longer (not necessarily better) than the ones in the director's cut, but they discovered he'd used most of the longer takes in his cut. It's no wonder to me that the broadcast networks stopped making movies.*

So why do I think the Radiosport Team Championships ought to be a genuine Olympic event? Here's the skinny, from the official Olympic rules: "Olympism is a philosophy of life, exalting and combining in a balanced whole the qualities of body, will and mind. Blending sport with culture and education, Olympism seeks to create a way of life based on the joy found in effort, the educational value of good example and respect for universal, fundamental ethical principles." *If that's not the essence of Ham Radio contesting, I don't know what is. Besides, we have tens of thousands of participants! And we don't take performance enhancing drugs (unless you count martinis). We just need some juice with the Olympics Committee!*

The half-hour film I made of WRTC-2000 is entitled The Ham Radio Olympics *and is available from ARRL or the Northern California DX Foundation.*

Phil Weaver, 9M6CT, picked me up at the airport in Kota Kinabalu for my trip over the mountain to the Hillview Gardens Ham Radio Resort. It's not at all unusual for Hams to pick up visiting Hams at the local airport. Every time I go to a film or TV festival at Cannes, France, I'm picked up at the Nice airport by my friend Pierre, F6HIZ in his BMW. Invariably, I try to arrive at dinner time. After dropping my bags, Pierre whisks me off to one of the multi-star restaurants in that part of the world and we catch up over a fabulous dinner and great wine. One of the memorable restaurants he took me to was on a cobblestone road so narrow that the Beemer was too wide to navigate it, so we had to walk up the hill to the restaurant, the only way to get there, unless there was a horse handy.

Wayne Overbeck, N6NB, one of the sparkplugs behind the record-breaking SCCC Field Day adventure in the late seventies, volunteered to measure the forward gain and front-to-back ratio of a five-element quad that I'd built and had used for years from my station in the Hollywood Hills.

To celebrate this nation's 200th birthday, the FCC allowed special callsign prefixes in place of the usual W, K, WA, etc. I got these AC6BVN cards made because I decided to try to get a Worked All States certificate with that callsign so of course I'd need QSL cards if I expected to get QSLs from Hams in other states.

I made WAS too. Note the multi-element Quad at the top of my big tower.

Wayne discovered that the Quad wasn't working very well, and in fact on 10 Meters had more gain off the back of the antenna than off the front! How ignominious! After those findings, Wayne and I co-authored an article for a new journal in the Amateur Radio publications field, Ham Radio which was about the superiority of Yagis (in our opinions). We caught a lot of flak from Quad owners. Passions about antennas and Ham equipment are easy to stir up. Fun too.

The "switches" refers to my changing from a Quad to Yagi
antennas, and I've used those Yagis ever since.

When I'm out on my one-man Field Day adventures, the reason I charge a penny for information about Ham Radio is that people don't appreciate things (including information) that they get for free, at least according to my father.

"Hemming and Hawing," which Don, K6IPV, was doing when I told him he'd have to move his trip to East Malaysia forward a week, is a phrase from the 15th or 16th century and it means "a throat clearing noise" while the brain attempts to catch up with the mouth. I told you that before, didn't I?

Brad Field described himself as a " fancy man" when he accompanied his wife to one of her "English as a Second Language" foreign assignments. For the record, one definition of a fancy man is: "a dashing, handsome, charming, and sophisticated man characterized by exquisite wardrobe, impeccable taste, and respect and good manners toward the fairer sex." That's Brad.

When I mentioned that we were "spotted," as you'll remember, that means that someone in the States posted our callsign and frequency on a so-called DX Cluster which is an Internet service that lists all of the DX stations on the air and their frequency. Instantly, every Ham needing a 9M6 multiplier was on our frequency calling. Mayhem hardly describes it.

The Malaysia DXpedition was a great adventure. The nights were so clear and dark that, unlike Los Angeles, you could see stars by the millions. I'm a member of the SETI League (Search for Extra-Terrestrial Intelligence) and with all of those stars, I had no trouble imagining intelligent life somewhere out there. Don't be surprised if some Ham is the first to hear a signal from outer space. It'll probably be Morse Code.

And finally, XYL is Ham Radio parlance for ex-young lady, or wife, but you figured that out, didn't you?

I've already said "73," but no good QSO ever ends with just one, so again, very best 73, and good DX.

Afterword

I've spent an entire book regaling you with my Ham Radio adventures. It should be clear to you that I really love this hobby. But why? What makes it so alluring?

I spent a lot of time wrestling with this question when serendipity arrived (as it often does), and presented me with an answer, written by a friend of mine, Brooke Allen, N2BA. I've never met Brooke as far as I remember, nor do I remember a specific QSO that we've had. But he and I are both contesters, and we've both gone on DXpeditions, so I'm sure we've made a connection sometime, perhaps several times.

Here's how Brooke explained Ham Radio to a non-Ham friend of his as they drove to a science convention and Brooke described the Ham station in his car.

"My rig is a magical box that will take a light-bulb's worth of energy from our car battery, modulate it with my voice, and direct it to a short metal stick on the roof of the car in such a way that magical invisible wave-like particles will boil off it and spread out in every direction.

"Some of those particles will go out into space but most of them will be absorbed by something; the ground, clouds, trees, and the like. A few will bounce off of things such as the upper atmosphere, the earth, and the oceans, before they too are eventually absorbed. A few will bounce off things more than once.

"Another magician like me in Italy or Russia or Argentina or Japan will have a piece of metal hooked up to his magic box. An unfathomable number of magical particles will be hitting his piece of metal from all kinds of sources; man-made, natural, and extra-terrestrial. Compare the cross-sectional areas of our two pieces of metal to that of the entire universe, and compare the power of things like lightning bolts, stars, and the big bang to my 100 watts, and you will realize that only an infinitesimal fraction of the magical particles he captures will have come from us.

"But he will direct his magic box to select just those few magic particles from me and use them to reconstitute my voice and he will answer me. It will be as if I flash my headlights and someone in Europe will see it and flash back. That other magician and I probably won't have anything in common except that we are both magicians, and that will give us plenty to talk about. The whole thing is magical, and there is no other word for it.

Dave Bell, W6AQ

"We talked to people in Florence and Moscow and Buenos Aires. The drive to the conference was quite long, but it wasn't long enough because Twenty Meters was still open when we arrived and I really wanted to work Japan.

"Most science teachers do it all wrong. Can you imagine a magician first teaching you how a trick is done, and then doing the trick for you? Similarly, most Hams explain their hobby all wrong. Stop that. Explain the magic, and then shut up and see what happens."

Brooke goes on to write; *"I have had many conversations like this one:*

She: *"Radio contests do not make any sense to me in the internet age."*

Me: *"Do you understand why people run marathons?"*

"Sure."

"But, why on earth would anyone run 26 miles and 385 yards in this day and age just because legend has it that that two and a half millennia ago some dude ran that distance to announce the results of a battle, and then dropped dead? If you want to go somewhere, just hop in your car.

"People run marathons because they are fun."

"Ham contests are fun in the same way that marathons are fun. But there is one difference."

"What's that?"

"You can run a marathon all by yourself. But you can't win a radio contest all by yourself. You can only win if you help your competitors try to beat you, just as they help you to beat them. How awesome is that?"

Try Brooke's approach the next time you have to explain a contest to someone. It works.

The above is excerpted with permission from a series of articles entitled *Game Design for Contesters* written by Brooke Allen, N2BA, for a quarterly magazine called the *National Contest*

Journal, published by ARRL. It certainly goes a long way toward explaining why Ham Radio, and especially contesting, is so alluring. All four of the articles in this series are online.

Ham Radio, for me at least, is all about connections, whether of the three-second variety as in a contest, or the hour variety as in a ragchew, or in person at a convention or club meeting. Often these contacts result in lifelong friendships. It's all about like minds making connections and having fun doing it. What you get from all of these connections is a support network. I have lots and lots of friends, all over the world.

I was looking for a final sentence to this Afterword when there was a knock on my front door. Who should I discover on my porch but Mike Schwab, OE6MBG, and his wife Sissy, OE6YWF, visiting Southern California from their home near Graz, Austria? They'd just been down in Encinitas, California visiting my friend Jim McCook, W6YA. I didn't know they were coming, and they didn't know if I'd be home (sort of the in-person version of getting on the band and seeing who's on.) We sat around, had some nice white wine and hastily assembled crackers and cheese, and discussed some of the many things we had in common. My friend Kitty Stallings showed up and among other things, took a group photo in my den.

Here we are, good friends as a direct result of Ham Radio. From left: Alice (Sam) Bell, W6QLT, Mike Schwab, OE6MBG, holding my QSL card in front of Sam, Dave Bell, W6AQ, and Sissy Schwab, OE6YWF, rarely on the air, but a big supporter of Mike's hobby.

Sissy and Mike invited us to visit them in Austria which we will probably do next summer after attending HAM RADIO, Europe's biggest Ham convention, held annually in Friedrichshafen, southern Germany on the northern shore of Lake Constance (Bodensee). I'll probably take my new Elecraft KX 3 with me and make a few contacts from Europe, maybe from Lichtenstein or Andorra—a couple of semi-rare ones. I can hardly wait.

END